HOWNING YOUR SPHERE

Michael E. Durgin

ISBN: 978-1-5356-1368-2

Contents

Foreword

BEING AWARE OF SO MANY motivational pieces of literature that grab the reader by flashing big name authors and mentors, I must apologize for alleviating that step in *Howning Your Sphere*—maybe next time, when this is a best-seller. *Howning Your Sphere* is purposely misspelled; you will hone your own sphere, as you do now, and come to understand that your ACTSYS or action system is the center force that drives all that is around you. We hope to give you tools that will permanently alter your life in a positive fashion. It will suffice me to say that this is about my experiences, and given my life, this is how I had to change my action system to reach my own optimized sphere.

Howning Your Sphere is an experiential real-life story of Michael Edward Durgin. Temporal and spiritual in scope, this work explains a journey through trials and tribulations that led to a spiritual awakening and inner peace along with marked accomplishments. The first part of the work starts in fictional autobiographical form, where the names are changed to protect me. Then the gloves come off, and at one point I realize the parallelism between Job's life in the Bible and mine. I know this to be the first story of its kind because it's mine. I am a member of the Church of Jesus Christ of Latter-Day Saints, and many of my experiences discussed in this momentous memoir have to do with being truly converted to what this life and the hereafter offer when you seek enlightenment and self-improvement through your spiritual eyes once opened. You will learn how to recognize messages and their messageurs, or deliverers, and how to act on promptings while developing faith that allows an increase in visitations and ministrations of angels. This is a real account of the ongoing blessings that come with change and survival in grief. The two works to follow to complete the trilogy are *The Psalm of the Messageur* and *Your ACTSYS, Your Sphere.*

My intent is to publish this trilogy and make a contribution towards building a cardiovascular weight room and pool facility onto the Caribou, Maine, recreational center to further bless my new community. In Doctrine and Covenants 123:11, it states "that we owe all the rising generation and to all the pure of heart. Therefore," in verse 13, "that we should waste and wear out our lives in bringing to light all the hidden things of darkness, wherein we know them; and they are truly manifest from Heaven." And in verse 14, "these should then be attended to in great earnestness." 7/31/07 (He's eleven years old, and I've had him since he was four.)

Hi. This is Jesse. If you're looking for a loving letter or something in that direction, you better put this down. I AM MAD!! I am sick and tired of all your stupid choices. I thought I was important in your lives, but you know what, I really don't think I am. You have constantly chosen drugs over me. If you think my mom is making me write this, she is not. Yes, I called her my mom because moms don't only give birth; they also have to love and care for their children. They have to make sure they are fed and sheltered. A real parent would choose their kid over drugs. But with you, it is the opposite. Drugs are bad! Drugs are bad. Drugs are bad. I want you to read that over and over. Guess what. I am getting adopted, and I'm happy about that. You have no clue how bad you have hurt me inside. You need to start acting like a real parent. You need to choose me instead of drugs. You need to take care of your kids. All you think about is drugs; you never think about how anyone else feels except for you. You don't think doing drugs affects anyone else, but it does. Stop being so selfish. Think about all I've said and about whether I'm happy.

Doing Drugs

Pros: Nothing, nothing

Cons: yellow teeth, bad breath, messed-up mind, poverty (because you have to pay for drugs), lung cancer, and many other things. Drugs, alcohol, pornography, war, gambling, immorality, and yes, even inactivity in the church can lead to this type of anger and disappointment. Fortunately, today Jesse is back with his real mom, who is not yet a member, is getting his Eagle, and gets himself up every day to go to seminary. He's also a straight "A" student. However, he's an exceptionally gifted young man as most go the direction of their parents. Now that you've heard some of the milk, it's time for the meat.

Introduction

THE TIME HAS ARRIVED TO implement your ACTSYS, or action system, that you will learn from the following work. The author is going through a journey. At this moment in time, I'm in Hawaii on the island of Oahu after adjusting all my means to ridding the world of its dependence on oil through design and corresponding installation of alternative energy. I'm ready to share *Howning Your Sphere*. The reason for the "own" in "hone" will reveal itself in the coming pages where a soul is reborn repeatedly in a continual series of blessings by trial and tribulation, leading to a discovery that we will share together in the hope that you, the reader, will be touched in a way to motivate you to act in a manner conducive to pursuing and achieving your life's intention.

First, we'll discuss a transformation from the natural man to the spiritual man. As you chip off your rough edges and become a creator of your own sphere, you, too, will come to realize that when your actions align with your beliefs and you center yourself on doing what you love, a sphere forms around you like unto what you speak and believe you are. Then and only then do heavenly providential forces work in your favor to bless you—or, in transgression, equally and opposite to destroy you. Each of you, individually, controls your own destiny. This was done by conscious design, and many great beings have visited humanity through the centuries to teach this principle. Some will receive truth and rise to a higher existence while others succumb to carnal worldly focus. The truth has been revealed and is ongoing today through revelation from a Prophet of God on the Earth, even Thomas S. Monson.

When the Savior appeared in the meridian of time, many were blessed with His great message, and others rejected the message because it was contrary to their behaviors, habits, and lifestyles. Many believe that the strength of a man has to do with his physical attributes and physics, but the real strength lies in his spiritual conviction and example. Without your Spirit, you are just a tabernacle of clay. So, it is with the natural man versus the spiritual man. The natural man would have you believe that your strength is entirely within yourself and that you can do whatever you want without consequences and not rely on the Lord. The natural man would have you lifted up in the pride of your own heart, boastful. The natural man is temporal and serves the world and the things that are in it by coveting material things while not having charity for those who struggle around him. You may know the natural man by his fruits as he leads a telestial existence. The natural man is a humanist and takes credit while uplifting men of position and bowing to the arm of the flesh, uplifting men instead of acknowledging the Creator's hand in all things great and small. The natural man is in a fallen state. The spiritual <u>man</u> is what God wants you to be, for God has only given you things of a spiritual nature and of the celestial order. He has never given you a law that would require you to live a lower set of standards. You must progress to be a spiritual being to reach the highest honor in the life to come.

The process of setting goals and declaring intentions is foremost in progressing to your highest honor in this life and the life to come. Your decision to integrate both hemispheres of your God-designed brain will make no sense to those around you until you reach higher ground and surround yourself with like-minded progressing souls. Remember, be careful from whom you seek advice, and also don't forget that if you buy an individual's opinion, you should be ready to purchase and live their lifestyle.

The primary concern of our future entity Motivate and Elevate U. (short for University) is to rise together and be part of SIGN (Sphere Influence Global Network): "A SIGN just in time." This will be the teaching and coaching side of my business. You must realize that your life runs in cycles, and like growing up and crawling, walking, and then running, that running too fast soon leads to a compulsive cyclical repeat of past mistakes. It usually can take an Earth-moving experience of cataclysmic proportions for your spiritual eyes to open long enough to catch a glimpse of yourself in the soliloquy of the mirror. You will need to acquire Me-power before you can empower others to come help you in your endeavors. You will operate at a vantage point of higher elevation with a raised sense of awareness and heightened excitement levels called eustress, which means good stress. I have found this while meditating in a treehouse; while on my knees praying and fasting; and swimming a mile in fresh or salt water. While I exercised and hiked up Wilhelmina Drive in Honolulu, the apex provided a immersive panoramic view of the mountains (mauka) in Manoa, Diamond Head, and the Waikiki Beach waterfront. A famous architect in the islands was named Vladimir Ossipov, and his house used to sit on this property; however, shifts in the land caused it to crumble over time due to its igneous foundation. Like Ossipov's home, you must have a rock-solid, immovable foundation of principle to survive in this world of wavering, ever-corruptible standards. Noticing how the incline of immense magnitude becomes easier each time we climb is a constant reminder that once your muscles are exercised, tasks that once seemed daunting become second nature. My wife, while making this hike the first time, said, "I can't look at the top because it seems impossible to climb." The best thing to do is just look in front of you and take a step, one foot in front of the other. Before you know it, you're at the apex enjoying the view.

This is my message that I will share with you and thousands of others one soul at a time. I will coach and mentor others like you with a custom-tailored game plan and a step-by-step mindset, line upon line, precept upon precept. You will realize that you've been designed to accomplish great things while in this life and in the next, both being interwoven with ancestors and progenitors. Remember, going uphill without knowing when it ends is the same as running without a destination. Going downhill can be equally as challenging. Your life, like mine, is full of ups and downs. When you know your destination, it gives meaning and purpose to the ups and the downs. To know is to have a plan and a roadmap of goals with a correlating action system. What follows is the format I used to get where I am in my progression with my ACTSYS to bless your life while completing my eternal sphere. Thank you and enjoy.

You were born unto greatness. Mediocrity is a state of mind. The sphere that circulates beneath your feet is a constant reminder that time is passing and that what you do with it will determine how you will be remembered and what will be written on your headstone. Your system of action and beliefs must be in line. When your actions align with your beliefs, you become one with the Universe around you. Cooperation moves into place on your behalf as your cube is honed into your own sphere, setting into perpetual motion momentum creating your own world around you and unleashing your hidden potential. Thus, your action system or ACTSYS becomes the center while you are still a cube, and life deals you glancing blows that chip off the corners and the rough edges, never to stop spinning whether you control it or not.

My birth, like yours, was intended for something great—a responsibility that only I have to create a world within a world that will house my body and spirit for eternity. Today I write from Beatrice,

Nebraska. The last six months, I was in Honolulu, Hawaii, after having just married my wife from Nova Scotia, Canada. In the midst of all this change, a star was born. Now step into where a sphere is being honed. I spell "honed" *HOWNED* because I found through my process that outside forces existed while howning my sphere and creating a world. Actually, I owned many of the difficulties at a certain point as if these glancing blows were necessary in some way to prepare me for the future. Now, join Adam Michael as he is being born in Japan.

The first thing on my agenda of goal-setting and howning my sphere was a hypnotic induction through great music and relaxing orchestra music. I think of the Savior Jesus Christ and his atoning sacrifice. While paddling on a surfboard the other day, I kept falling into the ocean. I can only imagine how Peter felt. You see by my dialogue the difficulty of writing and carrying through with goals. I've read Napoleon Hill's books over and over again. I put my goals on a positive affirmation disk, and I listen to them morning and night. I will write books to warn you, my brothers and sisters on this sphere, that you, too, can escape the chains and hown a new sphere for yourself. This is my life's contribution to you.

I am attracting success. Success is coming to me easily. Abundance and prosperity are flowing to me from all directions. It's easy to feel and to be successful. I only think positive thoughts. I'm in perfect spiritual and physical health. Record yourselves saying these things, and then record yourself speaking your goals and intentions. Goals focus your intentions and efforts while helping you to establish a different tilt on your ACTSYS to change your beliefs and align your actions with those beliefs. Think of five lifetime goals, followed by five annual goals, three professional goals, three interactive professional goals with coworkers, and three personal goals to make you happier. Constantly focus on the things you want by having a vision board and meditating. See yourself in the moment and feel how you will feel when you accomplish those goals. The best is still unwritten. My lifetime goals are that my children will serve missions, be married in the Temple, and be educated through example while howning their own individual spheres. I will be financially free at age fifty-five (I am now fifty). I will be a Mission President. I will bless lives with my authored books.

Since I've written these goals, they are all coming true. One of my goals was meeting my current wife, and she's happy and thrilled to be with me as I am in perfect health. AS I AM!

This year, I will earn twenty thousand dollars a week in income. My first book, *HOWNING YOUR SPHERE*, will be marketed and will be a best-seller. I will write the other two books to complete the trilogy, and I will be booked solid for one year on a motivational speaking tour and coaching individuals one on one. LIVE. This year, I will have a new all-wheel-drive fuel-efficient vehicle, and next year I will build my log home. I will be sealed to my current wife in the St. George Temple. I will weigh 250 pounds by April 23, 2011, and 205 pounds by June 23, 2011. I am a catalyst and a battery charger in all environments because attitude determines altitude. I AM STEAM, 212 DEGREES FAHRENHEIT.

The following poem is a wake-up call to me. I hope it helps you to go back and do what I've done on this page and then live it until you hown your sphere.

To Act or Not to Act
by
Michael E. Durgin

There are two kinds of apprehension:
The fear that we will fail in an endeavor
Or, even greater, the fact that we will
exceed in success beyond our wildest dreams.
Both can be equally paralyzing.
Like a football field,
Just put one foot forward, and the Lord
will run the other 99 yards to meet you.

Japan

It was early in the morning on April 23, 1961, when during a rain at Tachaikawa AFB, Tokyo, Japan, a loud cry rang out in the delivery room. The doctor grabbed the blood-covered infant, still connected by an umbilical cord, and handed this newborn baby boy to his mother as the father watched. "We'll name him Adam Michael," the mother said as she looked at the father with tears in her eyes. He nodded agreement with a look of confusion and anticipation at what this boy meant to this family. His firstborn was a boy, born of goodly parents.

The father had been given orders to come to Tachaikawa AFB as a military policeman. The couple were newlyweds; the mother gathered her things, and they both flew to Tokyo. Soon after arriving in Tokyo, the mother became pregnant.

There was much sorrow along with excitement as both Mary and Arthur Duncan prepared to leave their childhood home in New Hampshire to travel to the foreign country across the Pacific. Being in the military and on an American installation made the transition a little easier. Mary was an RN and had involved herself immediately in a nursing surgical technician job while Arthur was busy with responsibilities of a military nature.

This new birth of Adam would change their lives at home and professionally forever. For now, however, this was a joyous occasion. Arthur had just come home from wiping up the remains of a young soldier after a motorcycle accident. All that was left of this young man were his head in the helmet and a spread of flesh that needed to be swept up with hoses from a fire hydrant. Mary, being a nurse, had seen various trauma cases. Arthur didn't feel any discomfort during the delivery of the child and afterbirth.

Mary lay in her hospital bed as they took Adam Michael to be circumcised. This was a tradition in the family. Mary was Catholic in religious heritage, and Arthur didn't think much of religion. However, he had been circumcised, and they had agreed to circumcise the child. Mary knew when she heard Adam Michael crying distantly down the corridor that the circumcision was complete. About a half-hour lapsed before Adam Michael was returned to the mother in her room. Mary looked at Adam to see what the doctors had done. Her medical background prompted her to check the doctor's work. As she looked along with Arthur at the infant's penis, she cried out, "What have you done?" Most of the foreskin had been improperly removed. Arthur called the doctors in, and they explained that it would heal, and all was normal. Mary knew that too much foreskin had been removed, but at this point it was too late, so they'd just live with it.

After four days, Arthur, Mary, and Adam Michael were allowed to go home as a family. While Mary lay in the hospital recovering, Arthur had been at work during this day. Afterwards, as was tradition, he'd stop off at the NCO club for a few drinks and then go to the hospital to see Mary. This night was no exception except that Arthur was at the bar handing out cigars that said, "IT'S A BOY," on them. Everyone was buying him drinks, and he didn't want to refuse and hurt someone's feelings.

As he climbed in his car, he realized he was a little buzzed from the alcohol. He'd gotten to know Tachaikawa pretty well at work, and being an MP, he figured he'd be okay. He arrived at the hospital to pick up

Mary, and as he tried to get out of the car, he hit his head on the roof hard enough to make him dizzy. "Damn it!" he exclaimed.

He went to Mary's room and saw her nursing the child and leaned over to kiss her. Mary accepted and afterwards said, "Have you been drinking again?"

Arthur said, "No, I just had a few at the NCO club with the boys to celebrate."

Mary shook her head. Just then, the orderly came with a wheelchair and said, "Mrs. Duncan, are you ready to check out?" Mary sat up and handed the baby to Arthur, and he held the infant awkwardly in his oversized hands while Mary made her way to the wheelchair.

"Let's go home," she said. When they got to the car, Arthur put the baby in Mary's arms.

She said, "You're not driving us in this condition!"

Arthur immediately retorted, "I'm driving. Don't tighten my jaws!"

Mary said, "Okay, but be careful. I don't want us killed."

Weeks passed and then months. Adam Michael had a sitter while Mary worked swing shifts at the hospital. Arthur worked five days a week, eight hours a day, and usually got home around seven o'clock from the club expecting dinner to be ready when he got home. Mary had been working nights, so usually she would make dinner before she left for work. One day she was asked to work a double shift while at work, so she called the sitter and asked if she could stay. She said, "No problem, Mrs. Duncan. I can use the extra money."

When Mary got home, she was exhausted, but she knew that Arthur would be home, so she started making dinner. Chinese pie, she called it; it had three layers, corn, hamburger, and mashed potatoes on top. It was almost done when Arthur got home. He walked into the house and startled Mary at the stove. Adam Michael woke up and started crying when he heard the door slam. Arthur was drunk and came to the dinner table still in uniform. "Smells good," he said. "I'm starving!"

Mary could hardly stand up as she brought the dinner to the table. After quieting Adam Michael, she joined Arthur, who was already eating. "Where're the biscuits?" he asked.

Mary, hardly able to keep her eyes open, said, "They're almost done, honey. I had to work a double at the hospital."

"Damn it!" Arthur exclaimed. "You know I like biscuits with my dinner. I'm almost done now. Who wants biscuits when dinner's over?" Adam Michael shivered at Arthur's voice and began crying. Arthur looked at the crying baby and said, "Shut up, or I'll really give you something to cry about."

Mary said, "You don't talk to the baby like that! Why don't you go watch TV, and I'll do dishes?"

Arthur went to the fridge, grabbed another Carling Black label beer, and then went and turned on the FBI.

Mary took Adam Michael to their room and told Arthur on the way to the living room, "We're going to bed. I'm exhausted."

Arthur said, "Okay, I'll have a couple more beers and finish the show, and I'll be in."

This baby had changed their lives. Arthur pretty much did the same things as before the baby was born except sleep. As Adam Michael got older, he would cry for feeding usually at about two a.m. Mary would get up and wake Arthur. He was getting sick of it. Mary worked, kept house, cooked, cleaned, and took care of Adam Michael when she wasn't working. Mary had gotten pregnant once before; that baby was lost when Arthur came home drunk and pushed Mary violently.

The next day when Mary told Arthur what had happened, he wanted to cry. He didn't cry because that wasn't a manly thing to do, but he apologized repeatedly. Mary was angry and wouldn't accept, so Arthur left and went to the club to take the edge off. Arthur usually felt better after a few drinks. He always did this after his father would beat his mother. Adam Michael was almost two when Mary got pregnant with her second child. Mary and Arthur soon forgot what happened with the miscarriage and went on with their lives.

Arthur had his weekends off, and Mary had some leave from work, so they decided to have a picnic and go fishing. Adam Michael was two and a half years old, so Arthur got Michael a fishing pole. Arthur had a degree in fisheries and wildlife from UNH and really liked the outdoors. They arrived at the lake outside of the base, Mary heavy with child, walking hand in hand with Adam Michael, and Arthur struggling to carry the cooler full of food and beer, the fishing poles, and his tackle box. Mary spread a blanket on the ground as Arthur popped a brew and prepared the poles with bait. Arthur popped another beer and said, "Come on, Adam Michael, let me teach you how to fish." They walked down to the lake, and Arthur cast both poles out with bait and bobber. Twenty minutes passed, and nothing was biting. Adam Michael held his pole and concentrated on the bobber like his father had told him, waiting anxiously for it to move while watching gold fish go for the water bugs.

Arthur, realizing he was out of beer, set his pole down and told Adam Michael to watch the lines while he went up the embankment to get two beers—this time he wouldn't run out. Adam Michael saw his father put his pole down, so he did the same. Adam Michael wondered how the fish could swim so easily and jump out of the water to eat the water bugs. The gold fish were within reach, so Adam Michael reached for one. The bank was muddy; his foot slipped, and he went under.

Arthur came up to Mary, and Mary said, "Where's Adam Michael?"

Arthur said, "He's okay. I just came up to get a beer."

Mary looked down the hill and couldn't see Adam Michael anywhere. She told Arthur, "I don't see him."

Arthur looked and didn't see him anywhere. They looked at each other, and Arthur dropped his open beer and ran to the shoreline. He saw the footprints in the mud and bubbles coming about six feet offshore. He dove in and combed the bottom. Mary had come down to see why Arthur dove in. Just then, Arthur surfaced with Adam Michael. He was blue in the face, and Mary panicked. Arthur administered CPR for drowning victims. Soon Adam Michael choked up water and began crying as his color slowly approached normal. Mary grabbed Adam Michael, and Arthur hugged Mary, all three of them crying. It was a close call. Adam Michael should have died. The gold fish were so tempting, and Adam Michael was left alone while his Dad went to get beer. They felt very fortunate.

On September 8th, 1963, a brother was born for Adam Michael to goodly parents. "We'll name him James," Arthur said with tears in his eyes. This baby looked just like Arthur. Adam Michael was almost three now. After the family had gotten used to the new member, they decided to throw a birthday party for Adam Michael. Adam Michael spent many a day at the neighbor's house. A friendly Japanese gentleman had befriended Adam Michael and often let him come over when the sitter would allow. The man had spider monkeys that Adam Michael loved to play with. He was bored with the sitter and missed his mom and dad. This day, April 23, 1964, was a special day, special enough for Arthur to come home at five thirty—he skipped the NCO club because he knew he had beer at home, and this party was important to Mary. Mary was home already.

When Arthur walked in, he asked, "Where's Adam Michael?"

The sitter said, "He's next door playing with the monkeys."

Mary explained, "Over there again with those filthy animals."

"I'll get him!" Arthur said.

This party was very special, for Mary had baked a marble cake with chocolate frosting and had ice cream and party hats for all Adam Michael's friends, and there were presents. After singing "Happy Birthday" to Adam Michael, all the children had cake and ice cream, and then it was time to open presents.

Mary asked, "Where's Adam Michael?"

One little girl said, "He's on the porch with Renee."

"I'll get him," Arthur replied as he reached in the fridge for another beer.

Mary went out to the porch and saw Adam Michael kissing Renee. She grabbed her camera and took a picture. Mary explained what she'd seen, and Arthur rolled his eyes, spun his right finger, and exclaimed, "Whoopee!"

One year passed, and James was getting bigger. Mary was now pregnant with a third child. She hoped it would be a girl. Life was hectic for Mary, Arthur, and their two boys. On September 24, 1965, a third child was born in Japan at Tachaikawa AFB, and they named her Marie. During this time, Arthur received orders to come back overseas to Charleston, West Virginia, and continue his education to become an OSI agent. Preparations were made as Mary put her notice in at the hospital and began to pack things for the military movers. Prior to being given the OK to move, Adam Michael, James, and Marie were required to have physicals. All the children were assumed to be healthy; however, Adam Michael had developed a rash on his neck that week. The doctor said it was a rare parasite that would have to be treated with salve and antibiotics. This condition, they later found, was from the spider monkeys Adam Michael had befriended.

This delayed their plans as Adam Michael was under quarantine for one month during treatment. Arthur's orders were changed, and he was quite upset—but it was nothing a few drinks couldn't fix. Eventually, Adam Michael healed, and with the other children being given a clean bill of health, the Duncan's made ready to leave Japan and go back to the states. Mary and Arthur were having marital troubles during this time as Arthur had begun drinking heavily and on occasion would hit Mary or the children. Mary had decided without telling Arthur that she would take Adam Michael, James, and Marie and go to her mother's in Laconia, New Hampshire, as soon as they'd arrive stateside. Arthur knew nothing of this plan; he thought everything was fine with their marriage. After all, he'd always been sorry. He always apologized and promised it wouldn't happen again.

When they arrived in Patterson AFB in California, Mary told Arthur that it would be best if she and the three children went to Meme and Pepe's in Laconia while he went to Charleston and made arrangements to buy a mobile home and got it moved and set up. Mary said she would then fly back to join him. Arthur didn't think too long before he realized he needed a break: no kids or nagging wife for a couple of weeks. So, he okayed the deal, and they went their separate ways. Arthur waved goodbye to his family as they flew **off on the D.C.-10 to Manchester, New Hampshire, and decided to fly to Charleston, West Virginia. On his way to** temporary housing, he stopped off for a few drinks at Patterson's NCO club and went home to prepare to leave.

The Separation

Mary arrived in Manchester and was greeted by her mother and her sister June. They soon went up Interstate 93 by Weirs Beach at Lake Winnipesaukee and were in Laconia in about an hour.

After bringing the baggage in, Uncle Peter and Uncle Eddie, who was home on military leave, showed Mary and her children their rooms. The house was beautiful, a large green colonial with a two-car garage and finished floors. Mary looked into the room where she had found her father fourteen years before with his stomach blown against the wall by a self-inflicted shotgun wound. A tear came to her eye. She looked away as Remy, her stepfather, asked her how she was doing and invited her into the kitchen for some coffee.

Mary sat down with her mother and father and began to tell them about all that had happened since the delay with Adam Michael's skin condition. She told them she might have to stay a while and look for a place since things weren't working out with Arthur. The drinking and the physical abuse were getting in the way of progress with family, and the children were being affected. Mary's mother said, "You must go back and try again with Arthur. This isn't good for the children." Mary cried, and Remy got up and took Adam Michael, James, and Marie out to the yard with a blanket, so they wouldn't see their mother crying. Peter, Mary's stepbrother, brought out a camera and took some pictures of the children out on the lawn on a blanket.

After about two hours of conversation, Mary came out and called Peter to bring the children in for lunch. Adam Michael and Peter were beating Eddie and James at badminton while Marie, too young to play, watched intently. Lunch was delicious as Meme had prepared lasagna. Adam Michael ate three plates, and Meme exclaimed, "Adam, you're going to be very big someday if you keep eating like that!" She began talking to Mary in French as they would always do when they got together. Adam Michael was used to hearing Canadian French slang and cursing by Mary when he'd do something wrong. He couldn't understand, but he knew what she meant. This was far better than the beatings he received from his father with a belt whenever anyone of the children did something wrong because, in Arthur's words, he was the oldest and should have known better.

Adam Michael and James were asked by Uncle Eddie, "Would you boys like to see the train set I played with when I was a boy?" Unanimous was the decision, and they went into the basement. Mary, Meme, and Remy (Pepe, as the children called him) sat down to play cribbage. Halfway into the first game, Mary counted, "Fifteen one, fifteen two, fifteen three, and six is nine." As she moved her pegs in the board, the phone rang. It was Arthur calling to see if Mary and the children had made it safely. He was in St. Albans, West Virginia.

Catholic Obedience

Mary was handed the phone, and she knew it was Arthur by the look of concern on Meme's face. Mary didn't have anything to say, but after the eye was given by Meme, she said, "Hello, Arthur, how're things?"

Arthur said, "I've found a used trailer on a lot in a trailer park that we can buy within our budget. Of course, you'll have to get a job at a local hospital for us to make ends meet. What do you think?"

Mary couldn't believe what she was hearing. Arthur sounded like nothing was wrong. Mary, sounding a little irritated, said, "Arthur, you haven't apologized for your behavior during Adam Michael's sickness. Furthermore, I will not be banged around anymore during your drunken episodes!"

Arthur explained, "Honey, I told you I was under stress and that it wouldn't happen again. What more can I say or do?"

Mary thought for a moment and said, "Okay, Arthur, but we'll stay here a few weeks while you get settled and the military movers move us in."

Arthur said, "I miss you and the kids, and I need your signature on the lease and on the deed for the trailer. Won't you just get here as soon as possible?"

Mary was softening, and Meme smiled when Mary finally gave in and said, "Arthur, I love you and miss you, too. We'll be there in a few days."

Arthur said, "Great, now let me talk to the kids."

Adam Michael and James were in the basement playing with trains, and Marie cried because they wouldn't let her play. Mary yelled downstairs, "Your father's on the phone!"

James and Marie turned and ran up the stairs, yelling, "Yay, Daddy!" Adam Michael was sick of his father, so he stubbornly remained and watched the toy train going into the tunnel. Mary came downstairs while James and Marie took turns on the phone.

Arthur asked them, "Are you having fun at Meme's?" They said they were and that they loved and missed their daddy.

Mary said, "Adam Michael, don't you want to talk to your daddy?"

Adam Michael said, "No."

Mary got angry and said, "You get upstairs and say hello to your father!"

Adam Michael reluctantly obeyed. As he went upstairs, he thought of the welts on his bottom and legs that still hurt from the night Dad had come home drunk. He got on the phone and said, "Hi, Dad."

Arthur asked, "What took you so long? Don't you love Daddy anymore?"

Adam Michael said, "You hurt us and Mommy."

Arthur said, "Daddy's sorry, Adam. He's been under a lot of stress lately. I tell you what: when you get here, I'll take you and James fishing. Your birthday's coming up, and I have a special surprise for you, okay?"

Adam Michael replied, "Okay."

"Now let me talk to your mother," Arthur demanded. When she returned, he said, "Mary, I'll see you and the kids when you get here, okay? And I love you."

"I love you, too," Mary said. "Goodbye."

Mary looked embarrassed as she hung up the phone, but Meme smiled. "Do what's best for the children and go back to Arthur and make a go at it. You've been under a lot of stress lately. Here, have a scotch and relax," Meme explained, filling a jigger of scotch.

The day came when Mary and the kids had to leave and go to Charleston, West Virginia, from the Manchester Airport. Goodbyes and good lucks were exchanged along with hugs and kisses as the Duncans boarded a twin-engine Cessna to fly to Logan Airport in Boston, Massachusetts, where they would connect on United Airlines Flight 368 on a D.C.-10 to fly to a military air strip in Charleston. James and Marie sat quietly and slept most of the flight. Adam Michael threw up on the way to Boston in turbulent skies, and Mary took care of him. Adam Michael was very nervous about seeing his father again; though he would only be four years old in three days' time, Adam Michael had seen much dysfunction in his parent's relationship and was quite scared of seeing his father.

They finally arrived in Charleston, and the family was reunited. Arthur was very happy to see them. They all drove to St. Albans, West Virginia, to move into their new trailer. Upon arrival, Adam Michael saw the blue military car in the driveway and knew this was home.

Mary exclaimed, "This is nice! Arthur, this town reminds me of Laconia."

Arthur said, "Yes, and there is a nursery school and kindergarten just three miles away where the kids can go while we're at work."

Mary went to work immediately, unloading boxes and organizing shelves and cabinets, while Arthur prepared to go to TDY (a military term for "travel duty"). Adam Michael and James went out in the yard to play. Off in the distance, Adam Michael could see a creek and woods. This was different than Japan; it was kind of like Meme's backyard. Adam Michael knew he'd get in trouble if he left the yard, so he and James began exploring underneath the trailer. Just then, Adam Michael heard water running or dripping. He turned to ask James if he'd heard it.

James looked surprised when Adam Michael turned, for he was peeing in his pants. Adam Michael brought James in the house, where his father was getting ready to leave and his mom was in the cabinets.

Adam Michael told his mom, "Mommy, James peed his pants while we were under the trailer outside."

His father stopped, dropped his briefcase, grabbed Adam Michael by the wrist, and gave him a whipping with an open hand. With each whack came more advice. "You should have brought him IN if he needed to go pee! DON'T you know better than to GO under the trailer? You're old enough to KNOW better!"

Mary told Arthur to stop; Marie was crying in her crib. Arthur gave Adam Michael a dirty look, stomped out the door, jumped in his blue government car, and drove off. He'd be gone for five days to Maryland, they were told.

The next day, everyone got up for breakfast. The house was different with Arthur gone; everyone was happy except for Adam Michael. He couldn't sit down because the bruises on his bottom hurt, so he sat down on the couch and ate his breakfast on the coffee table. Mary got Marie and James ready for nursery school and Adam Michael ready for his first day of kindergarten. They got in the car and drove into St. Albans.

Soon, Mary stopped in front of a church and said, "Come on, kids, let's go."

Adam Michael was out first; Marie and James waited for their mom to remove their seatbelts. James and Marie were left in a gymnasium full of children. Mary consoled James and Marie, "You kids be good. Mommy loves you, and she'll be back after work to pick you up." Adam Michael and his mom said goodbye.

Mary then took Adam Michael, rushed back to the car, and took off to take Adam Michael to kindergarten, not worrying about seat belts. When they stopped in front of a large Victorian house, Mary said, "This is the place. Let's go and meet your teacher. Then Mommy has to go to work."

They walked up to the door. An elderly lady opened the front door, winked at Mary, and said, "You must be Adam Michael."

"You're going to have lots of fun here and learn with other children to get ready for the first grade in a year," Mary told him. "Thank you, Mrs. Parr. Bye, Adam Michael." Mary walked back to the car and took off for work; she was late.

Mary had almost become a Catholic nun until she met Arthur and decided to get married instead. She had earned an associate degree in nursing, which helped her get a job as an operating room technician. Arthur's military income was $12,000 a year with a housing allowance, so they decided they would have to work to maintain their lifestyle.

Adam Michael liked Mrs. Parr and enjoyed working on grocery-bag turkeys stuffed with shredded newspaper and construction-paper tail feathers. He still had a problem sitting because his butt was hurt badly from his daddy's whipping. Mrs. Parr was big on discipline. Adam Michael was told by his dad not to discuss anything that happened in his house with people outside the house or "THERE WOULD BE MORE WHERE THAT CAME FROM." So, Adam Michael tried to switch cheeks. Most of the damage was on the right side; because his dad was right-handed, he had to lift him with his left wrist to inflict more direct hits with no resistance. Adam Michael had learned to start crying before the pain—this usually made the beatings shorter in duration.

Mary finally came to pick Adam Michael up; it had seemed like such a long day. When she drove up with James and Marie in the backseat, Mrs. Parr said, "Goodbye, Adam. See you tomorrow!"

Adam Michael ran out and hopped in the car, and his mom sped off towards home. "How was your first day?" Mary asked.

Adam Michael said, "It was fun, but I had trouble sitting down."

Mary looked at him and said, "Oh, you'll get used to it. We'll go home and have beans and franks, okay?"

James and Marie looked at each other, and Adam Michael said, "Okay."

For the next four days, things went pretty much the same except Adam Michael's pain disappeared. On the fourth day, while the children were having breakfast, their mom explained, "Your daddy will be home today, and it is Adam Michael's birthday, so we'll be having a cake."

James and Marie said, "Yay!" Adam Michael felt scared that his dad was coming home, for he was tired of being beaten, but he didn't want his mom to be mad at him, so he said, "That's great, Mom!"

That evening, the twenty-third of April, the kids came home with their mom and saw their dad's blue government car in the driveway. James and Marie said, "Look, Mom, Daddy's home!"

"Yeah, and I bet he's got something for Adam Michael's birthday," Mary said.

Arthur was out in the driveway. When he saw Mary pulling in with the kids, he opened the trunk of the blue government car and pulled out a big box wrapped in paper with baseballs all over it and topped with a ribbon.

"I wonder what's in there," Mary said.

"Hello, kids, did you miss me?" Arthur asked.

James and Marie ran up to hug their daddy while Adam Michael waited in line. He really didn't feel like hugging his dad because he still felt the pain from before his dad left. "Adam Michael, you ready for cake and ice cream and presents?" Arthur asked him.

"Yes," Adam Michael said. They went inside, and Mary pulled the cake out of the fridge and the ice cream out of the freezer. She then opened the drawer, pulled out four small candles, stuck them in the cake, and lit them. "Make a wish and blow them all out, and you'll get your wish," Mary explained.

Adam Michael wished that his father would stop drinking and hitting him and his brother and sister. Especially, he wished that his mom would not be hit any more.

The Siamese cat that Mary had brought from Japan was playing in the paper and ribbon, and Arthur kicked it down the hallway. "Frigging cat," he said, and Marie began crying.

Mary asked, "Who wants cake and ice cream?"

Everyone forgot about the cat and said, "I do, I do!"

The party ended, and all went to bed. The next morning, they all got up to go to work and school. Arthur left on his bus before any of the family awoke. When Mary and the kids came out to get in the car, James said, "Isn't that Bingo?"

Mary looked and saw her cat crushed by double tires on the pavement. "You kids get in the car!" Mary cried as she grabbed a shovel out of the shed and scraped her cat's remains into the storm sewer. Arthur's bus must have run over Bingo. Adam Michael cried and asked his mom if Bingo was dead.

"Yes, Adam Michael, Bingo's in heaven."

"Cats go to heaven?" James asked.

"Yes," Mary said.

Well, you have learned from the forbidden fruit in the first chapter's fictional autobiography that something is lost when real-life testimony is not shared in the first-person perspective. I want you to know that what follows is a commandment of the Lord and that I do have a testimony of the Gospel of Jesus Christ and its restoration through the prophet Joseph Smith and the First Vision in New York in that sacred grove. Heavenly Father and Jesus Christ appeared together for the first time to man and helped us to understand the Godhead. I know that The Book of

Mormon is true, revealed scripture that has come from people upon this continent through their experiences with spiritual things and visitations. Christ was here on earth in the Americas, and He called disciples after His resurrection.

I know that Thomas S. Monson is our prophet today here on this earth and that I wrote this while President Hinckley was the prophet. He died in his nineties. There are great men upon this earth who have sacrificed their lives and paid nearly a one-hundred-percent tithe. They are called General Authorities. They sacrifice their time, money, and talents for the building up of the kingdom of God upon the earth, and I hope one day to do the same. The purpose for writing this work is as follows:

The little flowers that grow upon the lava in Hawaii grow on the rock. I may have not been the best soil in the beginning for planting of Gospel principles. I hope that my conversion will help others to come unto Christ. The Lord has a plan for your life. The forbidden fruit had to be partaken of, so you could prove yourself and exercise your own will and agency to see if you would return home better than when you left.

Like that flower that grows on that lava with so little nutrients, that seed clings to life and will grow with nourishment. I liken myself to this plant. I have grown wonderfully in the Gospel of Jesus Christ.

The Book of Mormon, 3 Nephi 23:9-11 states, "How be it that ye have not written this thing, that many saints did arise and appear unto many and did minister unto them." This speaks of the many saints who came forth from the grave following the Savior's resurrection. His atoning sacrifice and subsequent resurrection provided a way for us to overcome the grave. I am grateful that, with my family, I can live in an exalted state with Heavenly Father and his Son, Jesus Christ, and the Holy Ghost. You may find yourself wondering how to reconcile what happened back then into my life today.

The Book of Mormon, 3 Nephi 23:9-11 states, "How be it that ye have not written this thing, that many saints did arise and appear unto many and did minister unto them." This speaks of the many saints who came forth from the grave following the Savior's resurrection. His atoning sacrifice and subsequent resurrection provided a way for us to overcome the grave. I am grateful that, with my family, I can live in an exalted state with Heavenly Father and his Son, Jesus Christ, and the Holy Ghost. You may find yourself wondering how to reconcile what happened back then into my life today.

The Book of Mormon, 3 Nephi 23:9-11 states, "How be it that ye have not written this thing, that many saints did arise and appear unto many and did minister unto them." This speaks of the many saints who came forth from the grave following the Savior's resurrection. His atoning sacrifice and subsequent resurrection provided a way for us to overcome the grave. I am grateful that, with my family, I can live in an exalted state with Heavenly Father and his Son, Jesus Christ, and the Holy Ghost. You may find yourself wondering how to reconcile what happened back then into my life today.

The Book of Mormon, 3 Nephi 23:9-11 states, "How be it that ye have not written this thing, that many saints did arise and appear unto many and did minister unto them." This speaks of the many saints who came forth from the grave following the Savior's resurrection. His atoning sacrifice and subsequent resurrection provided a way for us to overcome the grave. I am grateful that, with my family, I can live in an exalted state with Heavenly Father and his Son, Jesus Christ, and the Holy Ghost. You may find yourself wondering how to reconcile what happened back then into my life today.

This obviously requires repetition. Remember that reiteration overcomes doubt and solidifies communication from deity.

Try to figure out what these true events have to do with us today. Is there any hope? I never read scriptures when I was Catholic. A whole new world was revealed to me as I likened the real-life experiences of people in the past to my life. The actual medium and timeframe disappeared when I realized that God and His Son Jesus Christ were speaking to me about my circumstances and that wisdom and happiness could be found by learning the path to happiness in this life from others in the past, as well as what happens when you choose to live contrary to revealed truths and principles. Universally, actions and consequences remain similar throughout history. Remember the Lord and be happy or forget him and be miserable. You have a choice, don't you?

In the Book of Mormon, 3 Nephi 10:14, after the Savior's death, many prophecies were fulfilled. Nephi writes, "And now, whoso readeth, let him understand; he that hath the scriptures, let him search them, and see and behold if all these deaths and destructions by fire, and by smoke, and by tempests, and by whirlwinds, and by the opening of the earth to receive them, and all these things are not unto the fulfilling of the prophecies of many of the holy prophets."

By raising your voice in prayer and song and by reading the scriptures with the discernment of the Holy Ghost, which allows for communication and proper fitting interpretation, you may learn the wisdom of those who already know the relationship between earth-life, death, and life hereafter. The mysteries of Christ are contained in the books which have been revealed especially: the King James version of the Bible, translated in crucial spots by Joseph Smith; The Book of Mormon; The Pearl of Great Price; and The Doctrine and Covenants.

You may have the truth of all things by reading The Book of Mormon. If you haven't picked it up, read it, and prayed about it, then I've wasted my ink. Again, start now! Read it, pray about its truth, and call the missionaries from The Church of Jesus Christ of Latter-Day

Saints. They're in the phone book, so do it. If you're a member and you think you know all there is to know and have a testimony, think again. Pick it up, read it, and pray alone and with your family. Share it with your friends and help others to come unto Christ and be sealed for time and all eternity in the covenant of the everlasting priesthood, which only exists with Christ's power and authority in this church and in this church alone. I had a minister from Baltimore tell me the other day that that was a bold statement, and I asked him if he'd read the book I gave him. Read The Book of Mormon now.

I wrote this narrative essay at Littleton High School in 1979. This will shed light on deception:

It was a beautiful, sunny, hot summer day in Saint Albans, West Virginia, at eight thirty in the morning as the dew was evaporating. Some of my friends and I decided, as we had before, to go into the field with our glass jars and lids with breather holes to pick up rocks and throw them at our ultimate conquest, the flying grasshoppers. The purpose of our day was to see which one of us could daze the most grasshoppers in between flights and put them in a jar. Very accurate throws were required as these beasts were only two inches long and would fly away if you got too close. I was winning as I had jarred three grasshoppers before my friends had gotten any. My confidence grew. Then out of the side of my eye, I spotted the ultimate prize, a monstrous three-and-one-half-inch-long army green king grasshopper. I yelled to my friends, but I was worried that if I yelled too loud, my ultimate prize would fly away. My friends couldn't hear me. Just then, the king grasshopper flew away under an old rotted platform. The three grasshoppers that were prisoner paled and became insignificant compared to the visualization of the king grasshopper in the jar. So, I released my advantage on my friends, the three locusts, and went after the largest grasshopper I had ever seen. Like a lion after its prey, I snuck up stealthily on the deck. I could hear them underneath. I thought to myself, *I won't even need a rock for this one!* I could just reach under and grab him. So, I reached under there and grabbed a large mass of what I thought was my king grasshopper. I later found out that I had done nothing more than irritate a large nest of mud wasps. The pain was immediate. The sun was in my eyes as I turned to run. I could hear them swarming above my head, and the stings were multiple. By the time I reached my trailer where I lived, it seemed like I had run miles. The wasps were imbedded in my skin and had perished from my adrenalin and blood flow.

The King Grasshopper and his soldiers had won the battle, but I was in the war of my life due to the multiple stings, twenty-six to be exact and the poison that had been injected in me by the wasps.

Fortunately, the doctor said that if I survived this, I wouldn't be allergic to bee stings again. My competitive nature would prove to be a blessing and a curse throughout my life. I was so busy trying to win a competition that I had created in my own mind. The temptation of the king grasshopper wouldn't have existed without the urgency of winning a competition that only I was aware of. The king grasshopper, instead of being the captured victim, became the victor.

Coincidence?

Well, you've heard about the king grasshopper and some of the things I did as a boy while being raised Catholic. I was an altar boy in West Virginia, the youngest in my archdiocese to be confirmed a member with a confirmed name of Paul, which is interesting because my patriarchal blessing in the Church of Jesus Christ of Latter Day Saints revealed that I was from the tribe of Benjamin. If you know about Paul, who was Saul of Tarsus, you know he was also a Benjamite. I've always thought that it was a really neat "coincidence." I have been talking to you about one of the reasons why I keep wanting to write this book, to benefit my family. I thought at first of a personal journal about the experiences I had planned to keep sacred. The commandment has come through prayer to reveal all these things as a convert to the church to give you a different perspective, without all the meat that I'm learning about now, such as: the parable of the fig tree and some of the great things in Jeremiah, Revelations, St. John, Matthew, and Mark.

I met Brother Kawasaki in line at a restaurant in Orem. We struck up a conversation, and he said he'd be interested in publishing my book. I just knew it wasn't coincidence. Last night the SPIRIT spoke through a family member, saying, "You need to write this book. It's the most important thing right now." So, I am going to sacrifice the time. I want to publish this before my birthday, April 23, 2011. Now, let's go back to the recurring dream.

I had many of those when I was young. I'm forty-nine years old now, but back at the time of the king grasshopper, I had this recurring dream that I could fly. I had wings and would get up momentum like a plane, running and flapping my wings. Just when I was ready to leave the world and fly off in the sky, these hands would grab me, hold me, and pull me back to earth. The frustration that I felt, I still feel today—that feeling of wanting to fly away and go to another place. That is the result of where we came from in the pre-existence, and when I interpret this dream, I believe it's the draw of earthly things that keeps us from flying off and experiencing spiritual things. I'm grateful for all I've suffered that I'm going to share with you. The adversities have helped me to have greater spiritual experiences. I pray for the Spirit of the Lord Jesus Christ to be with me in these proceedings, that His words may be my words and that I may do no injustice to him and that this may bless many lives. My opinions are not to be misconstrued as the opinions or doctrines of the church; these are mine alone. One of my goals is to be a full-time mission president, and to do that, I must be financially stable, hence this book.

I remember that my dad received a phone call once in West Virginia. He was an OSI agent in the Air Force. He was very secretive; he didn't talk very much and liked to have a drink at the NCO club on occasion. He received this phone call and started crying. I had never seen my father cry. He'd found out that his mother had just died. My dad did end up going to Vietnam and participated in cross-lines espionage in Laos and Cambodia. He went shortly after he found out about his mother's death. I remember suffering a lot of emotional abuse. My dad used to say, "You think I'm bad! My dad was a real prick."

One time I was so upset, my dad said, "If you're mad at me, hit me." I didn't want to hit my dad because he was so big. All of a sudden, I got up the gumption, and I just closed my eyes and swung. I hit my dad in the nose and broke it. I was just a little seven-year-old kid. He yelled, "Pat, look at what your son's done to me!" He gave me all kinds of emotional abuse after that. "You're not getting anything from me." That was one of my childhood memories.

After my dad came back from Vietnam, we moved back to Bowling Air Force Base in Washington, D.C. I ended up going to school in an eighty-five-percent black Catholic school in the southeast part of town on Fourth and Martin Luther King Avenue in Suitland, the homicide capital of the world. My mother worked at Cafritz General Hospital, and they dealt with the most homicides of any hospital in the world. So, I was living in this unfamiliar place after moving from rural West Virginia to the inner city in D.C. We had a lot of experiences there. Dad had just returned from Vietnam, and he wasn't himself. He was someone else. A lot of men died in Vietnam. I believe my father died there as well.

A big flood called Hurricane Agnes blew in. We were living on the Potomac river, and everyone was evacuated. We were able to return to our trailer as the waters receded from National Airport, which is now Ronald Reagan Airport. We used to go down to the river fishing. We'd catch white perch and all kinds of stuff in this nasty, polluted river, which has since been renewed and is now one of the best bass-fishing rivers in the world. Even the most polluted river can be renewed, becoming something new. I liken that unto me. As my life became more and more polluted, I started to stop it up, and when the flood receded, I found renewal through the gospel of Jesus Christ and through all these experiences.

We went down there fishing this one day with Kevin, my brother, and Taigue, who was a marine's son. My brother went to Boy Scout summer camp with him. We went down to the river, and they found this little wooden boat that had floated ashore in the flood. My brother and Taigue got in it even though I told them not to because it would sink. This river, you understand, is unpredictable. It's about half a mile wide, in front of the National Airport and across from Bowling Air Force base. There were white caps on the river from the wind, and we just had one of the worst floods in the history of the east coast, and here, my brother and Taigue decided to go out on this boat. Of course, I ended up getting blamed and beaten for it. The tide pulled them into the middle of the river, and I freaked out. I ran to the boat dock and talked to this guy. He called the National Guard, who came out and rescued them from the middle of the river with a helicopter before they capsized and died. It was an unforgettable experience. My dad showed up in his blue government car with yellow lettering. He'd just returned from TDY and was in his uniform. He proceeded to hit me, telling what a bad brother I was for letting Kevin do that. I always got blamed for things Kevin did. When he was a little kid, I used to take the blame for his peeing his pants. Life is interesting.

That was after dad had gotten back from Vietnam and would drink a little too much. My mom found that he was having affairs with other women, and I never doubted that I have brothers and sisters in Vietnam that are half-Vietnamese. He was two years away from home, with no gospel standards, coping with the war. War is hard; it's hard to see someone you love dead. He was debriefed and couldn't share very much, but he had a lot of friends die over there, and he saw a lot of brutal torture.

He came home one night, a holiday. Since it was just Thanksgiving the other day, here in Utah, I was reminded of one Thanksgiving in Washington, D.C., when my dad came home, and my mom had made this beautiful meal, but the biscuits weren't ready. My dad would always complain about what was wrong, and he was never grateful for what was right. I don't think I ever heard him thank my mom for anything; he just expected her to do all these things. I've tried to change that with my children.

He had come home from the NCO club. Thanksgiving dinner was on the table, and the biscuits weren't ready. That's all it took. My father ripped the door off the refrigerator and threw it through the bay window. I was just a kid when that happened, but ever since, I've never complained when something wasn't ready on time for dinner. It's weird how we learn, isn't it?

Yesterday, I got a pair of bifocals and had to accept the fact that I needed glasses to see, read, and drive. I notice that when I'm looking far off, I have to look at one part of the lens, and when I'm looking close to read, I have to look down into another part of the lens. I think the seer stones that the prophet uses are like the glasses. You have spiritual eyes and physical eyes; you can actually use them for both. You have to choose to look up, and you have to choose to look down. You need a bi-focus in your life, and you can have these experiences. I'm not sure why I've had so many of them—probably because the Lord knew I would write them down.

So, during Thanksgiving dinner, my father, home from Vietnam with post-traumatic stress disorder, rips the refrigerator door off and throws it out of the bay window of the mobile home. You've got to wonder what the reason for that was. As parents, we do and say things we regret.

I know why I turned down an appointment to the Air Force Academy: I didn't want to go to war because of what it did to my father. I know that war has a purpose, that the military has a responsibility to protect the good. I think that a lot of times, war is money-motivated. There were a lot of things that went on in Vietnam. I can't talk about them because it would probably get me arrested. My dad was debriefed when he came back, and sometimes he would tell me things. I've met a lot of Vietnam vets who have told me the government wasn't there for just one reason. Like everything else, there's always corruption, always ulterior motives, and that's all I'll say about that.

I'm having a hard time getting back to this, but this was the time I saw my father come home from the NCO club and drag my mom. My parents had separated, and he dragged my mother down the hallway, separated her shoulder, and raped her. She called his commanding officer, and of course, he had just broken a general's jaw at the officer's club. My dad was out of control with post-traumatic stress disorder.

My mom decided to get a divorce, and we left in our pajamas one night. We went to a hotel, and I remember telling my mom that I would take care of us. I remember looking in the backseat and seeing the faces of my little brother and two sisters. They weren't saying a whole lot. Of course, my mom was in the middle of what looked like the beginning of a nervous breakdown, and I was the oldest son. We had a lot of difficulties when we moved into the Meadows of Newgate in Centreville, Virginia.

Now, Centreville is a thriving place and has a big skate center. That's where I met one of my best friends in my life, this black guy named Clifford. We were playing football in between the townhouses, and he grabbed me by the back of my shirt and swung me around, causing me to hit my head on an electric post. I called him every name in the book except the one he expected because I don't use the word. I was raised in the inner city in D.C., and I believe the word is used by ignorant white people. None of us has the right on this earth to look down our snouts on any other race or act like we're better because this is a manifestation of our own insecurities. We're all children under heaven, and I think it's sad to continue teaching our families to be prejudiced against people who are different than us. Clifford and I became really good friends. Later on, he ended up dying in a racing accident. The last time I saw him was on my eighteenth birthday when I came home from Virginia Tech. We did everything together; we used to ride ten-speeds together, we played football together, and we went to Chantilly High School together. I still consider him to be my best friend, and I miss him.

My mom eventually took a job up in New Hampshire. We went up there to high school in Littleton, and a lot of things happened there. I was an All-State football player in New Hampshire. I met a guy, Scotty, whom I looked up to. He was an exceptional athlete, and he ended up going to Keene State University. He was home on break with Carol when he flipped backwards out of her convertible, broke his neck, and died.

That was one of the first spiritual experiences that I had besides the recurring dream: Scotty visiting me in a dream and telling me he was okay. Years later, I went to Littleton and told his brother Kim about the dream, but I'm not sure he understood. I dreamt Scotty visited me, and I wasn't a member of the Church of Jesus Christ of Latter Day Saints yet.

Years passed, and I moved back to New Hampshire. One night, I was at the Silver Bullet in Franklin, New Hampshire, which is where my dad was born and raised. I was driving home intoxicated on the interstate in fog, ice, and snow. I was in my Nissan four-wheel-drive, and I fell asleep, went off the road, and took out all these guard rails. I went airborne about three hundred yards and hit the side of a mountain down in this gorge. I was wearing my black leather biker jacket and dressed as a kung fu master because it was Halloween. That night, a guy had walked into the bar with a KKK outfit and a cross. This was in New Hampshire where there is no KKK. I lost it because I felt bad and beat this guy with his cross; that's why I was kicked out of the place, ended up driving, and had this accident.

I looked up from the gorge and wondered why my truck wouldn't move in four-wheel drive. That's when I noticed the rear-end axle and tires hanging in the guard rail wire. I walked away from the accident, went up unto the interstate, and hitchhiked. It was two a.m. in fog and ice and some girl picked me up and brought me to Tilton, New Hampshire, which is where my aunt and uncle live, closer to the Robies. There I called Uncle Ray. Ray died this last month of emphysema from smoking cigarettes. He had a tumor and some other problems, so he follows my father into the spirit world. I'm hoping I can do his work like I did my dad's. I'm going tangentially through these experiences without going into too much detail because I want to focus on the good things—I'm just trying to give you some background as to what led me to have the kind of life and conversion I have.

That accident totaled my truck. Things weren't going well for me. I moved back to Virginia. I'm going through my timeline in chronological order because I want to share these experiences with you. My brother stabbed this guy on the metro train and was facing murder charges; "Murder on the Metro" was the headline. TV cameras filled my mother's front yard. He killed Frank, and that messed me up, but not as much as it messed him up. He's still suffering for it, and he can't forgive himself. He's lost a couple of families over it. I actually had custody of his son for seven years. This was a life changing experience for all of us. I was at this party one night where we were all doing coke, and there was a girl who had a seizure. Everybody said she was going to die. I ended up saving her life with CPR. I realized afterwards that not only had I saved her life, but I had almost taken her life. That was one of my first turning points when I realized I needed to change.

It was shortly thereafter that I was in Maryland and saw a guy die in a car accident. His head was hanging in the windshield, and I could see his brains coming out of his eye sockets. I wondered, *What is this life all about? Is it a matter of these traumatic things happening to us, and then we leave this earth? There's got to be a better way to live.* We obviously didn't know that better way yet, but I started thinking there had to be something better.

Then one of my partners from Ireland, with whom I owned a house, embezzled an insurance company to buy a Trans Am. He was actually my girlfriend's cousin, and he owed me a lot of money for our townhouse. His father, who owned a company, had cut him off, and he lost his mind. One night, he came up, and we got into a fight. He ran down and got a twelve-inch survival knife, came back upstairs, and started slashing. I had forty-two stitches in my leg and twenty-seven in my wrist, and he cut my pinky finger open. I took the knife from him and ran outside. He went to prison for five years for malicious wounding. A lot of positive things have happened in my life, too; I'm just going through the ones that led to my spiritual experiences.

In 1992, I hit a tree head-on going seventy miles an hour, airborne in a Buick Regal. That was my first out-of-body experience; I saw myself in the car and wondered where I was. It felt really good. I was in between life and death because of the way I had lived my life. I was sent back immediately. I just experienced the separation; I didn't have any ornate experiences, but I spent six months in the hospital in traction on morphine, looking out the window and wondering if I'd ever see the light of day again. I had a lot of time to reflect. I was very angry, very upset, and that was what had driven me in football when I was young. I had gone back in 1989 and played football with Acadia University in Wolfeville, Nova Scotia. I played football in New Hampshire in high school and played one year at Virginia Tech.

After I left the hospital from that accident, I went to live at my mom's in Virginia Beach. She was in the church, trying to be a missionary. Now I'm trying to be a missionary to her because I've been to the Temple and married twice. My first wife died, and I'll talk to you about that later. Now, I'm trying to go to the Temple with my mother. She actually had a knee replacement this week and had a priesthood blessing. So that accident was life-changing for me and very humbling. I was very angry. I made a mistake. I knew something had to change.

I found out that my mother's father had committed suicide; that she had found him when she was seven years old; and that her mom blamed her for not calling her at work. Her dad was suicidal because he'd had an affair and was excommunicated from the Catholic church. Then I found out about my dad. He had a brutal upbringing. His dad was an alcoholic, and his mom died of cancer. His dad beat his mom all the time. At this point, I started to understand more of why my life was so messed up by my parents; they were coping the best they could with what they had. I didn't make the best decisions myself, either. I think that's the bottom line. I want to blame other people for what I do wrong when the blame is on me. In 1993, I had another accident, and I hit a lawyer's son and broke his arm running a red light. I had a federal judge in Norfolk, Virginia, as an attorney, and the police captain's son Mike was a friend a mine. They came and bailed me out. I had so many DUIs not on record. There was the DUI of 1994 where I just got pulled over in my truck for having a light out—I didn't have an accident that time, fortunately.

Let's go back in time to 1983. I was in a court room facing 160 years in prison for drug charges. I had sold some cocaine to a state narcotics agent, and that wasn't pretty. It was a really ugly situation, another life changing moment. After that DUI in 1994, I ended up going to my friend, Jack, in Virginia Beach. I stopped by a store and picked up a couple of warm pies. I knocked on his door and asked, "How do you do it?"

He said, "Those were the most expensive pies I've ever eaten."

I started going to AA meetings with him, and he was my sponsor. At all times we're supposed to be anonymous, but big deal. I'm not anonymous. I'm writing this book, and I'm grateful to the program. The first year, I worked those twelve steps and ended up sharing my fourth step with my sponsor, whom I was hanging out with, and I didn't even know he was gay. He was my eighth-grade teacher.

Conversion

In Norfolk, my sister had sent the missionaries to my warehouse down on Twenty-Sixth and Llewelyn. It was a bad neighborhood, full of prostitutes, crack, my Rottweilers, and my baseball bat and surrounded by Constantine wire. My life had deteriorated to a certain point, and I decided to give up. I said a prayer one night in the warehouse. "Lord, if You're there, show Yourself unto me."

And you, whomever is reading this book, I want you to know at that moment, an unseen force moved my arm, and I picked up a dusty Book of Mormon that my sister had sent me off the headboard of my bed. I read it cover to cover in seven days. I started talking to the missionaries. I moved to my sister's, put all my stuff in storage, and was going to AA meetings. It was time for a change. How many things had to happen to me before I was willing to change? How many things have to happen to you before you are willing to change? How many things do you have to suffer before you actually decide you are sick and tired?

And there were these church elders: Elder Davis from California and Elder Peterson from Illinois. We played basketball together. I was driving my one-ton truck one Sunday. At the time, I was living with my little sister Angie in Virginia Beach. I was cruising in my big four-wheel-drive with my long, curly hair and bib overalls when for the first time, I heard a voice say, "Go in there."

I looked around my truck. "Who's in here?"

"Go in there," I was told three times. I looked at a building and went in.

It was a Sunday, and I guess church was letting out. There was a Bishop and some missionaries, and I started talking to them. I don't know what I said, but they called me golden, and they pulled me into a room and started teaching me. They were Elders Davis and Peterson. Awesome things started happening in my life. I was going through something that I believe started when I was in that warehouse. I still had my free agency, but I had given my control over to the Lord and asked Him to help me. The elders invited me to a youth fireside, and while I was there I met Kree L. Koford, a seventy-year-old man who sat with me and taught me how to write using the spoke-and-wheel system they learned as General Authorities. I wasn't even baptized yet; they wouldn't let me get baptized. I met Mission President Hamula, who is in the First Quorum of the Seventy right now. I met Stake President McGill, who was from Detroit. I met Stake President Michael Roucher and his parents; his dad was the D.C. Temple President. All these people wanted to meet me because they'd heard my story. I started having these awesome spiritual experiences, and I told them about my past and how I came into the church.

President Hamula said, "Brother Durgin, you must have been really valiant in the pre-existence."

I didn't really know what that meant, but I do now. President McGill said he was from Detroit, was familiar with gangs, and had a lot of problems when he was a kid. We had similar backgrounds. Michael Roucher's father was the Temple president, and they were in my wife Paula's ward when she was a little girl. President Roucher was the one who ended up sealing us for time and all eternity in the Washington, D.C. Temple. For those who are not members, that means being married beyond this life, not just "till death do us part." Kree L. Koford saw me standing in the lobby at a youth conference, looked beyond the crowd, and walked straight to me. The Spirit must have led him to me because we had a good conversation. I've had many non-chance meetings with different general authorities since then, and I know the Lord leads me to these spiritual men through service. Like with my glasses, I must be tuned in and be looking through the right lens. It's nice to be able to see both, to do the best you can in this world, and to realize that everything has spiritual blessings or consequences. Everything that is physical is spiritual. You have to look through both lenses simultaneously, which can make things seem blurry if you're not used to doing that. My first testimony meeting, I went into the church building. I had not yet been baptized; they wouldn't allow me to be baptized because I had a DUI I was appealing.

My attorney was a Greek guy, Spanoulos, in Virginia Beach. He was friends with the federal judge, and he couldn't get me off—for the first time in my life. I had to plead guilty in order to get baptized, so I pled guilty to a DUI and spent my whole first year with a suspended license, going to AA meetings and living up on a mountain that I'll tell you about later, way up in Bluemont, Virginia.

My first testimony meeting in Hamilton Ward was amazing. I walked in and saw this lady blubbering. I wasn't a church member, and I thought *What is this?* I just knew I'd be hit by lightning when I walked through the door. There was a lady upfront crying. *Where's the priest?* I wondered. I was Catholic, and you can imagine what it feels like to go from one church to another and not understand what you are doing. I was sitting in the pew when I got shoved from behind. I thought it was my brother-in-law, Steve. So, I looked under the seat and slid to the end of the pew so that no one could do that again. When I got shoved in the back again, I looked around, and nobody was there. Then I was shoved a third time. This was weird. Somebody in spirit was shoving me, and then they put their arms under my arms and picked me up and walked me up to the podium. I wasn't even a member! I spoke for twenty minutes about parents, children, obedience, and the detriments to the kind of life I led. It was really weird, and I guess I took up the whole testimony meeting. The members came up and asked, "Brother, what's your name?" to which I answered, "I'm not your brother." I didn't understand.

They call each other brothers and sisters. They said, "That was a fantastic testimony."

"What's a testimony?" I asked. I didn't even know what I had done; the Spirit took me up there.

Then my sister invited me up to their house. She took me up to the D.C. Temple. This was life-changing for me. In addition to the voice I had heard that called me into the church at Virginia Beach, the missionaries had gotten to me. My sister, Sharon, worked for years sending the missionaries to me. I never wanted to talk to them, just like I hadn't wanted to talk to my mom when she tried to be a missionary after my accident. I wasn't ready yet. When the student is ready, the teacher will appear. I was finally ready.

I went up to the D.C. Temple to see the lights in Kensington, Maryland. The lights were beautiful, and there were all these pretty little sister missionaries. Of course, I was thirty-four years old, single, going to AA meetings, and I walked in there and looked up at these *creche* scenes, which is French for "manger scenes." We saw Christmas tree decorations from all around the world, decorated in the fashion of different countries and various traditions. We had these pretty little missionary girls showing us around, and I was thinking to myself, *I could have me one of those missionary girls.* Little did I know that I was going to have one later on! But that night was special. Looking at the lights, I walked up the hill thinking of this one pretty girl that I saw. At that moment, my feet were frozen to the sidewalk. I could not move, and I felt all that voltage go through my body, a power that I had never felt before. I looked to my left. It was dusk. It was as if the whole place lit up, and I saw the leaves churn like a tornado up off the lawn. They came towards me like this vortex, this little funnel, and hit my body. I saw the leaves fall, and a voice said, "Let Satan out, and let Me in." As you could imagine, I couldn't breathe. I couldn't walk. I think the student was ready. I looked to my right, and the same thing happened, except the leaves swirled in the opposite direction. The same funnel came towards me and hit my body. As the leaves fell, I heard the message again: "Let Satan out, and let Me in." I was losing it; I was totally lost in some other dimension. I looked up and saw the Moroni statue at the top of the temple, and I couldn't breathe. I couldn't believe this was happening to me, and it happened three times. This vortex of leaves, this tornado, just as it had come, it had gone.

I went to my sister and said, "Sharon, you wouldn't believe what has just happened to me."

After I related all that had happened, she said, "Oh yeah, that'll happen."

So, I had this awesome experience, and I knew then that I was going in the right direction. No matter what, I was in the right place. I want you to know that this is the right place, The Church of Jesus Christ of Latter-Day Saints, and the priesthood is restored. Joseph Smith, as a boy, had the same experience that I had. His was for everyone, and this one was just for me—I want you to know that this does happen. I want you to know that these things do happen. The Church is true. The Book of Mormon is true. You need to read it. We need to read The Doctrine and Covenants every day. Read it, learn it, and you, too, can have these experiences. Your spiritual eyes will open. I leave you this testimony that Jesus Christ lives, that not only did He die on the cross for us, but He lives and that all these people live, people we can't see spiritually. They talk to us. I will continue with baptism and confirmation on our next meeting. I leave you with these things on this date, Sunday, December 9, here in Orem, Utah, where I am now writing this book. This is Michael Durgin, a grateful convert, signing out on another chapter of my life.

Progressing

I'm picking it up here on December sixteenth. This is an important part of the book: my baptism. I'd finally gotten approval from President Hamula, the D.C. South Mission President, to be baptized and take care of my problem. I remember the dreams I had prior to my baptism, where I was reminded of so many things that I had done wrong, from which I would wake up crying. I would wake up feeling bad, feeling guilty. It was a part of my process of being able to be baptized. At the actual ceremony, Elder Harrison baptized me. He taught me how to tie my tie. I could only do it on one side, and he showed me a double Windsor. The confirmation was performed by my brother-in-law Steve. I received the priesthood. I remember what a great day this was. I was worthy to bless the sacrament and serve it. I remember the day I received the Melchizedek priesthood. Prior to that, I was learning about the authority of the Lord on earth, who administered the same power that Jesus Christ had when he healed the lame, made the blind to see, and healed the lepers. We have that power on the earth today. We have that authority, which is important because there are a lot of powers on earth, but only by the authority of the Melchizedek priesthood can we pronounce blessings in the name of Jesus Christ.

Then, I was preparing to have my patriarchal blessing. The day I was given the Melchizedek priesthood, I was in the bishop's office. Afterwards, I felt this impression that I was coming home. The Ozzy

Osbourne song rang in my head. Believe it or not, there was an Ozzy Osbourne song called, "Mama, I'm Coming Home." It was the weirdest thing I'd ever experienced. When I received the priesthood that day, I felt that I moved that much closer to returning from where I came. A couple of weeks later, I was getting ready to get my patriarchal blessing from Patriarch Jenkins, in his townhouse in Leesburg. I had this vision during my patriarchal blessing of my family. Today, nearly thirteen years later, many of them are here. There is one on the other side of the veil, my wife who has passed away. My wife has since died, but in my vision, I saw more children than I have now. I don't know if I'll have them in this life or the next. I found out I was in the tribe of Benjamin. I wanted to know why everyone else was from Ephraim. I had met a Levite from New Jersey who was Brother Abraham's wife. Where Brother Abraham was in the tribe of Zebulon and I was Benjamin, most people are Ephraim. There are twelve different tribes of Israel, and Judah is one. Basically, there are some members that are Manassah. I thought I'd be Manassah because I have Native American heritage. I found out about Benjamin's blessings and why I receive messages the way I do, like Saul of Tarsus and Alma in the Book of Mormon. Saul became the apostle. These were exciting times. I was in the young men's organization and doing young men's activities. My whole life had turned around. I was living in Purcellville, Virginia, and going to Hamilton Ward. My brother-in-law, sister, their kids, and I were living in a converted chicken coop. I went to get my endowments at the D.C. Temple to make covenants with the Lord. I was still single. We were living in the chicken coop, and prior to getting my endowment, we went to Palmyra for the pageant.

We had been up all night replacing a motor in the car we drove. My brother-in-law Steve and I drove the Valiant that we had put the motor in all the way to northern New York. We got up there that night. I had a suspended license because of the issue I had before I got baptized.

When we arrived in Palmyra, I really wasn't supposed to drive. We were so tired. We couldn't find our camping place or a hotel that had room, so we ended up sleeping in the Joseph Smith Farm parking lot, where it says when you drive in, "No parking at night." I had nightmares all night about mobs beating the windshield in with clubs. I didn't sleep well with my legs hitting the steering wheel.

I even drove that night. I was supposed to only drive to work and back, but you do what you have to do. We were getting ready to die because everybody was passing out. I ended up driving the last leg of the trip. The next morning at the break of dawn, a bus pulled up next to the Joseph Smith Farm. All these missionaries got out, and I decided to follow them. They went down this trail, over a little bridge into what I found out later was the sacred grove. I had a memorable experience in the sacred grove with the missionaries. I listened to the mission president talk; this was no coincidence.

We came home, and I went to the D.C. Temple in Kensington, Maryland, and received my endowment on April sixth. That was a great day. I had my Temple recommend. I was still single, but it wasn't too long after that I met Paula Barlow. Everyone was trying to hook us up, including the bishopric. She had just wrecked her car and was getting ready to go to another singles ward in Alexandria, Virginia. We were in the Hamilton Ward, a family ward in Virginia. She came up on the mountain to get her car fixed, and it seemed like we always got to meet each other in different circumstances. Neither of us admitted that we wanted to be with the other person. The bishop ended up sending Debbie, Paula, and me up to Kirtland, Ohio, for a Zion's conference. Elder Hartman Rector, Jr. was there. We went up to the Kirtland Temple for a tour and ended up having a choir. There was a dance for later. Our choir was singing "The Spirit of God." We went into the Kirtland Temple and sang while having a sacrament meeting. As we sang, the angels were all circling us, appearing in pastel colors and carrying long brass horns. Our choir wasn't really that good, but in there, we sounded like the Mormon Tabernacle Choir. It was as if thousands of people were singing. "The Spirit of God Like a Fire Is Burning" was part of the dedication of the Kirtland Temple in the 1800s.

That night there was a dance. I say Paula fell for me at the Whitney store because she was holding onto my arm when we were doing the tour of Kirtland. We came out the Whitney store, and she fell on the stone steps. She had heels on and bruised herself. I was trying to run away from her because there were a couple of other girls whom I was going to dance with that night. Instead of going to the dance, I ended up putting ice on Paula's bruises. She lay on the couch while I knelt down in the hallway.

The first time we met was at the Annandale Stake Center, we were going for a singles' conference, and I was a gentleman. I opened doors and got her a drink and a cookie. We were with some other friends who were in the church. Demetrius (somebody I'll tell you about later) and I were with Liz and going to the Annandale Stake Center to this get-together. I ended up being nice to Paula, and my hand ended up on her leg. I was new in the church, and I didn't mean to put my hand on her leg—someone else was doing it. She said the moment my hand hit her leg, she had an out-of-body experience. She was outside of the car looking in, and the Lord told her that I could teach her a lot about the gospel. It was really odd because neither of us felt like we wanted to be with each other, and then we ended up in several different circumstances. Up there in Kirtland that night when I was putting ice on her bruises, I ended up proposing, and she accepted. Then we set a date and came back to Virginia. We ended up being sealed for time and all eternity in the D.C. Temple by President Roucher, a friend of Paula's dad. He sealed us for time and all eternity, as opposed to a worldly marriage of "till death do us part." We believe that when you get married in the temple, it's sealed on earth and in Heaven and that you stay together beyond this earth life. It was really a great experience making those covenants. We moved to a little branch in Harper's Ferry, West Virginia.

I had a construction company called Top Notch Construction company. An investigator, Eddie, was a musician and a friend of Jack, whom I will talk about later. Jack, from Virginia Beach, was actually from Maryland, and he had an interesting experience there in West Virginia. I had five callings in that little branch.

We ended up leaving there with Bishop Grow telling us that we would be the last yellow dog with the tail wagging if we left. I really didn't understand what the bishop meant. We ended up meeting with the bishop in the temple and doing his family file. Everything was made right. I had people accusing me of going against the brethren, even the elder's quorum president. I couldn't believe it!

I was a new member and didn't even know what they were talking about. I was going to Independence, Missouri, because the Lord had told me to go. I had a circumstance before we left. We came out of one of the temple rooms, and I saw this lady running up the stairs towards the Holy of Holies and disappearing. I'll tell you later on in this work who that lady was and who she became.

"Did you see her?" I asked Paula.

"I didn't see anything."

It was similar to when I received revelation in the Residence Marriot on our honeymoon to go to Independence, Missouri. Someone was talking to me in the dark inside the Residence Marriot in Bethesda, Maryland. "Go to Missouri," they repeated three times. Paula didn't hear a thing. Later on, Paula had dreams and visions of the earth receiving its paradisiacal glory after Christ's reign. She saw all kinds of neat things. She saw our oldest son Isaiah being a lion. Interestingly, he's a Leo by his birth sign. I don't put a whole lot of weight into that stuff, but it's interesting just the same. We were in the Residence Marriot on our honeymoon, reading lectures on faith by Joseph Smith. The book was compiled in Kirtland, Ohio. I went to Missouri first, and Paula came a month after in the Bronco. I suffered huge losses in Virginia. I came home one night, and Elsie, my Rottweiler I'd had since Norfolk, Virginia, was dead. I found her outside on the sidewalk with blood coming out of her mouth. Someone had given her meat with antifreeze in it. Eddie had been possessed to sabotage my transmission line, so we couldn't leave.

We then went to Missouri without knowing a soul and without having jobs. I called President Wood. He was a Secret Service agent and bodyguard to five US Presidents, but I didn't know that then. Because he was the stake president, I called him to find out where we could find a place to live. He hooked us up with the Thiemes. We stayed with them when we arrived in Independence. I ended up meeting President Medina while moving a road show stage. Bishop Morgan had told me to get a job to heed to council and authority because I had been working for myself.

One night, I was reluctantly returning the stage that we had borrowed for a church youth play we'd done. I was supposed to be somewhere else. I got this tap on the shoulder and met President Medina, who's now the stake president in Independence, Missouri, as well as an executive at Hallmark. That night, I didn't know who he was, and I didn't know he was in the stake presidency, but I ended up doing a bunch of work at his house and getting to know him fairly well.

We stayed outside one night with shovels and a chain saw cutting roots out of the way just, so I could replace his main water shut-off. I re-piped his whole house and did some remodeling. President Medina became a friend of mine, and I learned a lot from him while I was in the Stake Young Men's Presidency. After I served in three YM presidencies, we went to summer camp together at Camp Naish. I was on the fast track for leadership in the church. Ultimately, I had some things happen that I'll talk to you about later, like the mobs in Kirtland; I had some resistance, and some bad things happened. I ended up working with public affairs, doing some great things with leaders in the church. It seemed like every time I was going to do good, something really bad happened. As I go further into my story, you'll understand that a lot of that goes on in these sacred places, especially Independence, Missouri!

My wife Paula is buried there in Independence, Missouri. She passed away suddenly. The trials and tribulations that destroyed my business, the people there, and my hardships there led me originally to title this book *Not Yet as Job*. I read that at Liberty jail. I thought, with all the things I've been through, I could understand Joseph Smith. I have since redirected my life to focus on positive recovery, discovery, and empowerment and hence changed the title to *Howning your Sphere*.

I want to leave you this testimony. I know that Jesus Christ lives, and He guides us. He guided me to write this book. I will continue to put it together for your benefit and my healing. From the perspective of a missionary, I, like Ammon and Enos, have come into the church. This work is beneficial to members and non-members alike. I was in the Elders' Quorum today and shared a story with them about retention. Individuals in the Church were talking about missionary work, and I said, "Retention is the biggest challenge right now because so many things of the world are creeping into the church." Divorce and pornography run rampant, and fewer and fewer young men are worthy to go on missions. With women outnumbering men in the congregation, there are not enough righteous priesthood holders. All these things were foretold in the scriptures.

Not Yet as Job

This is the most tangential book you have ever read; and although there are many feathers in my quill, I'll discuss that later. The Spirit has moved me to go into Job's section of the Bible. Later on, we'll discuss how this carried into Doctrine and Covenants Section 121, and that will probably be the conclusion on this subject. I have a lot of material to cover between now and then.

When I first joined the church, my brother said, "You're just like Job; you're so righteous. Just wait." I remember Satan speaking through my brother's body at what I call the tarring and feathering at Independence. I was beaten by the police there. I called 9-1-1 and was mistaken as the perpetrator. It says in Job chapter 1, "Job a just a perfect man is blessed with great riches. His property and children are destroyed and yet he praises and blesses the Lord." I'm sure we are responsible for some of our demise. Maybe it isn't good to be too righteous. I don't know how you feel about that. This was written by Job but sometimes in the perspective of someone else. I guess, like Joseph in Liberty Jail, this is the hard part to understand. How can we be doing so well, yet everybody blames us for making mistakes when the refiner's fire is lit? That's the only reason we can have these things happen to us. I believe that we do a lot of this to ourselves. Others hold us accountable; however, your demise is not entirely your own.

Sometimes, as in Job's days, "Job was one of the greatest men of the east" (Job 1:3). "He offered burnt offerings," in verse 5, "according to the number of them all. For Job said it may be that my sons have sinned and cursed God in their hearts, thus did Job continually." Verses 6-10 continue, "Now there was a day when the sons of God came to present themselves before the Lord and Satan came also among them."

Verses 7 and 8 read as follows: "And the Lord said unto Satan, Whence comest thou? Then Satan answered the Lord, and said, from going to and fro in the earth, and from walking up and down it. And the Lord said, Satan, hast thou considered my servant Job, that there is none like him in the earth, a perfect and an upright man, one that feareth God, and is eschewed evil? Then Satan answered the Lord, and said, Doth Job fear God for naught? Hast not thou made a hedge about him, and about his house, and about all that he hath on every side? Thou hast blessed the work of his hands, and his substance has increased in the land."

Satan was telling the Lord that Job was protected by the Lord, and that's why he was so righteous. During your mortal probation, you've been through the same thing—and you're protected, you're blessed, you're increased, and then all of a sudden, things start to unravel.

I marked four or five different things that happened to Job. In verse 14, "There came a messenger unto Job." The oxen were plowing and the asses feeding beside them. Verse 15 says, "The Sabeans fell upon them and took them away, and the oxen. And they had slain the servants by the edge of the sword." This was the beginning.

This is the second thing that happens in the first chapter of Job: "And I only am escaped alone to tell thee. While he was yet speaking, there came also another and said, The fire of God has fallen from heaven and hath burned up the sheep, And the servants, and consumed them; and I only am escaped alone to tell thee."

Same as the previous servant: "While he was speaking, there came also another, and said, The Chaldeans made out three bands and fell upon the camels, and have carried them away, Yea, and slain the servants with the edge of the sword; And I only am escaped alone to tell thee."

See, there was always only one person left to come tell him; Job was seeing everything destroyed in front of him, and my life's been the same.

"While he was yet speaking, there came also another and said, Thy sons and thy daughters were eating and drinking wine in their eldest brother's house. And behold there came a great wind from the wilderness, and smote the four corners of the house, and it fell upon the young men, and they are dead; and I only am escaped alone to tell thee" (verse 19).

Again, just one person survived.

"Then Job arose, and rent his mantle, and shaved his head, and fell down upon the ground, and worshipped."

He was humbled, and I'm not sure I could've handled this as well as he did. Job has unconditional love for the Lord. I think about the staphylococcus infection. I almost lost my leg five years ago before my wife Paula died. I am reminded of verses? in chapter 2 about boils: "Satan obtains leave from the Lord to afflict Job physically. He is smitten with boils. Eliphaz, Bildad, and Zophar come to comfort him. Listening to this is Satan the second time, and again there was a day when the sons of God came to present themselves and Satan came also among them to present himself before the Lord. And the Lord said unto Satan, from whence comest thou, and Satan answered the Lord, and said, from going to and fro in the earth and from walking up and down in it. And the Lord said unto Satan, Hast thou considered my servant Job, that there is none like him in the earth, a perfect and upright man, one that feareth God and eschewed evil? And still he holdeth fast his integrity, although thou movest me against him, to destroy him without cause. And he took him a potsherd to scrape himself and he sat down among the ashes."

"Then said his wife unto him, Dost thou still retain thine integrity? Curse God and die. But he said unto her, Thou speakest as one of the foolish women speaketh. What? Shall we receive good at the hand of God, and shall we receive evil? In all this did not Job sin with his lips."

Now when Job's three friends heard of all this evil that was to come upon him, and they came, everyone from his own place. You're going to find out about them later.

"Eliphaz the Temanite, and Bildad the Shuhite, and Zophar the Naamathite: for they had made an appointment together to come to mourn with him and to comfort him. And when they lifted up their eyes afar off, and knew him not, they lifted up their voice, and wept; and they rent everyone his mantle, and sprinkled dust upon their heads toward heaven. Job curses the day and services of his birth."

In Job asks, "Why died I not from the womb?"

REAL friends I have not is how I feel since my wife's death. "Why died I not from the womb?" I've questioned some of the things I've suffered. "With kings and counselors of the earth which build desolate places for themselves; who rebuilt mins." This is me. There is a whole section in chapter 3 that you want to read about the sorrow and questions. I had sorrow when I had my car wreck in 1992, resulting in a fractured pelvis and dislocated hip, putting me in traction for almost six months.

I wondered, like in Job 3:23, "Why is light given to man whose way is hid, and whom God hath hedged in?" It is good. This is why my biography was called *Not Yet as Job*. Job 3:20 reads, "Wherefore is light given to him that is in misery, and life unto the bitter in soul; which long for death, but it cometh not; and dig for it more than for hid treasures; I was not in safety, neither had I rest, neither was I quiet; yet trouble came."

He's wondering why this has happened to him. Wouldn't you?

"Eliphaz reproves Job. Is not this thy fear, thy confidence, thy hope, and the uprightness of thy ways?"

See, He's telling him what's wrong with him, which is what everyone has done to me, freaks. In Job 4:8, Eliphaz says, "Even as I have seen, they that plough iniquity, and sew wickedness, reap the same."

Here I get confirmation of the roaring lion in the experience on the West Virginia border that I will tell you about on the Appalachian Trailhead. Job 4:10 talks about "the roaring of the lion, and the voice of the fierce lion, and the teeth of the young lions, are broken. The old lion perishes for lack of prey, and the stout lion's whelps are scattered abroad."

The lion is Satan, the adversary. "How much less in them that dwell in houses of clay, whose foundation is in the dust, which are crushed before the moth, (verse 19) they are destroyed from morning to evening: they perish forever without regarding it. Doth not their excellency which is in them go away? They die, even without wisdom."

That's what the adversary does. The key is not to give up. Job chapter 5 continues, "I would seek unto God, and unto God would I commit my cause: which doeth great things and unsearchable; marvelous things without number: He disappointed the devices of the crafty, so that their hands cannot perform their enterprise" (verse 12).

And here's the pride of it in verses 13 and 14: "He taketh the wise in their own craftiness: and the counsel of the forward is carried headlong, they meet with darkness in the daytime and grope in the noon day as in the night." Verse 17 implores, "Behold, happy is the man whom God correcteth…despise not thou the chastening of the Almighty."

"Remember, despise not chastisement, for chastisement is the spirit of truth," Brigham Young says it in his priesthood manual. In Job 5:23, we see, "the beasts of the field shall be at peace with thee." This is important for you to know the Lord.

Verse 18 explains, "He maketh sore, and bindeth up: he wounded, and his hands make whole." I'm going to go to verses 18-27; I can't help it, this is awesome! "He shall deliver thee in six troubles: yea, in seven there shall no evil touch thee. In famine He shall redeem thee from death: and in war from the power of the sword."

"When I was stabbed I should have been killed. Instead I disarmed the perpetrator and fled."

"Thou shalt be hid from the scourge of the tongue: neither shalt thou be afraid of destruction when it cometh."

I walked in danger surrounded by weapons and I had none, no fear of death.

"At destruction and famine, thou shalt laugh: neither thou shalt be afraid of the beasts of the earth." Like the lion on the trail. Are you getting this? You need to read the Bible here, folks. Listen to this! You know the Book of Mormon is great, awesome revealed scripture, but the Bible is important, too—there's a lot in here!

"For thou shalt be in league with the stones of the field:" (The white stone) "and the beasts of the field shall be at peace with thee. And thou shalt know that thy tabernacle shall be in peace; and thou shalt visit thy habitation and shalt not sin. Thou shalt know also that thy seed shall be great, and thine offspring as the grass of the earth." This sounds like the promise made to Abraham, the sands of the earth.

"Thou shalt come to thy grace in a full age, like as a shock of corn cometh in his season. Lo this, we have searched it, so it is; hear it, and know thou it for thy good." That's faith!

In chapter 6, exclaims, "The things that my soul refused to touch are as my sorrowful meat. Oh, that I might have my request; and that God would grant me the thing that I long for! Even that it would please God to destroy me; that he would let loose his hand and cut me off!" I feel like that when I'm suffering. "Deliver me from the enemies' hand or redeem me from the hand of the mighty." Both Joseph Smith and I had this same experience in the sacred grove.

While writhing in pain on the ground, Joseph Smith said, "Deliver me from mine enemy." Oh, boy! Does that say a lot?

In Job 6:24, urges, "Teach me and I will hold my tongue, and cause me to understand where in I have erred." Remember, you can't exercise the priesthood in anger or confuse the mantle of the bishop.

"How forcible are right words! But what doth your arguing reprove; Do ye imagine to reprove words, and the speeches of one that is desperate, which are as wind? Yea, ye overwhelm the fatherless, and ye dig a pit for your friend. (chapter 7) …Why does thou not pardon my transgression so that my soul choseth strangling, and death rather than my life? (verse 15 and 20) I have sinned; what shall I do unto thee, oh thou preserver of men? Why has thou sent me as a mark against thee, so that I am a burden to myself?"

Here's an analogy. On Job 8:14 reads, "Whose hope shall be cut off, and whose trust shall be a spider's web?" I'm going to talk about the spider's web analogy later.

In chapter 9, says, "We cannot contend against him." That's Satan—remember, he was right up there with the Lord. We do have power, though, as verse says: "His roots are wrapped about the heap and seeth the place of stones" like an altar.

I'll tell you more about the white stone up on the Appalachian Trail in the near future. "We cannot contend against him," him being Satan, but we can "if He will contend with him, he cannot answer him one of a thousand." Just don't blame God when the adversary is having a field day on you!

Job 9:11 reads, "Lo, he goeth by me, and I see him not: he passeth on also, but I perceive him not." It's like grief, why me?

"Behold, he taketh away, who can hinder him? Who will say unto him, what doest thou?" Why me? You know, you're grieving. Job is grieving here, and this is Satan doing all of this, not God.

When you're grieving, you go through three stages: shock, anger/blame, and sorrow. I went through it, and so will you. Job is weary of life in chapter 10. He expostulates in verse 15, "If I be wicked, woe unto me; and if I be righteous, yet will I not lift up my head. I am full of confusion."

Again, Satan, not God, "Thou renewest thy witnesses against me, and increasest thine indignation upon me; changes and war are against me. Wherefore then hast thou brought me forth out of the womb? Oh, that I had given up the ghost and no eye had seen me." Job's not too happy here. He's mad at God. In verse 6 of chapter 11, his friend accuses him, "God exacteth of thee less than thine iniquity deserveth." He's telling Job that it is his fault because of iniquity, just like my friends told me. My father-in-law asked me, "Is this working for you?" Basically, he was saying that everything in your life is your fault.

Obviously, things were not working well for me at that time. When you grieve a loss like that, things don't usually work very well. Sometimes you've just got to get through it because, as ____ says, "Thou shalt forget thy misery and remember it as waters that pass away." That's where I am now.

Listen to this: "Also thou shalt lie down, and none shall make thee afraid; yea, many shall make suit unto thee. But the eyes of the wicked shall fail, and they shall not escape, and their hope shall be as the giving up of the ghost. I am not inferior to you" (Job 12: __) This is when his friends are giving him heck. The Lord is in control. " I a m not inferior unto you (Chapter 13) Do not control with me (Verse 19) Who is he that will plead with me? For now, if I hold my tongue, I shall give up the ghost." Job is contending with the Lord.

In chapter 14, "Job testifies of the shortness of life, the certainty of death, and the guarantee of a resurrection... The Lord's call to come forth from the grave." Yes, I'm looking forward to the resurrection. Verse 13 reads, "That thou wouldest appoint me a set time, and remember me!" The word "remember" is written 118 times in the Book of Mormon, and there's a reason for that.

In chapter 15, "Eliphaz sets forth the disquietude of wicked men." All his friends are giving him ideas here. Wait until you hear the end!

"What knowest thou, that we know not? What understandest thou, which is not in us?" Basically, it's a testimony that we know. Verse 31 reads, "Let not him that is deceived trust in vanity: for vanity shall be recompense." That's the pride and money you see a lot of here. (verse 9 chapter 16)

In Job 16:9, Job refers to Satan: "Mine enemy sharpened his eyes upon me." Remember, I said my demise is not entirely my own. Verse 17 continues, "Not for any injustice in mine hands: also, my prayer is ours."

Chapter 17 reads, "The Righteous also shall hold on his way, and he that hath clean hands shall be stronger and stronger. But as for you all, do ye return, and come now: for I cannot find one vise man among you." This is Job talking to his friends.

"Bildad tells of the damned state of the wicked." Of course, you know, here he goes again. "Wherefore are we counted as beasts and reputed vile in your sight?" Judge not lest ye be judged. "Surely such are the dwellings of the wicked, and this is the place of him who knoweth not God." So Bildad is talking to Job. "Job tells of the ills that have befallen him.

In chapter 19, Job proclaims, "I know that my redeemer liveth." He still has a testimony. In verse 14, he refers to fair-weather friends: "My kinsfolk failed, and my familiar friends have forgotten Me." I know all about that; that's what happens when you go through tribulation. Sometimes, there are friends who want to help you; you just don't know how to let them help you because you're grieving. "They that dwell in my house, and my maids, count me for a stranger: I am an alien in their site. I called my servant, and he gave me no answer; I entreated him with my mouth." See, fair-weather friends forget you pretty quickly, don't they?

(Chapter 19 verses 14,17,18) "My breath is strange to my wife." Oh boy! "Though I entreated for the children's sake of mine own body. Yea, young children despised me; I arose and they spake against me." This is Independence all the way. You, down there in Independence, listen to me because I'll tell you what you are suffering.

"Oh, that my words were now written! Oh, that they were printed in a book!" (Job 19:23). This is my reason for waiting this book. Okay? So now they're written twice, both in the Bible and in my book. This is my reason: "That they were graven with an iron pen and lead in the rock forever! For I know that my Redeemer liveth." I have a testimony of Jesus Christ. (Chapter 20) "Zophar shows the state and portion of the wicked. The triumphing of the wicked is short, and the joy of the hypocrite but for a moment." So, he's telling Job that he's just like all my friends. "The heavens shall reveal his iniquity; and the earth shall rise up against him. (Verse27 chapter20) The increase of his house shall depart, and his good shall flow away in the day of his wrath. This is the portion of a wicked man from God, and the heritage appointed unto him by God."

Sometimes, good men suffer. It's not that we're bad when we're going through this. Stop judging each other, and learn to love each other because, like reads, "There, if not by the grace of God, go I." I'm going to do very well in life now. I am ready for the restoration, just like Job. (Chapter 21) "Behold I know your thoughts, and the devices which ye wrongfully imagine against me." I thought about that a lot when my father-in-law asked, "Is this working for you now?" Anyway, back to Job.

"How then comfort ye me in vain, seeing in your answers there remained falsehood?" There's false doctrine. (Chapter 23 verses 15-17) "Therefore, am I troubled at His Presence: when I consider, I am afraid of Him. For God maketh my heart soft, and the Almighty troubleth me: because I was not cut off before the darkness, neither hath he covered the darkness from my face."

You'd be afraid, too, if you went through what we went through. (Chapter 26) "He divideth the sea with His power, and by His understanding, He smiteth through the proud, my lips shall not speak wickedness, nor my tongue utter deceit." Job is still righteous; righteousness endures, and "will not let it go, (Verse 6) My heart shall not reproach me as long as I live," (Chapter 28). This is the white stone.

"But where shall wisdom be found? And where is the place of understanding?" Man knoweth not the price experience I had with the white stone. (Verses 20-21) "Whence then cometh wisdom? And where is the place of understanding?"

I've seen wisdom when I experienced that white stone. I've seen the Celestial kingdom, and I want everyone to know it. It's not pride; it's here, right around us. It's a matter of being in that frame of mind, that meditation when you can be shown these things if it's the Lord's will and if you're looking for it. You've only to ask. Ask, believe, receive; that's how it works. Then in verse 21: "Seeing it is hid from the eyes of all living and kept close from the fouls of the air (Verse 28) and unto man behold the fear of the Lord, that is wisdom; and to depart from evil is understanding."

Reverence, that's the trail where I heard the lion's roar. In chapter 29, "Job recalls his former prosperity and greatness. He was blessed because of his righteousness, his charity, and his good deeds." I've helped a lot of people, but I've suffered also. Stop judging that when you suffer you're doing something wrong. Sometimes you're not. In verse 12, Job says,

"Because I delivered the poor that cried, and the fatherless, and him that had none to help him." He continues in verses 15-16, "I was eyes to the blind, and feet was I to the lame. I was a father to the poor: and the cause which I knew not, I searched out." This is Independence missionary work.

In verse 21, Job says, "Unto me men gave ear, and waited, and kept silence at my counsel. After my words they spake not again; and my speech dropped upon them. And they waited for me as for the rain; and they opened their mouth wide as for the latter rain." These are fair-weather friends and acquaintances. Verses 9-11 read, "And now am I their song, yea, I am there by word. They abhor me, they flee far from me, and spare not to spit in my face. Because He hath loosed my cord, and afflicted me, they have also let loose the bridal before me that was Satan. What did I do to deserve this? (Chapter 31) if I had walked from vanity, or if my foot hath hasted to deceit; let me be weighed in an even balance, that God may know mine integrity." This is what happened to me in A-1 Master Services in Kansas City.

"Then let mine arm fall from my shoulder blade." This is charity. You cannot worship the money; you need the money to help and bless people. Don't worship it. (Verse 39) "If I have eaten the fruits thereof without money or have caused the owners thereof to lose their life, let thistles grow instead of wheat and cockle instead of barley. The words of Job are ended." (verse 40 Chapter 31).

In chapter 32, another friend, amen, "Elihu in anger answers Job and his three friends-he says: there is a spirit in man, and the inspiration of the almighty gives understanding; also, great men are not always wise." He's got that right—there are a lot of these guys. A lot of people think they're wise, but they really don't know a lot. You try to tell them, and they're just not ready to hear it.

"But there is a spirit in man: and the inspiration of the Almighty giveth them understanding. Great men are not always wise: neither do the aged understand judgment." The mouths of babes! Remember that children sometimes give us the most. Remember when the Savior said, "Suffer the children that they come unto me." I may do a poor job of paraphrasing, but I'm feeling the Spirit as I write.

Verses 21-22 read, "Let me not, I pray you, accept any man's person, neither let me give flattering titles unto man. For I know not to give flattering titles; in so doing my maker would soon take me away." My father taught me that we all put our underwear on one leg at a time. We're all the same. He said, "Don't ever bow down to any man," and I never will.

Chapter 23 tells us, "Elihu says: God is greater than man. He speaks to man in dreams and visions." I've had them; I know He does, and there's hope for you. You just have to turn it around and do what the Lord tells you to do. The gospel is on the earth; if you spread it and are anxiously engaged in a good cause. It says in Doctrine and Covenants that you will be blessed. (Verses 9-17 Chapter 33) I'm doing less interpretation of these verses and am more focused on giving you the meat of what's in Job.

Job and I are so much alike. Joseph Smith was told by the Lord that he was "not yet as Job." If I believe I could be anything close to these men, if I could have a lace in their shoe, I would be honored. I revere these men who have died for their cause, for the truth.

"I am clean without transgression. I am innocent; neither hide their iniquity in me. Behold He findeth occasions against me, He counteth me for his enemy, He putteth my feet in the stocks, He marketh all my paths. Behold, in this thou art not just: I will answer thee, that God is greater than man. Why dost thou strive against Him? For He giveth not account of any of His matters."

I want to let you know that I'm at the Salt Lake City airport in the cargo area. All of this has been recorded waiting for some New Zealand corned beef from the Islands to San Francisco to here. This has been written in spare moments, the way the Spirit has impressed upon me in different places. I want you to know that when you read this book, like it says in the Book of Mormon, "if it be wisdom that ye shall read these things." I hope that it will lead you in the right direction and that you realize that the things I'm telling you are true.

Job 33:14 reads, "For God speaketh once, yea, twice, yet man percieveth it not." A lot of us either aren't in the mood to listen, or we are so caught up in the world that we don't hear Him when He talks.

"In a dream, in a vision of the night, when deep sleep falleth upon men, in slumbering upon the bed; then he openeth the ears of men, and sealeth their instruction." That's the only time he can talk to themsome people. "That he may withdraw man from his purpose and hide pride from man." I've been guilty of pride.

Chapter 32, reads, "Elihu teaches: god cannot be unjust, nor commit iniquity, nor pervert judgment, nor respect persons. Man should bear chastisement and bear iniquity no more."

Brigham Young said, "Learn to accept chastisement as the spirit of truth." When people give you a hard time, don't blame the church. Sometimes you need to be told what's wrong with you by someone with authority. You need to be reproved and corrected as part of your repentance process. Too many people have left the church because they have been offended. As Elder Bednar said in a General Conference Talk, "Some of us have the propensity to be offended," and when that happens, we leave the church. Elder Bednar said something like, "Now let me get this straight. You mean that you gave up Temple blessings and permanent inheritance with your family in eternity because somebody made you mad or said something wrong to you?" It doesn't make sense, does it? "Therefore, hearken unto me, ye men of understanding, far be it from God that he should do wickedness. And from the Almighty that He should commit iniquity." Satan does all that in chapter 35.

Elihu contrasts weakness of man with the powder of God; our wickedness hurts other men, and our righteousness helps them. You should trust in the Lord.

Chapter 35, verse 8 reads, "Thy wickedness may hurt a man as thou art; and thy righteousness my profit the Son of Man."

Chapter 36, reads, "Those who are righteous are prospered." That's happening to me now. I'm not the best person on the face of the earth, but prosperity is right around the comer. I will be a mission president; I want to sit with Thomas S. Monson. I want them to know who I am. I have met several General Authorities and talked with them, and I know that the Lord is aware of me. I had a special experience in the St. Louis temple with President Monson, and if I told him, he'd remember it.

"But if they obey and serve Him, they shall spend their days in prosperity, and years in pleasures." This is the probation period. (verse 11 chapter 36) "For by them judgeth he the people; He giveth meat in abundance." So, remember, "to him who much is given, much is required." When you have been warned, it behooveth you to warn your brother. (verse23 chapter 37) "Touching the Almighty, we cannot find Him out: He is excellent in power, and in judgement, and in plenty of justice: He will not afflict." It's not the Lord who afflicted Job; it's not the Lord who caused the planes to crash into the Twin Towers; it's not the Lord who flooded New Orleans. "Hast thou perceived the breadth of the earth? Declare if thou knowest it all." This is the Lord speaking to Job in Chapter 38, asking questions. You have much to learn. (Chapter 40) I'm just going to read verses 6-20.

"Then answered the Lord unto job out of the whirlwind and said, gird up thy loins now like a man: I will demand of thee, and declare thou unto me. Wilt thou also disannul my judgement?

"Wilt thou condemn me, that thou mayest be righteous? Hast thou an arm like God? Or canst thou thunder with a voice like him?

"Deck thyself now with majesty and excellence; and array thyself with glory and beauty. Cast abroad the rage of thy wrath; and behold everyone that is proud and abase him. Look everyone that is proud and bring him low; and tread down the wicked in their place. Hide them in the dust together; and bind their faces in secret. Then, will I also confess unto thee that thy own right hand can save thee."

This reminds me of the whirlwind experience outside of the D.C. temple before I was a member of the church. The whole time, we have the ability to step out of the misery and save ourselves. You won't listen to anyone until you go through the grieving period. You can use your right arm to protect yourself.

"Behold, now behemoth, which I made with thee; he eateth grass as an ox. Lo now his strength is in his loins, and his force is in the navel of his belly. (Verse 17) He moveth his tail like a cedar; the sinews of his stones are wrapped together." Here you go with beautiful blessings: "His bones are as strong pieces of brass; his bones like bars of iron. He is the chief of the ways of God: He that made him can make his sword to approach unto him. Surely, the mountains bring him forth food, where all the beasts of the field play." Everything's better when you have faith. "The Lord points to his power in Leviathan, all things under the whole heavens," in chapter 41.

In chapter 42, Job sees the Lord with his own eyes while in dust and ashes. "He chastises Job's friends, accepts him, and makes his later end greater than his beginning." Verses 7 and 8 say, "It was so that after the Lord had spoken these words unto Job, the Lord said to Eliphaz the

Temanite, my wrath is kindled against thee, and against thy two friends; for ye have not spoken of me the thing that is right, as my servant Job hath. Therefore, take unto you now seven bullocks and seven rams, and go to my servant Job, and offer up for yourselves a burnt offering; and my servant Job shall pray for you; for him will I accept; lest I deal with you after your folly, in that ye have not spoken of me the thing which is right, like my servant Job."

You go closer to me with your lips, but you deny the power and authority thereof. This reminds me of all my friends and everyone I knew thinking it was my fault, that everything that's happened to me meant I had to be doing something wrong. Well, listen to this: "And the Lord turned"—this is me today; it is good— "and the Lord turned the captivity of Job, when he prayed for his friends; also, the Lord gave Job twice as much as he had before. Then came there unto him all his brethren, and all his sisters, and all they that had been of his acquaintance before and did eat bread with him in his house; and they bemoaned him and comforted him over all the evil that the Lord had brought upon him; everyman also gave him a piece of his money, and everyone an earring of gold." This is what is happening to me now.

"So, the Lord blessed the later end of Job more than his beginning; for he had fourteen thousand sheep, and six thousand camels, and a thousand yoke of oxen, and a thousand she-asses. He had also seven sons and three daughters. And he called the name of the first Jemimah; and the name of the second Kezia; and the name of the third, Keran-Heppuch and, in all the land, were no women found so fair as the daughters of Job; and their father gave them inheritance among their brethren. After this lived Job a hundred and forty years, and saw his sons, and his sons' sons, even four generations." I just covenanted with the Lord; I will love to live two hundred years more. "So, Job died, being old and full of days." I'm sure that will happen to me soon enough. It's hard to pray for friends that despitefully use and accuse you when you need them most.

Title

I AM DRIVING IN A snow storm in Utah Valley and speaking into my portable recorder. The Prophet, President Gordon B. Hinckley, passed away last night at about eight p.m. and rejoined his wife, Marjorie Pay Hinckley, on the other side of the veil. I'm going to miss him as he has been the prophet of the church since I converted. He has accomplished great tasks as more temples have been built during his time as prophet than during any other term by a president of the church. I liken President Hinckley unto great like The Savior, Joseph Smith, Brigham Young, and all the great men who've ever walked on this sphere. Thomas S. Monson is the next in line, and I know that I will help him. President Hinckley, God be with you until we meet again.

We were in a priesthood meeting last night, a priesthood preview with my nephew, Jesse, after a baptismal interview. When the bishop got up and told us of the prophet's death, I was somewhat melancholy. I know we went to Missouri for a purpose. President Medina, who is now the stake president in the Independence Stake, was the first counselor when we met. My wife was called to run the road show, a youth play for the church, and I had reluctantly returned the stage to the stake center. We were struggling financially at the time, and my attitude was sub-par. Just then, someone taps on my shoulder and said, "I heard you're a plumber."

He needed work done at his house, and because of the lack of a functional entrance valve, we dug under a tree in the front yard five feet deep, chain sawed roots out of the way to find the curb shut-off and shrouded it for future access. We talked about many things that night, and I found he was a Hallmark executive; however, I didn't know his position in the church. I put a shower in his basement, re-piped his water, and added a washing machine rough-in. He jumped rope like a pro boxer down there, and I believe that jumping on concrete all those years caused him to need a knee replacement. The stake president at the time was previously a Secret Service agent who guarded five U.S. Presidents during his tenure. I grew to love these men and studied under them through much of my trials and tribulations. I have a picture of them awarding me my Wood Badge Leadership Award in Boy Scouts of America.

While in Independence, I was driving home in a hurry to get some young men home from an activity in my company van when this black chow dog ran right under the van. The dog went under the front and out the back, hitting the undercarriage several times. I knew he was dead. I didn't know why I was impressed to go back. The young men and I walked up to the dog, and his tongue was out. It was stiff, not breathing, and blood was rolling down the sidewalk. I felt impressed to put consecrated oil on the dog's head and pronounce a priesthood blessing in the name of Jesus Christ when in front of the young men and me, the dog jumped up and ran away. This helped these young men's testimony of the gospel and many of them served two-year missions.

These true stories are faith-promoting, and it is my hope that they will strengthen your resolve as you read. Jack is a friend of mine who was there for me when I needed to start changing my life in Virginia Beach. Jack was investigating the church in West Virginia, and on this day, he was sitting in our yard reading The Book of Mormon. The missionaries were teaching him the discussions and the gospel of Jesus Christ and had tried committing him to baptism. He exclaimed, "You'll have to show me a sign! My grandpappy took me fishing, and I told him if I caught exactly five fish, I would join his Southern Baptist church. That day I caught exactly five fish." He hadn't finished the lesson in Alma about being a seeker of signs. To keep a long story short, Jack had made an agreement between himself and the Lord to live the Word of Wisdom and endorsed a fifteen-step agreement to help him. Needless to say, he never received the sign he was looking for and broke the contract by going and buying cigarettes, smoking more than he had before. His lungs collapsed soon thereafter, and he went to the Naval Hospital in Bethesda, Maryland.

I remember giving him a blessing with the elders to help him quit, and we all felt the Savior join the circle. It's only fitting to mention the Savior on this day where President Gordon B. Hinckley slipped out of this life and into the next. I want you to know that all of my experiences in this work really happened, and similar and unique experiences will occur in your life when you start on the straight and narrow path.

One evening, I found myself sitting at the dinner table in Independence, Missouri. We had just put the meal and the settings down and began to bless the food. Suddenly, I felt an impression that I needed to go to the Salt Lake City temple. I told my wife about it, and we ended up setting a date to do just that.

We decided that we could kill two birds with one stone and pick up her belongings at her parents' house in Orem that she hadn't brought with her to Virginia before we met. Our first attempt to go fell short as a motor blew that was supposedly replaced by my bosses' mechanic in lieu of a raise. We made it north of St. Joseph with all our luggage and the children in car seats when the motor shot a rod. It was a big disappointment to all of us and our extended family. The boss made good on it and replaced the motor.

We then traded the Explorer for an Expedition and went to the mountains of Utah and Sundance.

I still didn't know what the Lord wanted me there for. I decided to turn off and take Paula and the children on four-wheeling a motorcycle trail. We almost flipped down the mountain thousands of feet when I was barely able to keep the truck on two wheels while turning around. It will never happen again. I realized how irresponsible and selfish I'd been in going off road with little children and my wife in the vehicle—never again.

By the way, Paula was pregnant with Rebekah at the time, and the other three were four and under. If you know anything about Robert Redford's Sundance property, you know there are no guardrails, and the drops are life-ending. If we would have rolled, there was nothing between us and a thousand-foot drop. I was ignorant.

We prepared to go to the Salt Lake temple as I had been told. We did a live endowment session, and after, we went upstairs following promptings. These promptings are spiritual feelings of influence, and you learn to listen, as it says in Matthew, when your spiritual eyes and ears are opened.

We sat in a sealing room, and I felt to go elsewhere in seeking guidance and the purpose of our trip. We went out in the hallway, and just then an elderly gentleman said, "You belong in here." It seemed as if they knew I was coming. I followed him into another sealing room and a voice said, "You are a High Priest in Heaven." I guess I must have been really valiant in the pre-existence, as President Hamula had said when he was the D.C. South Mission President. My patriarchal blessing said that I fought alongside Michael in the war in Heaven. If you want to know the meaning of some of what I've just discussed, follow

Jesus Christ's example and be baptized by one holding the authority of the Aaronic Priesthood and endure to the end. I realize these things I discuss are sacred or may be totally unknown to the reader. This is not meant to offend or confuse but to enlighten and make you more aware of my path. I want my family to know of the importance of making temple covenants and of having an eternal family. Listen to the Lord, pray, have family home evening Monday nights with your families, and have daily scripture study, along with meaningful communication with your Heavenly Father through earnest personal prayers. It is in these meditative moments that such experiences I share will occur in your life. We left the temple on a spiritually higher ground and decided to go get sushi. As we were driving, my wife's head turned backwards, and she was looking straight up into the sky. A grand mall seizure graced our day. We had a tough time on the way home to her parents' house. I'd like to back up in time now to discuss my daughter Naomi's birth (insert picture) in January of 2000.

We were in the delivery room, knowing that my wife was epileptic and subject to convulsions.

Her labors were always induced using Pitocin, so children would not cause her seizure increases in mid- to late-third trimester. I often wondered why the Lord wanted us to have children when she suffered more than other women; all she ever wanted was to be a mom. She was holding my hand when she looked up and past me and asked, "Grandpa, where's Michael?"

I asked, "Grandpa Lisonbee? Paula, you're talking to someone else, and I'm right here."

She was visiting with her dead grandfather right in front of me, and I couldn't see him. He was her mother's father. Paula felt like she needed to go to the bathroom, and she got out of her bed and went. Just then, a nurse came in and asked where she was. I told her in the bathroom, and the nurse panicked and said she could drop the baby in the toilet. She was dilated and almost delivered in the toilet. Naomi was delivered; however, during every contraction, her heartbeat would stop because the cord was wrapped around her neck twice from the internal aversion and corresponding external move to get her out of breach position before they burst the amniotic sack with what looked like a long crochet needle. We had difficulties with every delivery. Although Isaiah was the only full-term pregnancy she had, his high febrile seizures were the hardest for my wife to see.

I was in Kansas on a sales call when I received word that my son was in an ambulance, not breathing and not responding. Paula was panicking as she'd never seen someone she cared about so closely have a seizure. She had seizures. This time she would get insight as to how others feel helpless watching convulsions take their course. I was praying and dying, flying down the highway doing eighty-five miles an hour with emergency flashers on. When we arrived at the hospital, we weren't sure Isaiah was going to pull through. We were lucky, and he lived; however, we were informed that he was susceptible to high fever spike convulsions, and we would need to be very watchful and careful to use fever reducers with him quickly to avoid this happening again.

We later went home from Salt Lake, and it was time for Rebekah Loreine Yvonne Durgin to be born. This was our fourth child, and Paula was having more recurring seizure activity than she'd ever had previously. The doctors decided to take Rebekah six weeks early, even though her lungs were not fully developed. They found she was also inverted, or breach, and had to do another internal inversion where they grease the mother's abdominal area and turn the unborn from the outside. It's very painful for the expectant mom. The Pitocin and crochet needle, again—get the picture? The water broke, and the contractions started, and we were waiting for dilation when Rebekah turned 180 degrees back in breach, and suddenly, we needed an emergency C-section. Paula was panicking as we were being wheeled into surgery. I was giving her a priesthood blessing, and they told me I didn't need to be in with her, and I told them I had a strong stomach, so I prepped to be sterile in the operating room.

They cut her all the way across and removed what looked like a large wrinkled rugby ball, and they couldn't get Rebekah out, so the doctors T-cut the uterus and removed her. She was blue and non-responsive, and her mother was fading fast. I was almost a single dad that day, and I almost lost my wife and her newborn. I believe the priesthood blessing while going down the hall to the E.R. saved both. When Rebekah finally arrived, the doctor handed her to me, and they stabilized my wife.

We were actually prompted again to have another child. We would hear an infant crying every time we were to conceive another. I decided to stop and pursue fixing the problem first, epilepsy. The Lord took her home on February 25, 2003. This was the most devastating occurrence in my life; however, we are in a temple covenant eternal marriage. She's with the Lord to suffer no more until we meet again at Jesus's feet, and I call her forward from the grave. I have had experiences with those on the other side, and so can you, if the Lord's will be in alignment with your state of mind.

One of my acquaintances in Littleton, Scottie, fell out of Carol's convertible and died instantly. He was one of the best athletes in our high school. Children were always drawn to him. He played hockey, basketball, football, and baseball; he was a star in all. I didn't know him that well. What I mean is he was a year ahead of me in school in a town where many believed they needed to know everything in detail about everyone. We knew each other best from the football field. One night I was praying for him, and he appeared in a dream that night and said he was okay. I was not yet a member of the church at the time and did not fully understand the purpose of that dream.

Jeff is another one I felt at his passing. He was a prodigy student fellowshipping at Virginia Tech, and I had been dating his sister Kathy. Her father was a head of education at IBM. I was on my Virago motorcycle on my way to her house after hearing her brother had been in an accident. All I was hoping was that this wouldn't keep us from our plans to move in together. Jeff had been hit by a drunk driver down on the New River in Blacksburg, Virginia, where VPI&SU is located. I was sitting at a stop light on Route 7 when I felt a swoosh through my body and saw Jeff's face right in front of me. Something told me he was gone. When I arrived at her parents' in McLean, I tried to explain what happened at the light, but they were distraught. The phone rang, and they were told Jeffrey had died.

There have been highs and lows, and I'm certain you've experienced similar setbacks. Those highs and lows are necessary to knock of comers and hown our spheres of influence so as to find our way back from whence we came. Finishing milestones in my life have been the highs where I've accomplished goals like joining the true church, receiving and completing my Wood Badge Leadership Training, and being awarded in stake priesthood meetings by men I respected. When I reflect back on all I've known who are no longer living, I often wonder why I have been spared. Have you ever sat at a funeral and pondered your mortality? My gratitude is to these experiences that have led me to expound to you the message of hope. The wise learn from others' experiences. The ignorant will put their hand on the stove just to see if they really will get burned. Most of us are a little of both. Myself, I'm a chameleon.

The next experience has to do with my daughter, Elizabeth, my oldest girl. When she was two years old, we were in the living room looking at pictures. Let me preface this. My wife and I were coming out of the

D.C. temple when I saw a full-grown woman standing on the stairs. When she realized I could see her, she disappeared into thin air. I asked my wife if she had seen it, and she said she hadn't. I'd always wondered what that was about. Elizabeth, who could hardly speak and enunciated poorly at the time, stood in front of us and in perfect language informed us that she had seen us in the temple. So, I asked her, "Do you mean in this picture?"

She said, "No, I was on the stairs."

I had goosebumps on my arms and was immediately teleported in spirit to the moment in the temple. She had been checking us out as her parents before she was ever born. Believe this—it is true.

Another instance was with a lady named Laveda. She was an elderly sister whom I had been assigned to home-teach. I helped her solve a problem with the city of Independence as they wanted to tear down her childhood home. The neighbor had set it on fire illegally to try to expedite a grandfathered property line dispute. Her father had helped this guy out by selling him the house and land below market years before, and he was showing little gratitude by burning down a building that supposedly infringed on a property line by one foot. I ended up restructuring the damage, so the city wouldn't charge her to tear it down. We went to her house to challenge her to come back to church. She said she had to work on Sundays, so we gave her a blessing which stated that she would be blessed if she would take Sundays off and go to church.

Q

The next weekend, we were putting dinner on the table, a nice, juicy twenty-ounce rib eye, medium rare. Just as I was preparing to bless the meal, I felt an impression to go to the Stake Center. This was almost identical to the incident at the table where I was told to go to Salt Lake City. I told Paula I needed to go. When I arrived at the Stake Center, a baptism was being performed, so I sat down and looked around, wondering if this was the reason I left dinner. No, it wasn't, and I felt to get up and look. I saw my friend Ifo from Hawaii and asked him if he needed me for something. He said," No, why?"

I was trying to figure this out when I saw the bishop's door open, and I inquired of him if he needed me for something. He said he didn't. Suddenly, the high priest group leader came running in and explained that Laveda had fallen at work and broken her hip. We had just suffered a terrible ice storm, and she needed a ride to the surgeon in Kansas, and I was able to drive her in my four-wheel-drive expedition as the one the Lord had chosen to help her to the hospital in Leawood. Brothers and sisters, these things happen all the time. Would you have had the discernment to leave the table without the gift of the Holy Ghost?

I'd like to share a feather in my quill if you will allow me. Rick was a coworker from Liberty, Missouri. We were plumbers at the same company, and he was walking by my service van and saw a copy of the most important book in the world, The Book of Mormon. He turned to me and asked, "You're not a member of that church, are you?" I sensed his disapproval and asked him what he knew of the church.

He proceeded to tell me that everything I believed was a lie and that his ancestor, Jacob Whitmer, was a witness in the book and that his great-grandmother, lying on her deathbed, had said it was all a hoax. I told him he had been misinformed. I asked him where he lived, and he told me he lived with Becky in Liberty. I told him that if he was willing to go to the Liberty Jail Historic Site right near his house, the missionaries could help him find out for himself.

Becky and Rick went to the jail, spoke with the sister missionaries, and started taking the discussions. Becky chose to be baptized first; of course, they would either marry or separate as chastity outside the bonds of matrimony is one of the commitments for baptism in The Church of

Jesus Christ of Latter-Day Saints. They moved into separate houses. She was baptized in the third ward in Independence, Missouri.

About a year later, Rick called me and asked if I'd be a witness at his baptism. Tears of joy ran down my face as I realized I had been an instrument in the hands of the Lord to help restore an important family in the history of the church to activity. I hope I can meet Jacob Whitmer on the other side.

Later after his baptism, I was helping him with a water treatment display booth in Excelsior Springs. He was going to meet this girl he'd been talking to on a dating site. She came to our booth and wouldn't leave, even when Rick asked her to. I pulled Rick aside and asked him if he wanted to get married in the temple. He said he did. I asked, "How do you think that's going to happen? Let's say you meet a non-member and decide she's the one. You would need to get her the discussions, and she would need to convert. Then you would need to date with total chastity for the entire year-plus it would take her to get to the temple. What're your chances?"

He asked what he should do, and I told him to go on ldsmingles.com, which is a site where single members hook up with matching profiles and religious beliefs. He met Sharon from Idaho and was married in the Idaho Falls temple. When we went together to the St. Louis temple to get Rick's endowment, the president remarked, "It's about time one of you Whitmers made it back here."

Then, there was Highland, a Samoan who was my home-teaching companion, right after his mother died, who was not active in the church. He told me his dead mother wanted him to do his home-teaching. He had been inactive for years, and he, his wife Joy, and their children had not been to the temple. We sat in his parking lot one night after home-teaching, and I felt impressed to ask this three-hundred-pound guy,

"Who's going to marry your wife if you die? Who's going to marry your wife in the temple?"

He said, "I know she wants to go to the temple." I think he was taken aback by my line of questioning.

We talked about how rough our lives were and how tough we were back in the day. I asked him if he wanted to condemn his sons to the same things we went through. He asked," What do you mean?"

I said, "Well, if you're not teaching them correct principles and being a living example, and they see you deviating and not putting the church first, don't you think they'll do the same thing?"

Great things happened to Highland after that. He became active and was asked to talk in church. He gave his talk that Sunday and had a massive heart attack that night. He ended up on the transplant list, and the priesthood worked on his house to address some unhealthy conditions. Elder Johnson, one of the regional authorities, visited while we were working with Imo in the basement when Highland and Ron called me up to give a blessing. Highland was told in the blessing that if he and his wife would move forward to get to the temple and be sealed with each other and their children for time and all eternity, the heart transplant would be unnecessary. He ended up needing a ring installed and avoided the transplant, and I was there in the St. Louis temple with the entire family dressed in white, where they were sealed as an eternal family before moving to Denver.

The Lord will use you to bless others also. President Clayton, an attorney who served as Mission President in Independence, and President Rodgers asked me to submit a plan to better utilize dinner appointments to increase investigator attendance and to encourage member participation in missionary work, and I did so. The plan incorporated helping the ward with home-teaching and serving the ward and its auxiliaries. I will use it when I become Mission President. When someone is set apart and holds the keys of the priesthood for that position, they alone are entitled to revelation for the group. That has not been my position yet.

The Savior taught in parables, and I have found them to be quite effective in relaying messages to those who are spiritually in tune. Two of mine are the hourglass parable and the spider web parable. You've read the narrative excerpt of the king grasshopper. I've always loved analogies, allegories, and the Book of Isaiah and its clarification in Second Nephi in The Book of Mormon. You will read The Book of Mormon at some point and understand why Joseph Smith said that a man can grow closer to God by living by the precepts taught in this book than by any other. I'll conclude in the next several pages by quoting scriptures from The Doctrine and Covenants and the section that my family and I are reading now in the mornings, Third Nephi, which envelops the period that Jesus Christ visited the ancient peoples in the Americas. I am revealing this book for individual edification, and these are my views as a grateful convert. I know that the reader will be blessed if called to action to read the works previously mentioned.

Now let me share with you a couple of my parables as given to me in times of need. The parable of the hourglass: A young man came to me after his wife with whom he'd been married in the temple was kicked to death by her horse as she tried to free it from entanglement in a fence. He was the brother of a coworker, and we had taken up a collection to send in a card. I didn't know him, but I knew what he was going through. I wrote in the card that if he ever needed someone to talk to about losing a wife suddenly and what lay ahead for him, he could call me. I never received a phone call; however, we did get together while in a Walmart parking lot in Springville, Utah. This young man walked up to me as I was leaving for a service call, and he looked pale. I knew it was him. I asked, "You're Dave, aren't you?" After he acknowledged that he was, we sat down on the bumper of my truck. I could tell he was in shock after having just buried his young wife. They were in their early twenties! I had an impression come into my mind of an hourglass and saw a teaching moment to help this guy with his grief. I told him that he had filled his life up like the sands in an hourglass and that at this point he was in the narrow neck.

His actions from this point forward would determine his path for the rest of his life. I'm positive you, too, will go through life-changing moments such as this—maybe not as extreme, but they will be just as difficult for you even if you're living the Gospel. I asked Dave if he had served a mission, and he said that he hadn't. So, the PARABLE BETWEEN THE SAND AND WHAT WE FILL OUR LIVES UP WITH IS THAT THE GRAINS ARE GOING TO CONTINUE TO FALL, REGARDLESS OF WHAT THEY MAY BE, AND THAT THE BETTER YOUR CHOICES, THE MORE FULFILLING YOUR LIFE WILL BE IN THE HEREAFTER!

He had chosen to not serve a mission, which I believe is the most important assignment from the Lord that a nineteen-year-old can fulfill. I felt that something that was missing, if corrected, would help him by serving others to overcome his devastating loss. The hourglass was a perfect way to explain in a parallel universe that his life would go on with or without his approval and that he needed to set new goals and attract a new wife to protect the covenants he had made as opposition would increase and adversity would attempt to sway his standards and testimony just as they had mine. Refining in the Finisher's fire is a lot like going down a funnel where only the objects you allow in that fit will follow you and define who you are.

I told him that his wife was dead and that if he could serve a mission, it would keep him from being tempted and from breaking his eternal covenant with the wife who was now waiting for him on the other side of the veil. He would have to protect himself by getting involved in institute and singles activities again. Serving others on a mission or at home would be a great way to travel through the grieving period, which includes initial shock, anger and blame, and then acceptance with its accompanying pain and sorrow. I know that The Lord used me as a massager and that you will also have opportunities to help others through anguish based on your experiences of painful trials and tribulations. I think one of the reasons we suffer trauma is, so we can comfort others in their times of need. The Savior suffered the ultimate consecration so as to be our Redeemer with the Father. To mourn with those who mourn is one of the beatitudes.

Another parable of mine likens your life unto a spider web: The strategic spider chooses a well-lit night spot where he can habituate and catch food. Then the spider begins with one gossamer thread at a time, spinning a geodetic somewhat-symmetrical web, depending greatly on the distance to the anchor spots that will hold the web in place. This can take time to complete, each thread having significance, for the web is only as strong as the weakest link or anchor. The web is woven by the conscious built-in ability of the spider. However, have you ever walked into a web and (if you're a fellow phobic black-widow- or brown-recluse-hater) been in sheer horror at being bitten by the spider or, worse yet, not being able to get it off your face? Instinctively, you may run, wiping your face frantically, not realizing that you've just destroyed this spider's home, life's work, and means of survival all at once. This can happen to you in your life, just like the spider.

Do you think the spider gets depressed and goes down the wall and digs a hole to crawl in and waits to perish? Of course not! Instinctively, the spider relocates and starts anew, and some even return to the scene of the crime and start over. Either way, your web will be tom down at some point and your sphere of influence damaged beyond repair. Just do like the persevering spider and start anew; it's easy! Just spin the first gossamer thread and attach it at two points like an anchor, and spin with renewed vigor, and your web will be even better and magnanimous than the one you lost. My web was wiped out through my wife's death and embezzlement. My world spun backwards for a while. If it HADN'T BEEN FOR THESE TRIALS AND TRIBULATIONS, I MAY HAVE NEVER WRITTEN THIS BOOK FOR YOU! You can never afford to give up or in. And be careful whose advice you take in times of hardship; they may be more screwed up than you are. Seek a mentor who is where you want to be, doing what you want to do, and strive to apex them through your ACTSYS (Action System), and your cube will become a transparent sphere with centrifugal momentum sufficient to emulate light, love, and blessings to all who enter.

I have been told that this work is somewhat disjointed and lacks flow and continuity. To the critics, I say, "You're exactly right." Spiritual right-brain living will not make complete sense to the left brain. That is why the Lord created us with bicameral brains. Some reach astral plains of greater understanding in this life by understanding that the natural man is an enemy to God and hinders himself in a strictly temporal, scientific mentality. If this is you, start praying, and read The Book of Mormon and The Bible, along with The Pearl of Great Price with The Doctrine and Covenants. Be baptized and follow Christ's example of full immersion by holding the authority of the Aaronic Priesthood and lifting your natural man's eyes and seeing what you've been missing. I highly recommend it. Call the missionaries of The Church of Jesus Christ of Latter-Day Saints and receive the Gospel into your life. When you have received these things, having been warned it would behooveth you to warn your brother and your family, seek higher ground in temple ordinances as you seek to do the work of Elijah prior to Jehovah's second coming.

The most important paragraph I could impart to you was the last. What you do now is up to you. Let me share with you another experience that happened in Saint George, Utah. I was talking to Mike about expanding his service business into Saint George and having recreational vehicles as mobile billboards and offices. I felt that I needed to go down there and that I would meet someone named Jake or Jacob. I drove a company truck down a four-hour trip from the valley and went to the Better Business Bureau after having driven to Arizona by mistake as I thought Saint George was a city. On the way, I stopped at a McDonald's restaurant with a busload of people from California. This place was packed with elderly people. I had been told Saint George was a big retirement community due to temperate weather year-round. I then headed towards downtown to the licensing bureau and I was driving slowly because I didn't know where I was going. Then, this big construction truck passed me and cut right in front of me, and I noticed SHARP on the license plate. I didn't give it a thought at the time. I figured I deserved it and I wasn't in a hurry. I needed to rely on the Spirit, which I call my radar. I went into the Chamber of Commerce and got my paperwork along with the city court building, and when I left, I saw The St. George Temple with the Gothic arched windows open all around the top floor. The top sashes were down, and I'd never seen a temple like that. It was old. So I drove around the temple, thinking I would meet a Jake or Jacob there. I had an impression before I left up north that Jake or Jacob would be a contractor. I drove around the temple, and I saw a contractor going into to a house with tools, and I asked the Lord in prayer if it was him, and I felt nothing. So, I asked prayerfully, "Where do I go?"

The Lord prompted me to drive towards the mountains to a stop light, which I did. I was at the light. "Where now?" I felt an impression to go left 1.1 miles. I did. I thought this was weird as I crossed over the Interstate fifteen and stopped at a stop sign 1.1 miles exactly from where I turned left. I looked to my right and there was a Jack-in-the-box restaurant and I laughed to myself, Jake, Jacob, Jack?

Could it be this restaurant where I would meet my purpose for the trip? When I pulled in the parking lot, it was about two thirty in the afternoon, and I saw the truck with SHARP on the license plate that had cut me off earlier, and I knew I had to talk to the owner of the truck. I went in the restaurant to get some food, and I saw the guy who cut me off, and I told him the story of my trip and that I felt it was all to meet him, and he believed me and gave me his card. He said he did a lot of the churches' work in the area and most of the heating was boilers. Larry told me he had thought that I was asleep at the wheel earlier. I told him again that I had traveled four hours to meet someone I didn't even know, and I asked him if he thought it was coincidence. I told him we were looking to expand into his area and to do a national venture. He was excited. I asked him again if he thought any of this was happenstance, and he gave me another business card. I asked him if he was a member of the church, and he wasn't. You, too, can experience these non-coincidences as if they manifest themselves and materialize right before your eyes. You will need the companionship of the Holy Ghost, which is conferred upon you after proper baptism.

I am totally engulfed in the Spirit as I write these pages, and I realize this will be unlike any other book you have ever read. Isn't it wonderful? I've worked on tills for fourteen years, and there have been challenges to inspiration and periodic procrastination. I want to talk to you about church callings. For those of you who are not yet members, this means the bishop and his counselors prayerfully select individuals the Lord would have in certain positions of responsibility and service to the church. We are not paid, and neither are our clergy or leaders. I was TAUGHT TO NEVER TURN DOWN A CALL AS THEY COME

FROM Jesus Christ who stands at the head of this church. I have many times felt inadequate, but the laying on of hands and being set apart always helped me to be up to the challenges. You'll have callings in life, too—husband, wife, father, mother, son, daughter, brother, sister, friend, and professional. Do your best to remain worthy of the companionship of the Holy Ghost. You will be as Job at times in your life. The key is hope and the good news and comfort The Gospel of Jesus Christ can bring into your life, if you choose to live it. Every member of the church is a missionary, and every missionary a member.

Momentum to Finish

In Moroni 10:5 in The Book of Mormon, it states, "Behold, I would exhort you that when ye shall read these things if it be wisdom in God that ye should read them, that ye would remember how merciful The Lord hath been unto the children of men from the creation of Adam even down until the time that ye shall receive these things and ponder it in your hearts. And when ye shall receive these things, I would exhort you that ye would ask God, The Eternal Father, if these things are not true; and if ye shall ask with a sincere heart, with real intent, having faith in Christ, He will manifest the truth of it unto you, by the power of The Holy Ghost. And by the power of The Holy Ghost, ye may know the truth of all things."

There are things in your life that you overcompensate for and try to control. One of mine was to cure Paula of her epilepsy. I thought that if priesthood blessings and prayers wouldn't heal it, certainly surgery would. I was tired of watching her suffer in front of the children. I hope someday you feel the helplessness of watching someone you know dying slowly with grand mal seizures. Actually, I pray you don't. Paula was scared literally to death of having the surgical procedure done, and I just kept moving along. The Lord was telling us to have another child; however, I kept remembering the difficulties she had with the previous births, and I couldn't put her through that again. I didn't want to lose her. Who knows what would have happened had I been obedient to the

Spirit instead of my own wishes for us. I don't hold myself accountable for that, for I know she is not suffering anymore and has been reunited with her guardian angel grandpa in the Spirit World, awaiting the resurrection.

This may seem as a stretch to some, but I've drawn a comparison between this previous experience and the cause of an ingrown toenail. I call it the ingrown toenail parable. Our toenails are supposed to be clipped even with the end of our toes and straight across to avoid tearing the cuticle area. I've clipped mine wrong my whole life and have rounded them similar to my fingernails. The problem is when you clip into the quick, sometimes the toe bleeds and can cause infection when the nail grows sideways into the dermal skin layer. When I almost had my leg amputated in 2005, an ingrown toenail along with a leg ulcer caused the staph infection that took two weeks of intravenous antibiotic treatment to finally ward off the infection. So, you can lose great things in your life by doing seemingly minute things wrong. I know this may sound weird to you, but I fought those ingrown toenails for years before finding out that I just needed to learn a better way to clip them. Sometimes you may feel you're doing the right things when all along you're doing them the wrong way for the wrong reasons!

Sometimes you race around the track until exhausted only to find you're not even on the right track. Being under construction for thirty-six years, I liken this journey at a life-changing junction unto two ladders set up in front of you. You run up rung by rung to reach the top only to look over the edge and realize it was the other ladder you needed to climb. You go down the ladder and up the other one to get on the path you wanted, if prompted, to recognize your mistake—or like many, you may exit the top of the wrong ladder, never to travel the path intended, blinded by the craftiness of men and their coinciding opposition and adversity.

I remember being in Ireland on the Wicklow Way in in 1989. The hail and rain on this mountain ridge were relentless. I saw the Schlessinger House designed by Frank Lloyd Wright. I also looked over the Guinness Lake. This was a twenty-six-mile hike, and prior to the hike, an Irish gentleman saw me putting on my big boots and he asked in Irish brogue, "Do you walk much, Michael?"

I said, "I'm an athlete, and I've played football in Canada. I don't need your advice on footwear."

I couldn't believe when he was putting on plastic bags and running shoes they called "runners." I told them I could waste them on the trail with these snow boots, and my feet would be warm, unlike theirs. By the end of the hike at the Thatched Roof Pub, and after forging a swollen river with a human chain to avoid making the hike thirty-two miles by going to a bridge, my feet were sloughing skin and one big blister. This creek was usually only three feet across, but with the rain, it had swelled to a muddy torrent with white caps. I found some rocks protruding and risked my life to avoid hiking further and helped all across. My feet in those snow boots were squelching with every step. The only blessing was that the cold water in the boots soothed the burning, all-encompassing blisters. How I wished I'd used horizontal wisdom techniques and listened to the gentleman and worn plastic bags over my tennis shoes! I had to learn the hard way. Have you ever not listened and suffered the consequences?

There was an apple orchard in Virginia we took on to go prune as a service project by the priesthood and the youth that had been neglected for years. We had a professional tree expert there, and I had taken Forestry at Virginia Tech. The orchard was grown over, and the branches uncontrollable and unreachable, even if they did bear fruit, after fourteen years with no attention and no maintenance. You can imagine what a mess we had.

Our lives can be a lot like these apple trees. If not monitored and kept in check and given the love and attention you need, you can become grown over and infested with the things of the world. This may not bug you, but it sure did the trees. All their ability and talent to produce delicious fruit was lost through neglect and ignorance. Like this orchard, which could not be salvaged, you have to start all over, and that's much more difficult than managing what you already have. This orchard could have produced beautiful McIntosh apples and cider for twenty years, and now it would take ten years and a small fortune invested to get it producing again. Your life may be okay, but mine wasn't. However, through the atonement of Jesus Christ, my orchard was producing almost immediately without all the pain. It's never too late to change your ACTSYS and start over, recreating yourself and your sphere of influence.

I told you about Jason and Jill in Texas and about Demetrius, the young man I met in Pam's store in Purcellville, Virginia, who later served a mission for the church. He stood up in his farewell address to the ward and said he wished he could be more like me. In my past life, nobody in their right mind would have wanted to emulate me. My buddy Rick, who is a direct descendant of Jacob Whitmer, a witness of the Book of Mormon's authenticity, and I worked together to help him join the church and get married in the temple to Sharon from Idaho. He and I had a rough time at the end before I left Independence. My wife died, and he was in a near-fatal car accident. Brian and I decided to not put him on the corporate charter, and I had tears in my eyes when I had to tell him. This may have been a blessing for him as we toppled due to an embezzlement by a partner he never trusted. I wish I would have listened to you, Rick.

Laveda's hip that she'd fractured after the priesthood blessing told her she would be blessed if she quit working in Sunday's and would bring her son to church. Eventually this did happen. I was told to go to the Salt Lake temple from my dinner table in Independence and told that I'd been a high priest in Heaven. I saw the death masks of the prophet Joseph Smith and his brother Hyrum in that lady's laundry basket while on a service call—no coincidence. I saw the cotton stuffed in the bullet hole in Hyrum's face as this lady was a descendant of the man who made the original death masks after these two brothers' fates were sealed in the Carthage Jail by an angry mob. I've had the recurring dream to do missionary work as people are falling off my legs as I'm flying to celestial existence asking, "Why didn't you tell me?" their voices tailing as they distance themselves. This is why I've written this work, punching keys with single fingers because I've forgotten how to type. This work is for you, the reader, and I would recommend a plan of action: that you read this over and over again like I did Napoleon Hill's books until you form a new ACTSYS and begin to gain momentum centrifugally and then help others, so you are not asked, "Why didn't you tell me?" I am informing you and I will continue testifying of Christ's divinity and of the truthfulness of all revealed scripture, especially The Book of Mormon. In the recurring dream, each time I get my wings, someone drags me back. Never again, Lord; for that I am grateful.

Scottie, one of my friends in high school, fell out of a convertible and broke his neck. In a dream, he visited me and said he was okay. I was worried about his death as I always looked up to him in sports. My best friend was this black guy, Clifford. We didn't see each other after ninth grade when I moved to New Hampshire. When I was eighteen and home on break from college, I had a birthday party and Clifford showed up as a surprise from my mom. I didn't really spend quality time with him that night. Later on, I heard from my Native American friend Mitch that Clifford had died in a racing accident where his transmission blew up, and he was consumed in the fire. All of these experiences brought me to my knees and led me to come unto Christ. I challenge you to get moving in the right direction and to love and serve your fellow man with the talents you've been given and to develop those that need nurturing just like the apple orchard.

I, too, have plead with the Lord like Joseph Smith and Enos day and night and have highlighted scriptures in The Doctrine and Covenants section 121. This is when Joseph Smith was in the Liberty Jail on March 20, 1939. Every effort he'd made to be freed failed. Petitions to officers and judiciary failed to get them released from their wrongful imprisonment. Joseph, being selfless like the Savior, pleaded for the welfare of others. I find it hard while suffering to be more concerned about others. How about you?

It states that he asked, "O God, where art thou? And where is the pavilion that covereth thy hiding place? How long shall thy hand be stayed?" And in verse three: "How long shall they suffer these wrongs and unlawful oppressions...stretch forth thy hand." Joseph Smith asked The Lord to take action. "Let thine anger be kindled against our enemies." At this point he's begging. "And, in the fury of thine heart, with thy sword avenge us of our wrongs."

And then The Lord answers, "My son, peace be unto thy soul; thine adversity and thine afflictions shall be but a small moment." It's this way for all of us and you, if you listen the Mormon Pioneer Trail Exhibition (with photos).

I was with Martin C o o p e r , H u g h W. Pinnock., Kenneth Cope, Glen H., Judith Rix, and the Midwest Regional Presidency, along with President Wood. The Governor of Missouri and his wife were with us before he and his son were killed in a plane crash six months later. I was sitting in church, and the bishop announced these firesides with exhibitions and famous artists that were to be held across the state, and I thought to myself, *I can only wish. That would be something I'd like to be part of.* I had just started a new job in Kansas, and I probably wouldn't be able to get the time off as I was in the first ninety days. The firesides would have art and music from church members and would be held in Jefferson City, Columbia, Liberty, and Olathe. It had been planned by the church for a long time to signify the welcome back to Missouri by the governor after having been kicked out of the state by Governor Lilburn J. Boggs in church history and the extermination order being rescinded in 1976. It was legal to kill a Mormon in the state of Missouri until 1976!

I didn't hold any hope of being involved until Judith R., the Regional Public Affairs Director, called me and said she'd heard I had a truck that would be good to move the paintings in. I had step vans, and she said they were willing to pay for the van, either to rent or to pay me to drive, gas, time lost at work, etc. My income wasn't very good at the time, but I told her I would let her know after I talked to my boss. When I told my boss Leroy about the charitable church-oriented week, he asked how much time I needed, and it was done. I told Judith that I would take no pay and that I'd volunteer. I then told my bishop and asked him for a blessing prior to the trip to Martin's house in Clinton to pick up all the original oil paintings. The blessing stated that I was to be on guard as adversity would be apparent as certain forces didn't want this to come to fruition. Liz and the actors who were chosen for these paintings were set apart by the prophet so as to better feel, express, and understand the emotions of the original pioneers. The individuals who portrayed Joseph and Emma Smith were also with us, and I met them. I delivered, crated, and uncrated these original oil paintings that were priceless in their ability to stir viewers.

Hugh W. P., who was a regional authority at the time, wrote Ancient Hebrew Literary Forms. We got to know him and his wife somewhat on this trip. My wife and I were celebrating an anniversary, and because of the Independence Visitors Center, we were always having the missionaries in our home to teach investigators and have dinner. I even kept a freezer full of thick steaks that I bought discounted from Rodney's guys at Steakhouse. I have just been called as Assistant Ward Mission Leader in my ward in Orem, Utah, and I'm excited to get involved again. I'll never forget the dinners with the missionaries. We still do it once a week up here in Caribou Ward in Maine. All the different missionaries from the world over have graced our home, and really neat things happen when they're around. There is a three-fold mission in the church: proclaim the gospel, perfect the saints, and redeem the dead. We are to bring people unto Christ by our example and testimonies.

I just had surgery; the veins were stripped out of my left leg due to thrombosis and ulcerations, and I had a hernia in my belly button caused by throwing a three-hundred-pound stone out of a ditch at work. My brother showed up at my house and was wasted on alcohol and drugs. I was on pain-killers post-surgery, and my leg was full of staples. I called 9-1-1 to get him out of my house as he wouldn't leave and was spouting filthy, foul language in front of my wife and children. He saw my step van keys and grabbed them, running towards the van. I had just been to several pawn shops to get the tools back he'd stolen from me. This was the last straw. I threw down my crutches and pursued him. As he stuck the keys in the ignition, I leapt from the concrete wall through the sliding side door of the van and tackled him on the floor of the van.

We both saw a hammer lying within reach, and I grabbed it so he wouldn't hit me with it. The police showed up outside, and I was screaming, "Give me my keys!"

I heard someone say, "Come out of the truck with your hands where we can see them. Police! We are the police! Come out now and get on the ground."

I wasn't about to let go of the hammer for fear he'd hit me with it. The police grabbed me, and I told them I was the homeowner who'd called them. They tore my bib overalls to my feet as my stomach was overlapping the seat, keeping me from coming out. I let go of Kevin and the hammer and quickly came out towards the officers and told them the perpetrator was in the van with my keys, trying to steal my truck and tools.

They immediately started spraying my eyes with pepper spray, telling me to get on the ground. I told them I couldn't because I'd just had surgery on my leg. My brother then told them I was telling the truth. Then one of Independence, Missouri's, finest proceeded to mess up my leg for life by repeatedly hitting the stapled leg with a night stick until I collapsed. Officer McPhee, I pray for you; you must have been an abused child. Go back to S.W.A.T. school. They dragged me down my driveway in front of all my neighbors who, when questioned later, saw absolutely nothing. Like the mobs of old, the persecution was just beginning. They asked me if I wanted to go to jail or the hospital. I told them the hospital as I was in severe pain after the flogging that happened while my wife watched from my office window. My leg was bleeding, swelling, and black and blue and causes me problems to this day as I almost had an amputation from complications caused by a staph infection.

This young officer messed up big time. I filed a lawsuit with a firm in Liberty, and they told me my life would be miserable in Independence if I sued. I went into the police chief's office, and he asked me how I'd gotten in, and I told him I walked in through the motorcycle area overhead door. I told him I was there to file a citizen's complaint. He told me he was sorry but that I needed to see what the officer saw and know that sometimes they don't make it home to their families.

I asked him, "You know what they did to me was error in judgment, don't you?"

The prosecutor had said they would settle out of court, and I was seeking two million in damages. I received a call from President M. about attending a Regional Public Affairs meeting. I went, and the meeting was about being an example in all places. I felt impressed to drop the suit. The police drummed up false charges to cover their back by charging me with feloniously interfering with the arrest of an officer, which to this day still comes up on background checks. The system is broken, dishonest, and corrupt. In court, they tried to plea for twelve months suspended sentence and anger management counseling. I told my attorney that there was no way I would plead guilty to something that was a total miscarriage of justice. He argued, and the judge dismissed the case. But it was far from over.

My wife had watched from my office window the entire chain of events, and a few months later I was out with the missionaries, and this guy and his daughter committed to baptism. I had an impression to go home, and I decided to stay. I figured Paula would be thrilled with the results of this evening. I called home on the way back to tell her about the baptismal commitment, and there was no answer. I came home, and everyone was asleep already. I must have screwed up because my wife and I had plans this evening. I loaded the Gem Pack wood stove and the neo-angled glass wood stove in my self-created Juniperina granite hearth and went upstairs. I looked in the girls' room, and they were all sound asleep. I checked Isaiah's room, and he was snuggled up with his Woody doll, so I went in our room and said, "Paula," as I opened the door.

My wife was lying face down on the bed wrapped in a towel, and I rose my voice to wake her up and asked, "Paula, are you okay? What's going on?"

She didn't move, so I turned the light on, and her legs looked like purple fishnet stockings. I rolled her over, and her eye sockets were black and her face purple as she was stuck to the bed by her mouth with dried blood. I began cardio-pulmonary resuscitation and called 9-1-1 on my cell. While continuing CPR, I prayed in shock and horror for her to come back. At one point she blew breath out, and I screamed, "Paula, Paula!"

The 9-1-1 people kept asking me questions. It seemed like forever before the emergency people arrived, and I watched as they tried to revive her. I still had hope, but somehow, I knew. I was taken downstairs to talk to a homicide detective. Through all of this, the miracle is that the children never woke up! I was up all night, and Bishop U. showed up, and we went to the hospital and waited in a room for the news. She was gone, and I broke down. They asked if I'd like to see her, and I went up and walked in, and she wasn't there, only her still body, so I left.

The next morning, the children woke up; all five of them were seven and under. First, Isaiah asked, "Where's Mommy?" I told him Mommy had gone home to Heavenly Father and wasn't coming back. He was only five years old. He said, "You're kidding, right?"

I said, "No, son, your mom died last night. She had a seizure while I was out with the missionaries."

I had been in the refiner's fire before, but this was more than I could handle. You, too, will go through things in your life that seem impossible to bear, and then you'll find yourself on the other side of the gauntlet of grief, looking back trying to make sense of it all. The key is to look forward, like Job, for the best is yet to come.

Family and friends flew in from everywhere for the wake and the funeral with internment. Friends were offering help, like Rick (insert letter and picture), and all I knew how to ask for was for him to hold my coat at the funeral. I had single ladies from the relief society all through my house helping. It just seemed to cause more stress for me as I didn't feel at home anymore and would run out a seventy-five-gallon water heater crying in the shower so hard, so the children didn't see me torn up. I couldn't sing for a year, and I slept eighteen hours in the next thirty days. Bishop U. came to my home the day before the funeral and said it was not okay for me to stay single and that I needed to find a wife within ninety days, which he later denied, costing me a lack of integrity with Sandra's dad in Edmonton. She was my fiancée, and we had set a date. It took me four months, and I remember coming home and stopping in Utah to meet one of Rick and Sharon's single sister friends. What a mess—the whole time I was gallivanting around, my business was being toppled from its foundation by dishonesty and embezzlement. Isn't Satan creative?

Isaiah stood up at the funeral (insert letter) and talked to his mom as if she were standing right in front of him. I don't doubt she was although I couldn't see her. He said, "Mommy, I'm sorry you died." There wasn't a dry eye in the house. She was in the open casket in front of him. I thought he was such a man. She had blessed many with her organs, and I received letters from recipients of her eyes and other organs.

There was a huge attendance at the funeral, and President W. said, "There are a lot of men in the stake who are appreciating their wives more as a result of your tragedy." I'll never forget the feelings I had while dedicating the grave that still is short a headstone. We had a great experience at the viewing. Paula had always said it would take someone dying to get her family all together again. We were all in a circle, and everyone in her family took turns talking about her, and I saw her walking around the circle. She was there, and no one could see her but me.

My grieving period would prove my demise as what followed resembled an old-fashioned lynching which would eventually lead to me losing my house, business, credit, friends, and assets, not to mention my leaving Independence with the television station in my front yard. I was on top of the world, doing everything I thought to be right, though, like Job, I would be slandered by those closest to me.

There was money being stolen from my business and tax documents being falsified; to this day, eight years later, it still affects my integrity with others. To top it all off, I suffered ulcers and a life-threatening staph infection in the leg the police messed up. I had also gained 170 pounds and was diabetic. I'm not a whiner—when the going gets tough, the tough get going, right? Have you ever felt like what people say has no bearing on your situation or that if they could walk a mile or even a moment in your shoes, they'd put a shoe in their own mouth instead of a foot?

After my leg was saved by a rare disease specialist, two weeks of intravenous antibiotics, and a blessing with many prayers, my partner Brian started swimming with me. When I left Independence, he said, "I thought you were my friend." Brian, I couldn't deal with my situation and your constant belly-aching, and I'm sorry for that. When I went into the hospital, my leg was two times its normal size, hot, and skin molting off; I was twelve hours from death. Before, while I was traveling to Edmonton, my flight into Denver took a nose dive and almost crashed, and when I finally arrived I was in the middle of a lady on medication, an ex-boyfriend, and a counterproductive, over-protective family who kept Sandra from happiness. I was engaged to Sandra in Edmonton, Alberta, and after that crumbled, I came home crying. I had tried to do what the Lord wanted me to do, so I laid it in His lap and went home, where I belonged, with my children and what was left of my business.

Years ago, I had a patriarchal blessing given by Patriarch Keith B. J. in Leesburg, Virginia. This blessing is the only time you get a direct channel from Heavenly Father to tell you of your lineage and your mission and tendencies and talents you're expected to expand upon while in this life. He spoke, and his voice changed, and the words he spoke that I later received in written form had little to do with the spiritual impressions and the weeping tears streaming down my face without my crying. I felt a closeness with someone I could not see, and I saw a vision of my family in the future, many of which have already manifested themselves in this life now. When I came back from Canada, I just left my situation in The Lord's hands. Bishop U. had told me to find a wife within ninety days and then denied ever having said it to Sandra's father. Here I was, ready to move on. Next, Leano came to my house and said that she knew she belonged with the kids. I prayed about it, and we got married on a family home evening. You could call it a slingshot—heck, whatever you call it doesn't matter. It's my life, not yours. Offended? I hope not.

In my patriarchal blessing, I saw Leano up front. Pending life's circumstances, she'll still be there. Even though we're divorced, we were sealed for time and all eternity in the Nauvoo temple. I had a real great experience a year later with one of Hyrum Smith's direct descendants, Chris F., who played Joseph Smith in the Nauvoo pageant for nine years. He was my partner in security, guarding the perimeter and the murals from vandalism. We were in the Holy of Holies in the top room of the temple, just he and I, the night before the dedication, and it looked similar in finish to the upstairs in the Kirtland temple in Ohio which our church no longer owns. We worked with President W. after his second hip replacement, and I saw Hartman R., Jr. It was great watching the covert individuals' countenance and spirits change while going through the open house. One guy had a radical anti-Mormon T-shirt on, and I was asked to follow him. When he came out, he was asking questions like an investigator. It's amazing what the spirit of a temple even before dedication can do. The time-period architecture and the whole scene as it was in the eighteen hundreds there at the top of the hill overlooking the mighty Mississippi River, the bats circling the bell tower and the cauldron of light emitting from the skylight in the Celestial Room. I've had experiences at the Nauvoo temple that were earth-shaking. Faaleanoano and I were sealed there for time and all eternity. This was my second temple marriage in ten years and not my last as it's turning out. We just bought our first house in Orem, Utah, in the Cascade Second Ward. We rented a Tahoe and drove to Palmyra for the pageant and the Fuimoano family reunion. Brian, my partner, helped us out financially in the trip, and for that I'm grateful. There are some wonderful people in Independence, Missouri, whom I met over the twelve years there. I also met very spiritual patriarchs of the Polynesian persuasion such as Siale V. and Tom T.

Leano and I were walking in a supermarket when a diabetic issue caused her to faint and fall into the deli area freezer. She went into a coma, and we had to take her to the hospital. I was out in the parking lot, the same one I was in when Paula died, feeling the same feelings over again when Ron drove up and said, "Mike, you're just like Job." He had been with me during the death of Paula and now this. I heard Ron's now the stake young men's president, and I wish he and Viva all the blessings of the Gospel.

Then we moved to North Carolina. We left Independence, received a release from the Lord, and went there to help a bishop increase his beach house in my sister Sharon's ward. I became a deacons leader, and a couple of young men whose mom was divorced were under my stewardship. I had some challenges at my sister's house and got to know Bishop Robert S. He helped me out on my financial crisis somewhat and helped me get a license through PSI exams to help him build commercial buildings. I believe he's still using me as a qualifying individual for S. Custom Builders. He would have made a fortune on All Service Network had his son not interfered. Oh, well, that's how the ball bounces; I have no regrets.

While in Carolina, I met this African American girl with the missionaries named Shawna. We were sitting in her living room teaching her, and the Spirit told me to give her my scriptures to keep. I'd just bought them, and I told Shawna, "The Spirit just impressed me to give you these scriptures."

She exclaimed, "No, I can't take them from you."

I said, "Go ahead."

This young lady was a wonderful, beautiful person, and she had those scriptures all read and marked before too long. Her friend Laron is her daughter Lashonda's father. He is from Washington D.C., in the inner city where I grew up.

PRESQUE ISLE and SQUAPAN - Edward A. Durgin, Jr., sixty-six, died October 26, 2004, at the Maine Veterans Home in Caribou. He was born February 21, 1938, in Franklin, New Hampshire, the son of Edward A. and Pauline (Johnson) Durgin. Ed was a member of the Presque Isle Congregational Church. He was most recently employed at the Aroostook Area Agency on Aging. Ed served in the U.S. Air Force 1958-1979, spending most of that time as a special agent in the Air Force Office of Special Investigations. During his service career he was awarded a Bronze Star, a meritorious Service Medal, the Air Force commendation medal, Vietnam Service Medals, and a Good Conduct Medal. Ed was a lifetime member and currently the service officer and treasurer of D.A.V. Chapter 8 and was also a life member of the Hayward-Frazier Post No. 2599 VHW and the Ray Gooding Post No. 88 American Legion. For the past several years, Ed was greatly involved with Hospice of Aroostook and was once honored as Hospice Volunteer of the Year for the State of Maine. Surviving him is his wife, Janet Lee Durgin of Squaw Pan; two sons, Michael Durgin and his wife, Leano, of Missouri, Kevin Durgin of North Carolina; two daughters, Sharon Bosley and her husband, Steve, of North Carolina and Angela Hambright and her husband, Jim, of Virginia; a brother, Richard Durgin of New Hampshire; two sisters, Pat Robie, her husband, Ray and Debbie. He ended up getting married to her and he was also baptized the same day. I enjoyed their conversion and friendship for the short time I knew them before they went back to D.C. I heard they later returned to Wilson, North Carolina.

One of the highlights, besides building the beach house, before going to Texas was going to the Apex temple in Apex, North Carolina. As I walked through the entry, I heard, "I am here," and this was before going through the recommend desk. I wondered to myself, *who could that have been?* I went through the recommend desk with my sister as we had planned to do an endowment session, eat, and go straight home. I didn't have a clue what we would end up doing that day. We were able to get a ticket printed for my deceased father and do his initiatory, endowment, and sealing of him to his parents for time and all eternity. The temple presidency stayed after hours to help us get it done. I testify to you that no earthly experience can compare to the feeling of representing a loved one at the altar in the sealing room, giving them eternal blessings and families to live together with after this life. I would highly recommend it to anyone; however, first you must follow the Savior into the waters of baptism and live worthily for a year to enter the temple. It's not secret; it's sacred. I'll never forget the feeling of performing ordinances vicariously on behalf of my deceased father to help him to progress where he now awaits the resurrection.

Then when we'd finished my part of the ocean house trials, tribulations, and challenges, we left for Texas as we felt prompted by a call for help from Jill in Frost, Texas. They were friends who had joined the church in Independence and had two daughters with a third on the way.

So, like the Beverly Hillbillies, we left for Texas to meet Jill and Jason, who were struggling in many ways. Jason was working out of town with a plumbing company, and they were drinking, partying, and carousing. I went to work and saw the environment. I then told Jason he needed to choose between this foul existence or his family. He said, "You know, you're just like a preacher. You don't need to preach to me."

I retorted, "Maybe I do, and if this bothers you, maybe it should. Do you know that what you're doing is wrong and that it will keep your wife and daughters from the temple?"

It had only been ten months since he and Jill were baptized in Independence Second Ward. He ended up changing jobs and got on in Corsicana as a plumber on the Corsicana High School football stadium. We started attending church at the Corsicana Branch where we met some nice members who fellowshipped them and helped all of us.

Jason and I were working on the football stadium. I was a working superintendent, and he was an apprentice. He decided to go back to church as he had figured out his previous job was detrimental to his family. We were working on a concession stand setting fixtures when Jason suddenly fell and was having convulsions on the concrete floor. I asked in panic, "Jason, are you okay?"

He put up one finger and said, "Wait a second."

I took him to the hospital, and they diagnosed him with double pneumonia. They explained how he might have died within twenty-four hours had he not come in; it was bad. The doctors kept him, did more tests, and determined he had Hodgkin's Lymphoma. He needed biopsies done to determine the extent of the cancer. They sent him to specialists in Tyler, Texas. And he was dying at only twenty-eight years old and with a third child on the way. It was a hard time living in this house in a small town with no work and struggling financially along with life-threatening illness. I worked at a Sterilite Plant in 119-degree floor temperature, three twelve-hour shifts to make four hundred dollars before taxes. Jason was given blessings by his previous bishop in from Riley, Texas. He was healed but not completely. One of our ward's sisters was a mayor for a small town nearby and got the community in Dallas to help Jason and his family. Some local farmers and businesses began contributing to help fix their house and help with expenses. Jill's father and some of the brothers of a prominent family in our branch leveled the home and redid a terribly difficult steep, multi-layered roof. There were great outpourings of charity, the likes of which I had never seen before. We saw them be sealed for time and all eternity in the Dallas temple with their three daughters.

When we left the temple in the chaos of the moment, pictures, paperwork, and all items necessary to prove the temple work was accidentally left on the roof of our Chrysler Town & Country minivan; they were blown all over before we realized on the highway that we didn't have it. The camera fell on the highway, and we later found it disintegrated with the film barely saved. We went back to the temple, and someone was standing there with the paperwork. Adversity had come to put a damper on a sacred occasion. You will remember that we were told by the Spirit to go help Jill, not knowing any of this was to occur. The Lord works in mysterious ways, doesn't He?

After leaving Texas and living at my previous in-laws for six weeks in Orem Cascade Second Ward, we were able to rent a house in Orchard Third Ward, and I was asked to give a talk in sacrament meeting. I chose to talk about being an instrument in the hands of the Lord. I told of many instances where I was used as an instrument in the hands of the Lord, many of which are in this book you're reading. President Summerfelt and his wife came up to me with tears in their eyes after the talk and said, "We need you here."

We chose later to transfer to a Polynesian ward in the Polynesian Stake, returning home late one night with the children after the Manti Pageant. We taught the youth and twenty-seven two-year-olds in nursery along with my Cub Scout position. Then I felt it was time to go back to the Cascade Second Ward where my in-laws from my deceased wife went to church as we had bought a distressed property in that ward boundary, so we left President Makai's stake. We met great men in Utah and amazing leaders of men, these two Presidents especially. We signed our papers to buy the house on February twenty-ninth, the leap year. March first is on Saturday, and I thought I'd have this book published by April. I sought inspiration from the Lord to bring me someone who could transcribe my recorded voice into text, and I met a gentleman in the Orem Recreational Center whose daughter helped me. I'm editing that work now for you. My nephew, Jesse, was kind enough to lend a letter to his natural parents that defines much of my struggles in similitude. Thank you, Jesse, for being part of our lives.

I met a partner, Robert, who owns a local construction company, and I have learned much from him of the Lord's law of health or the Word of Wisdom. He suffers with physically debilitating ailments, as do I, and we're moving forward with joint ventures in health and business. He brought me to an herb shop in Springville, and I've had revelations and visitations there, not to mention much healthy advice from Dave.

I was sitting in the herb shop when Dave, the son of a world-renowned herb specialist, John, sat down. I discussed my health issues, and he taught me the benefits of apple cider vinegar and cayenne pepper. That, along with my sister's teaching me about the benefits of garlic, has changed my health and helped me wade through much temporal warfare with my body. There's one guy who works and is a partner in Ginger's Café, which is downstairs from The School of Nutritional Healing, who feeds the missionaries for free once a week. I was sitting in the café when these two older gentlemen seemed to be listening to me on the phone. These two were unusually conditioned physically even though they looked to be in their seventies. When I finished the phone call, they came over to my table and started telling me things about my life that no one knew.

I asked, "Who are you guys?"

One said, "I am John."

The other said, "I am James."

I asked and immediately knew who they were, if they were indeed the sons of Zebedee and the Brothers of Thunder. I was whisked away in the Spirit and saw them leaving. I had a sacred visit and was not prepared. I sat in awe of the experience, and I know I'll be ready next time.

I went camping with Robert, Jesse, and Isaiah up in Diamond Fork Canyon to help Jesse finish his Arrow of Light scouting requirement. I took Jesse on one of Robert's four-wheelers the next day, and on our way back to the camp, gravel on this one turn caused us to slide, and I tried to accelerate through the turn. We went straight up a cliff, and the 698-pound machine fell on me from fifteen feet up the cliff and see-sawed on my hip. Fortunately, Jesse landed on the road under me and only had road burns. My hip that had me in traction after my car accident in '92 now supported the teetering four-wheeler. I had a protrusion the size of a baseball on my left leg and numbness up my back and in my feet and lower legs that still plagues me today. I was able to flip the machine over and drive myself back to camp. Jesse was in shock and just walked the short distance to camp. Robert said it was impossible for this to happen without me breaking my neck or being paralyzed and didn't believe me as there wasn't even a scratch on his machine. I took him to the cliff and showed him the tire marks on the face of the cliff. He just shook his head and said, "Somebody's watching over you." For you, the reader, I want you to know that until you've done what the Lord would have you accomplish, you, too, will be preserved. I have personal knowledge of that.

The bishop came over with seven tickets from the General Conference of the church today. I saw President Hinckley in what would turn out to be his last session of his life. We got there late with some member friends, the Wrights. When I returned home that night, I experienced a recurring dream that has been happening throughout my life. In this dream, I'm trying to fly away. I begin by getting a running start like a swan, crane, or albatross. Just when my momentum and lift are great enough to take off, people start grabbing me and won't let me fly. Each time, I awake frustrated, unable to be free and unhindered by the things of this world. I've finally found my wings through the Church of Jesus Christ of Latter-Day Saints. Like Job, my friends can say anything they want. I don't blame myself, for my demise is not entirely my own.

"And then, if thou endure it well, God shall exalt thee on high; thou shalt triumph over all thy foes. Thy friends do stand by thee, and they shall hail thee again with warm hearts, and friendly hands."

"Well, thou are not yet as Job." This was Independence, Missouri, what I suffered there, and what I put others through.

"Thy friends do not contend against thee." My friends did. Some members of the church did charge Joseph Smith with transgressions, and his Masonic brothers plotted and carried out his assassination. There were disgruntled church members in that group also that stormed the Carthage jail illegally and mortally wounded the Prophet and his brother Hyrum while leaving others for dead. The Lord says, "Their hope shall be blasted." Just as Job's friends, "their prospects shall melt away as the hoar frost melteth before the burning rays of the rising sun."

Doctrine and Covenants, section 121, verse 12, says, "Blind their minds, that they may not understand His marvelous workings, that He may prove them also and take them in their own craftiness," and The Lord talks like Abinadi and Noah.

"You reap what you sow willing to bring upon others corruption and love to have others suffer, that may come upon themselves to the very uttermost." So just like Abinadi when he told Noah, the evil king, that this decision to burn Abinadi at the stake would seal Noah's fate to die by the same means. It was foretold by the prophet Abinadi, and then it came to pass. Simple, isn't it?

"That they may be disappointed also, and their hopes may be cut off; and not many years hence, that they and their posterity shall be swept from under Heaven. Cursed are all those that shall lift up the heel against mine anointed and cry they have sinned when they have not sinned before me, and cry transgressions of sin," the devil. And those that swear falsely against my servants," in verse 18," that they might bring them into bondage and death."

They accused me of bearing false witness in Independence when I tried to get help without sending a brother and returned missionary with seven children to prison. "Woe unto them; because they have offended my little ones they shall be severed from the ordinances of mine house." That means no temple recommend. "Their basket shall not be full; their houses and their barns shall perish."

The last yellow dog with the tail wagging like Bishop Grow told me I would be if I went to Independence and left West Virginia. "They themselves shall be despised by those that flattered them. They shall not have right to the Priesthood, nor their posterity after them from generation to generation." And verses 21 and 22 read, "It had been better for them that a millstone had been hanged around their necks, and they drowned in the depths of the sea." Verse 23 continues, "Woe unto all those that discomfort my people, and drive, and murder, and testify against them, saith The Lord of Hosts; a generation of vipers shall not escape the damnation of hell." That's why I left Independence. "That's the judgment," God shall give unto you knowledge by His Spirit," in verse 26," yea, by the unspeakable gift of The Holy Ghost, that has not been revealed since the world was until now.

On February 10, 2008, the Spirit spoke to me while in prayer. Prayer allows an interface with the Holy Ghost, Jesus Christ, and

Heavenly Father every day. "Our forefathers have awaited with anxious expectation… Minds were appointed by the angels," and in verse 27, "as held in reserve for the fullness of their glory. Which our forefathers have awaited with anxious expectation to be revealed in the last time." To Saul, to Alma, and to you and me. I liken myself unto these men as I've had similar experiences.

"A time to come in the which nothing shall be withheld, whether there be one God or many Gods, they shall be manifest. All thrones and dominions, principalities and powers," and in verse 29, "shall be revealed and set forth upon all who have endured valiantly for The Gospel of Jesus Christ." This is the sealing ordinance in the Temple. I think of President Hamula when he said, "You must have been really valiant in the pre-existence." President Hamula was the Mission President in the D.C. South Mission when I joined the church. He's from Mesa, Arizona, and is now a Seventy in the church leadership. He's a great man and helped me transition as a new member of the Church of Jesus Christ of Latter-Day Saints.

"And also, if there be bounds set to the heavens or to the sea, or to the dry land, or to the sun, moon or stars…" This is Nauvoo and all the ancient things on the Nauvoo temple: the sun, the moon, and the star stones representing the varying degrees of glory available to us based on how we lived this mortal probation (life). "How long can rolling water remain impure?" And in verse 33: "What power shall stay the heavens? As well might man stretch forth his puny arm to stop the Missouri River in its decreed course, or to turn it upstream, as to hinder The Almighty from pouring down knowledge."

The Mississippi River was turned upstream one time for three months after the eruption of a sedimentary fault under North America called the New Madrid fault. Brothers and sisters, this happened in the early 1800s, and 140 people disappeared, along with an entire town that folded into the earth. The Mississippi River was turned north. If you know physics, you know that had to be a cataclysmic event.

One of the strongest deflated and jumped into Officer McPhee. He used brutality as he repeatedly hit my stapled leg with his night stick while his partner emptied a can of pepper spray in my eyes. This was my driveway at my house where I had called 9-1-1 and reported a perpetrator. The whole time, I was telling them who I was. They were so scared of my size, they didn't listen. I was dragged down the driveway in front of all my neighbors, who saw nothing when questioned afterwards, and given the option of jail or the hospital. I had to go to the hospital as everything in my body hurt with excruciating pain. Then I was urged to drop the lawsuit as it would have been a negative reflection on the church.

"Let thy bowels also be full of charity towards all men, and to the household of faith, and let virtue garnish thy thoughts unceasingly; in the presence of God; and the doctrine of The Priesthood shall distill upon thy soul as the dews from heaven. The Holy Ghost shall be thy constant companion"—that is what the Church of Jesus Christ of Latter-Day Saints offers when you get baptized— "and thy scepter of righteousness and truth; and thy dominion shall be an everlasting dominion, and without compulsory, means it shall flow unto thee forever and ever." I add amen and my testimony. If I will be half the man Joseph Smith was, I shall count myself truly blessed. I am as Job and continue to be as I reach the end of this story and prosper with my time left on this sphere.

Doctrine and Covenants 123 states in verse 5 that we will, "present the whole concatenation of diabolical rascality and nefarious and murderous impositions that have been practiced upon this people." That's why I'm sharing my experiences with you. They are all true.

"That we may not only publish to all the world but present them to the heads of government in all their dark and hellish hue, as the last effort which is enjoined on us by our Heavenly Father. It is an imperative duty." And in verse 7: "That we owe to God, to angels, with whom we shall be brought to stand, and also to ourselves, to our wives and children, who have been made to bow down with grief, sorrow, and care, under the most damning hand of murder, tyranny, and oppression, supported and urged on and upheld by the influence of that spirit which has so strongly riveted the creeds of the fathers, who have inherited lies, upon the hearts of the children, and filled the world with confusion. Therefore, it is an imperative duty," in verse 9, "that we owe, not only to our own wives and children"—this is why I'm writing this work—"but to widows and fatherless, whose husbands and fathers have been murdered under its iron hand. It is an imperative duty," as it states in verse 11, "that we owe all the rising generation and to all the pure of heart. Therefore," in verse 13, "that we should waste and wear out our lives in bringing to light all the hidden things of darkness, wherein we know them; and they are truly manifest from Heaven." Verse 14 reads, "These should then be attended to with great earnestness. Therefore," in verse 17, "dearly beloved brethren, let us cheerfully do all things that lie within our power, and then may we stand still, with the utmost assurance, to see the salvation of God, and for his arm to be revealed." I have withheld many scriptures purposely to share some most important doctrine at the end.

In third Nephi, chapter 23, the Savior's on the Earth and says, "And whosoever will hearken unto my words and repenteth and is baptized, the same shall be saved." Brothers and sisters be baptized by one holding the authority of the Aaronic Priesthood as John the Baptist held. The restoration of the priesthood has happened through John the Baptist. The priesthood of Aaron was conferred upon Oliver Cowdery and Joseph Smith by John the Baptist. Peter, James, and John, three of the original apostles, restored the Holy Melchizedek Priesthood by conferring it through the laying on of hands to Joseph Smith and Oliver Cowdery.

You may wonder how dead people show up to do these ordinances to fulfill prophesy; you need only look to the Atonement of our Savior, Jesus Christ. The great and dreadful day of the coming of Elijah happened in the Kirtland temple in Ohio. Malachi speaks of turning the hearts of the children to the fathers and the fathers to the children, hence genealogy and vicarious temple ordinances done for the dead as Paul asks, "Why have we need to be baptized for the dead if the dead rise not at all?" in his letter to the Corinthians in The Bible. Jesus Christ and His Father did appear to Joseph Smith in the sacred grove in New York, and Jesus Christ did appear to Joseph Smith during the dedication of the Kirtland temple in Ohio. I've witnessed unexplainable phenomenon at dedications of the Nauvoo temple in Illinois and the Saint Louis temple in Missouri. I've been in many temples, and I testify to you that the Spirit resides inside and that nowhere else exists where more is done to bring immortality and eternal life to the children of men. We get as close as we can in this life to God and His Son in the temples of Our Lord and Redeemer, Jesus Christ.

And now it came to pass that when Jesus had said these words, He said unto them again, after He had expounded all the scriptures unto them, in third Nephi, chapter 23, verse 6, "Which they had received, He said unto them: behold, other scriptures I would that ye should write, that ye have not." This is why I felt prompted to work on this for the last seventeen years, so I can let my family and my children's children know that the scriptures live, that Jesus is the Christ, and that you, too, can have spiritual existence and experiences right here once you've chosen to follow the Savior. It's real; He lives! "And it came to pass that He said unto Nephi: bring forth the record which ye have kept. And when Nephi had brought forth the records, and laid them before Him, He cast His eyes upon them and said," in verse 9, "Verily I say unto you, I commanded my servant Samuel, the Lamanite, that he should testify unto this people, that at the day that the Father should glorify his name in me that there were many saints who should arise from the dead, and should appear to many, and should minister unto them.

"And He said unto them: was it not so? And His disciples answered Him and said: yea, Lord, Samuel did prophesy according to thy words, and they were all fulfilled. And Jesus said unto them: how be it that ye have not written this thing, that many saints did arise and appear unto many and did minister unto them? And it came to pass that Nephi remembered that this thing had not been written. And it came to pass that Jesus commanded that it should be written; therefore, it was written according as He had commanded."

The Lord has commanded me to write these things for my progenitors and all who will read these words like yourself. This is not scriptures to the world. I have not been divinely appointed. These personal experiences are mine, and I do not say that the church and its leaders agree or disagree with this work. This, I have done on my own, so don't hold the church or anyone else responsible for perceived errors as I have written this for the benefit of those, like yourself and my family who shall read this and develop an ACTSYS to attain a sphere of influence that leads to eternal life and not just immortality in a lesser kingdom. Ye have been warned. Now, it behooveth you to warn your brothers and sisters to read the Book of Mormon and to ponder its message and to be baptized. "And now it came to pass that when Jesus had expounded all the scriptures in one, which they had written, He commanded them that they should teach the things which He had expounded unto them." From just being obedient and teaching the principles that have changed my sphere.

Now, I will testify to my sons and daughters of a similar experience that I've had while adhering to the admonitions and following Alma. In Alma 36, it states, "My son, give ear to my words; for I swear unto you, that inasmuch as ye shall keep the commandments of God ye shall prosper in the land. I would that that ye should do as I have done, in remembering the captivity of our fathers, for they were in bondage, and none could deliver them except it was the God of Abraham, and the God of Isaac, and the God of Jacob; and He surely did deliver them in their afflictions. And now, O my son Helaman, behold, thou art in thy youth, and therefore, I beseech of thee that thou wilt hear my words and learn of me; for I do know that whosoever will put their trust in God shall be supported in their trials and their troubles, and their afflictions, and shall be lifted up at the last day. And I would not that ye think that I know of myself not of the temporal but of the spiritual, not of the carnal mind but of God. Now, behold, I say unto you, if I had not been born of God I should not have known these things; but God has, by the mouth of His holy angel, made these things known unto me, not of any worthiness of myself." I want you to know that I would be the last person on the Earth who would think I was worthy to have these experiences. I am certain that Alma felt the same way.

In Alma 36: 6, it says, "For I went about with the sons of Mosiah, seeking to destroy the chinch of God; but behold, God sent His holy angel to stop us by the way," just as He did Saul, my ancestor in the tribe of Benjamin, and behold, he spake unto us, as it were the voice of thunder, and the whole Earth did tremble beneath our feet; and we all fell to the earth, for the fear of the Lord came upon us. But behold, the voice said unto me: arise. And I arose and stood up and beheld the angel. And he said unto me: if thou wilt of thyself be destroyed, seek no more to destroy the church of God. And it came to pass that I fell to the earth; and it was for the space of three days and three nights that I could not open my mouth, neither had I the use of my limbs.

I remember saying that prayer in the warehouse on 26th and Llewelyn in Norfolk, Virginia ("and the angel spake more things unto me my brethren"), and this happened to me at the D.C. temple when I was spoken to by Jesus Christ. I did not hear the words "if thou wilt of thyself be destroyed, seek no more to destroy the church of God." I was told, "Let Satan out, and let Me in."

Three times in a row, the same words shook my soul as the vortex of fall leaves spun like tornadoes back and forth, falling as they hit my body in alternating directions with each expounding of the exact words above. I wasn't a member of the Church of Jesus Christ of Latter-Day Saints as of yet. In Alma, he says, "I was struck with such fear and amazement lest perhaps I should be destroyed, that I fell to the earth and I did hear no more. But I was racked with eternal torment, for my soul was harrowed up to the greatest degree and racked with all my sins. Yea, I did remember all my sins and iniquities." This is how I felt leading up to my baptism, being reminded consciously of sins I'd forgotten I'd even committed layered over with years of dysfunction.

Before and leading up to my baptism, I was reminded in dreams and visions of recollection of things I had done to myself and others that I'd forgotten ever happened. In Alma, he says, "For which I was tormented with the pains of hell; yea, I saw that I had rebelled against God, and that I had not kept His holy commandments. Yea, and I had murdered many of His children, or rather led them away unto destruction." I had done that in my past life by taking people down the path of drug addiction and alcoholism and many other unmentionables.

Alma _____ continues, "And in fine, so great had been my iniquities, that the very thought of coming into the presence of God did rack my soul with inexpressible horror. Oh, thought I, that I could be banished and become extinct both soul and body, that I might not be brought to stand in the presence of my God, to be judged of my deeds. And now for three days and three nights I was racked, even with the pains of a damned soul. And it came to pass that as I was racked thus with torment, while I was harrowed up by the memory of my many sins, behold, I remembered also to have heard my father prophesy unto the people concerning the coming of one Jesus Christ, a son of God, to atone for the sins of the world. Now, as my mind caught hold upon this thought, I cried within my heart: O Jesus, thou Son of God, have mercy on me, who am in the gall of bitterness, and am encircled about by the everlasting chains of death."

That's what I did in that warehouse in Norfolk, Virginia. I prayed and pleaded, "Lord, if you're there, show yourself to me because I cannot live like this anymore."

And my hand was pulled by an invisible being to pick up the dusty paperback Book of Mormon that my sister had sent me months prior, and the rest is history. That day my life took a 180-degree turn. I instantly became someone else with a new action system (ACTSYS) in a new sphere of influence. Some corners had been knocked off my cube, and I began spinning with purpose.

Alma then said, "And now, behold, when I thought this, I could remember my pains no more." I picked up a dusty copy of the Book of Mormon and read it in seven days.

"And oh, what joy and what marvelous light I did behold; yea, my soul was filled with joy as exceeding as was my pain!" My life has never been the same since reading the Book of Mormon and getting with the missionaries. Brethren and sisters in and out of the church, do this!

Alma continued, "Yea, I say unto you, my son, that there could be nothing so exquisite and so bitter as were my pains. Yea, and again I say unto you, my son, that on the other hand, there can be nothing so exquisite and sweet as was my joy. Yea, me thought I saw, even as our father Lehi saw, God sitting upon His throne, surrounded by numberless concourses of angels, in the attitude of singing and praising their God; yea, and my soul did long to be there. But behold my limbs did receive their strength again, and I stood upon my feet, and did manifest unto the people that I had been born of God."

That's what I do now, brothers and sisters; I witness to everybody whom I meet through my example, prayers, testimony, and especially in this work. Alma further exemplifies, "Yea, and from that time even until now, I have labored without ceasing, that I might bring souls unto repentance." I've been an instrument in the hands of The Lord and helped many souls find their way onto the straight and narrow path that leads to the Tree of Life. I'll continue to do so, for it's not over until it's over.

Alma exclaims, "That I might bring them to taste of the exceeding joy of which I did taste." It states in The Doctrine and Covenants that "if ye have been warned, it behooveth you to warn your brother." And in Alma again: "That I might bring them to taste of the exceeding joy of which I did taste; that they might also be born of God and be filled with The Holy Ghost. Yea, and now behold, o my son, The Lord doth give me exceedingly great joy in the fruit of my labors, for because of the word which He has imparted unto me, behold, many have been born of God, and have tasted as I have tasted, and have seen eye to eye as I have seen; therefore, they do know of these things which I have spoken, as I do know; and the knowledge I have is of God. And I have been supported under trials and troubles of every kind, yea, and in all manner of afflictions; yea, God has delivered me from prison, and from bonds, and from death."

This has happened to me. This has happened to me.

Continuing, Alma testifies, "Yea, and I do put my trust in Him, and He will still deliver me. And I know that he will raise me up at the last day, to dwell with Him in glory; yea, and I will praise Him forever, for he has brought our fathers out of Egypt, and He has swallowed up the Egyptians in the Red Sea; and He led them by His power into the promised land; yea, and he has delivered them out of bondage and captivity from time to time. Yea, and He has also brought our fathers out of the land of Jerusalem; and He has also, by His everlasting power, delivered them out of bondage and captivity, from time to time even down to the present day; and I have always retained in remembrance their captivity; yea, and ye also ought to retain in remembrance, as I have done their captivity. But behold, my son, this is not all; for ye ought to know as I do know, that inasmuch as ye shall keep the commandments of God, ye shall prosper in the land; and ye ought to know also, that inasmuch as ye will not keep the commandments of God ye shall be cut off from His presence. Now, this is according to His word."

And I do this in the spirit of fasting as I complete this work for the good of all who will read it. I am not yet as Job and am a grateful convert to the Gospel of Jesus Christ. It is my hope that you will enjoy reading this as much as I did writing it along with the appendices. The final assembly is taking place in my life. Till we meet again in second book of the trilogy, *The Psalm of the Messageur*, enjoy *Howning your Sphere* as much as I am myself.

The Lord whispered to me in a treehouse in Orem, Utah, that it is now time to prosper. Several messages led me to the Hawaiian Islands after marrying my wife, Dana, from Nova Scotia who took on my five children and me. I am forever grateful for her sacrifice as a great nurturing mother and look forward to her joining our eternal family soon in the Temple of our Lord through the sealing power of the Holy Melchizedek Priesthood which has been restored to the Earth through the prophet Joseph Smith. My Nephew Jesse has returned to help his real mom in Ocean View, Virginia; I had custody of him for eight years, and in the front of this book is a letter he wrote to my brother, his father, and to Debbie, his mother, that emulates how I felt growing up after Vietnam destroyed our family. Dana, Jesse, Isaiah, Elizabeth, Naomi, Rebekah, and I were in Hawaii for six months, and then we moved to Nebraska, so I could work on this book, and now we reside in Caribou, Maine, where my father is buried in the Veterans' Memorial Cemetery.

This book is about reinventing yourself as I am doing and changing values at your core to open up new perspectives. Last night I prayed to the Lord to relieve my extreme joint pain and numbness in my feet from all the accidents and traumas. I woke up from a dream I was having, and in the dream, my back cracked. While lying there, my back actually popped in three places, and my neck as well, without moving, and the pain and numbness I've suffered since 1992 was gone.

What legacy do you want to leave your children? Are you condemning them to suffer through the same trials you've faced by repeating the behaviors of you and your parents? What are your actions doing to your world and theirs? What will be the phrase on your headstone, and how will they speak of you when you're gone? Not to be morbid, but these are all questions I've asked myself. Right here and now, I forgive all who have wronged me as I seek forgiveness from all I have wronged. I forget all that has been wrong in my life and seek to help the souls around me to come unto Christ. Many ideas in this book have hidden spiritual meaning, and I challenge you to change your ACTSYS and begin spinning in perpetual improvement and become one with the good, creating a better sphere of existence for all who read this work. Thank you, and may you be blessed through these pages. The song by Rascal Flatts, "I'm Movin' On," comes to mind. Please read the verses of *The Psalm of the Messageur*, and au revoir.

The Magnolia

The *LIRIODENDRON TULIPIFERA* AND THE *Liriodendron acuminata* are the Latin genus and species names of the magnolia trees that have fascinated me as early as my days in dendrology at Virginia Tech. These trees are beautiful and have deep, shiny leaves, flowers of extreme tropic-like appearance, and seeds that look like small beehives. The magnolia trees are full, and the leaves are thick, luscious green. I don't think any tree is so attractive, except some in the tropics. I've seen these trees often on jobs digging up water lines and sewer lines, and I started to figure out that aside from their beauty, these trees were very aggressive in their root system and predatory beneath the ground. Many times, the roots of the magnolia are two to three times larger underground than the tree itself, and often a root, drawn to any source of moisture, will travel hundreds of feet.

On one job, a root traveled two hundred feet and dove fifteen feet straight down to a breached six-inch terracotta clay pipe hub, penetrated the mortar connection, and expanded into finer roots inside the pipe to feed the tree above with moisture and nutrients from the sewage. I was on an extending backhoe digging the area to put in a new sewer line to the street as the homeowner had had no use of plumbing for forty-eight hours.

The reason I am discussing this unique tree with you at the beginning of *Psalm of the Messageur* is many times what you see is not what you get.

When you receive counsel or advice from any source, make sure through developed discernment that beneath the surface the advice or message is not only to ensnare you in the future. The adversary goes to great lengths to rob you of opportunities to receive truth, and like that root, he will exploit your weakness. Once it's penetrated, it's difficult to get flowing in the right direction again, no pun intended.

On jobs like this, there are rules and codes governing the installation of the new pipe which make it unlikely to be penetrated again, and any piping lying between the break and the street must have a means of accessibility provided to snake and remove any future blockages. You and I in our lives are no different. Codes and rules may change with time. They have to in order to keep these types of incidents from occurring. However, there are universal rules of conduct and codes of behavior that should never change.

Like with finding a method to win over this root system, you are helpless without studying the information (or, even better, having a mentor or anyone whom you discern has greater knowledge and is willing to impart wisdom to you) to avert future pitfalls and hardships in your life. I have had many messageurs come to me and impart wisdom and advice when I've needed it. Non-coincidental meetings, many times with total strangers, have become more frequent since I was baptized and received the gift of the Holy Ghost from one holding the authority of the Melchizedek Priesthood. These sacred visits increased even more in frequency after having made sacred covenants in the temples of our Lord.

Often, like Adam Michael's experience with the goldfish in "The Forbidden Fruit" chapter in *Howning Your Sphere,* the first book of this trilogy, we become deceived by the appearance of things that are dangerously attractive. Like the magnolia tree, we, too, can be impaired temporarily and sometimes for a lifetime by misinformation and what lies beneath. In your ACTSYS, you must have good motives.

The tree has no malignant reason for its God-given root system; it simply needs it to survive. Satan is no different. His purpose is to keep you from Christ, His Spirit, and the principles of peace, joy, and happiness that can be had in this life if you become worthy to hear the promptings from holy messengers and servants. Tradition in your families and history can keep you from following the path of the restoration.

Often, you may do all the things I'm challenging you to do and then later have blockages in your life that hinder progression. The Savior's atonement provides accessibility to clean and purify again, restoring the flow of messages from His Spirit through appointed means. In the next section of this work, I will discuss the various ways I've been approached in my life by both Earthly beings and Heavenly beings on my quest to come unto Christ. Many times, audible messages come from unseen individuals also. And, no, I'm not mentally ill. Remember, just because you haven't experienced these things doesn't make them any less true. Reading the Book of Mormon and abiding by its principles will get you closer to God than by reading any other book as Joseph Smith declared as the first Prophet of this dispensation.

Spiritual awareness and sensitivity are reached when you set time aside to escape your Earthly business and allow time to meditate, close your eyes, and have up-time or what some would call down-time. You can actually be lifted to another state of existence in another dimension right here and travel an educational journey without physically going anywhere. In Psalms 45: 1, you read, "My heart is indicting a good matter: I speak of the things which I have made touching the king, my tongue is tire pen of a ready miter." When you are ready and willing, the teacher will appear, and like me, you will begin anew on a path less traveled, like I did on the Appalachian Trail with the white stones and the effortless moving through time and space while learning a valuable new perspective on how the Spirit will whisk you away and return you to report to others who are like-minded. You'll be moved by unseen beings to gain access to information that is life changing. In Virginia Beach, a voice told me three times to "go in there," and "there" turned out to be an LDS Stake Center where a Bishop and two missionaries just happened to be walking out of a sacrament meeting and were able to immediately teach me. A coincidence, I know it wasn't. I saw my yet unborn daughter at the D.C. temple, and she told me it was her as soon as she could talk. The woman I saw was fully grown into adulthood. So how could that have been my daughter, who is now twelve years old? I know that there is more to this life than what meets the eye, and many of life's mysteries can be erased in the temples of our Lord. The only way in is through repentance and baptism and living obediently to LDS, THE LORD'S principles taught in gospel instruction and in the temple. In Psalms 51:11-12, David pleads, "Cast me not away from thy presence; and take not thy holy spirit from me. Restore unto me the joy of thy salvation; and uphold me with thy free spirit." When you receive the gift of the Holy Ghost by the laying on of hands by a priest holding the Melchizedek Priesthood after being baptized by a priest holding the Priesthood of Aaron by full immersion, you will have the constant companionship of the third member of the Godhead, the Holy Ghost. He will remain your companion as long as you keep the commandments and continue to repent and partake of the Sacrament worthily.

This is the reason that I want *The Psalm of the Messageur* put to accordion and organ music to resemble a carousel or merry-go-round because life's noise gets in the way of the message that comes in a still, small voice. The chorus will be only in unison with the sound of crashing waves as this sound brings peace to the soul whether you can swim or not. The wave comes in as the Lord giveth and out even stronger as the

Lord taketh away. In Psalms 33:3, David commands, "Sing unto him a new song; play skillfully with a loud noise." Also, in Psalms 40:3, it states, "And he hath put a new song in my mouth, even praise unto our God: many shall see it, and fear, and shall trust in the LORD." To further help you understand, in Psalms 119, GIMEL, verse 19, it states, "I am a stranger in the earth: hide not thy commandments from me." The footnote for stranger in HEB says, "Sojourner, i.e., not of this world." The question asked in Psalms 137:4 is, "How shall we sing the LORD'S song in a strange land?" In the next book of the trilogy, you'll be able to realize how all the books tie together through the Acts of the apostles and the Book of Mormon; in Psalms 150:2-4. you hear David expounding, "Praise him for his mighty acts: Praise him according to his excellent greatness. Praise him with the sound of the trumpet: praise him with the psaltery harp. Praise him with the timbral and dance: praise him with stringed instruments and organs."

Again, the greatest of all messages from God to man are contained in their purest forms in the Book of Mormon and in Psalms 85:8-13. This is reinforced by David when he states, "I will hear what God the LORD shall speak: for he will speak peace unto his people, and to his saints: but let them not turn again to folly. Surely his salvation is nigh them that fear him; that glory may dwell in our land. Mercy and truth are met together; righteousness and peace have kissed each other. Truth shall spring out of the earth; and righteousness shall look down from heaven. Yea, the LORD shall give that which is good; and our land shall yield its increase. Righteousness shall go before him; and shall set us in the way of his steps."

Therefore, you have the great messageurs and the not-so-great opposition to them. Which you choose to listen to will have and has had a great bearing on who you are and how you experience and understand yourself and others. Psalms 1:3 explains, "And he shall be like a tree planted by the rivers of water, that bringeth forth his fruit in his season; his leaf also shall not wither; and whatsoever he doeth shall prosper." The opposition in Psalms 91:13 states, "Thou shalt tread upon the lion and adder: the young lion and the dragon shalt thou trample under feet. In other words, the serpent or Satan shall be able to bruise your heel, but you shall be able to crush his head. Celebrate your life thus far and clear yourself of all wrong-doing through repentance and start over a new being in Christ." Alma, while speaking to his son, Helaman, in Alma 37:21 in the Book of Mormon, states, "And now, I will speak unto you concerning those twenty-four plates, that ye keep them, that the mysteries and the works of darkness, and their secret works, or the secret works of those people who have been destroyed, may be made manifest unto this people; yea, all their murders, and robbing's, and their plundering's, and all their wickedness and abominations, may be made manifest unto this people; yea, and that ye preserve these interpreters." He speaks of the Urim and Thummim which help men understand God's language and allow men to speak to God through His Son Jesus Christ who is Jehovah of the Old Testament. Also, these interpreters allow men who are chosen to become prophets, seers, and revelators able to translate ancient languages. I believe these are the philosopher's stones that the Freemasons sought from the Knights Templar when they slaughtered them. In the chapter of Alma, verses 24-27, Alma further explains to Helaman, "And now, my son, these interpreters were prepared that the word of God might be fulfilled, which he spake, saying:

"I will bring forth out of darkness unto light all their secret works and their abominations; and except they repent I will destroy them from off the face of the earth; and I will bring to light all their secret works and abominations; and except they repent I will destroy them from off the face of the earth; and I will bring to light all their secrets and abominations, unto every nation that shall hereafter possess the land.

"And now, my son, we see that they did not repent; therefore, they have been destroyed, and thus far the word of God has been fulfilled; yea, their secret combinations have been brought out of darkness and made known unto us.

"And now, my son, I command you that ye retain all their oaths, and their covenants and their agreements in their secret abominations; yea, and all their signs and their wonders ye shall keep from this people, that they know them not, lest peradventure they should fall into darkness also and be destroyed."

Alma reinforces the need for ongoing revelation and for translation of ancient ways so that history will not repeat itself. David states in Psalms 1:3, "And he shall be like a tree planted by the rivers of water, that bringeth forth his fruit in his season; his leaf also shall not wither; and whatsoever he doeth shall prosper." This means that the righteous shall have lasting success while the wicked will eventually perish. In Psalms 2:2-3 as David speaks Messianically, he explains, "The kings of the earth set themselves, and the rulers take counsel together, against the LORD, and against his anointed, saying:

"Let us break their bands asunder and cast away their cords from us." The bondage of royalty in the world is not as favorable as fellowship in the Church of Jesus Christ of Latter-Day Saints. In Psalms 132:9-18, it reads, "Let thy priests be clothed with righteousness; and let thy saints shout for joy.

"For thy servant David's sake turn not away the face of thine anointed.

"The LORD has sworn in truth unto David; he will not turn from it; Of the fruit of thy body will I set upon thy throne.

"If thy children will keep my covenant and my testimony that I shall teach them, their children shall also sit upon thy throne for evermore.

"For the LORD hath chosen Zion; he hath desired it for his habitation.

"This is my rest forever: here will I dwell; for I have desired it.

"I will abundantly bless her provision: I will satisfy her poor with bread.

"I will also clothe her priests with salvation: and her saints shall shout aloud for joy.

"There will I make the horn of David to bud: I have ordained a lamp for mine anointed.

"His enemies shall I clothe with shame: but upon himself shall his crown flourish."

As you see, these things are happening now as a result of thousands of years of prophecy and revelation, all of which still exist on the earth today as a result of Joseph Smith's First Vision and the keys of the Melchizedek and of the Aaronic Priesthoods and their authorities, and powers are conferred and exercised under the Divine Will as manifested through a prophet on the earth today, even Thomas S. Monson. I testify of this in the sacred and holy name of Jesus the Christ from whom all blessings flow. There is a line of authority from which all things flow, and these messageurs come when the Lord decides. Alma explains in Alma 12:28-30, "And after God had appointed that these things should come unto man, Behold, then he saw it was expedient that man should know concerning the things whereof he had

"Appointed unto them;

"Therefore, he sent angels to converse with them, who caused men to behold of his glory.

"And they began from that time forth to call on his name; therefore, God conversed with men, and made known unto them the plan of redemption, which had been prepared from the foundation of the world; and this he made known unto them according to their faith and repentance and their holy works."

So, you see, there have been messageurs all along, and missionaries who share the truth have existed since the beginning of man, and 52,000 of them currently serve all over the world wherever they are sent to bring the truth of the everlasting Gospel to those who are ready. I work with missionaries in the church currently as a ward mission leader and enjoy their company as we find ways to bring individuals and families unto Christ. Every member of the church is a missionary; however, as David states in Psalms 115:5-7, "They have mouths, but they speak not; eyes have they, but they see not: they have ears, but they hear not: noses have they, but they smell not: they have hands, but they handle not: feet have they, but they walk not: neither speak they through their throat."

We possess a pearl of great price, and yet many in the church fear men and do not share the truths of the gospel, and so many who would accept still wait to be informed. Many times, we are warned to leave and go elsewhere like the saints in Hahn's Mill of Missouri. They didn't listen to the Prophet, and many died. Ammon was told when inquiring of the Lord in Alma 27:12-14, "Get this people out of this land, that they perish not: for Satan has great hold on the hearts of the Amalekites, who do stir the Lamanites unto anger against their brethren to slay them; therefore, get thee out of this land; and blessed are this people in this generation, for I will preserve them. And now it came to pass that Ammon went and told the king all the words which the Lord had said unto him. And they gathered together all their people, yea, all the people of the Lord, and did gather all their flocks and herds, and departed out of the land, and came into the wilderness which divided the land of Nephi from the land of Zarahemla and came over near the borders of the land. When you have a prophet, who speaks to God and gets answers, you will listen if you're a believer. The Lord speaks to us individually in prayers if we've learned to listen and know his voice. In families, parents are to receive promptings and revelations for their well-being as well as their children's. Pray often and listen!

The next subject is one that I've struggled to learn, especially on the listening side: the art of communication. You might think you're a great communicator, and I hope you do because if you don't believe in yourself, who will? In communications among and between mortals, we send messages and receive messages constantly; however, your awareness and skill in discerning between the lines is what will key in your response that helps the receiver know you truly empathized with the message your compatriot sent. One of the most effective tools of influence for me was neural-linguistic training, which taught me to use non-verbal communication skills along with body language and mirroring to establish rapport with business clients, helping them feel better while doing business with me and allowing my agenda-setting to be most effective. How this relates to *The Psalm of the Messageur* is we're all singing different tunes as diverse as the songs of birds. Birds sing almost constantly, and as we know, whether we're there or not, there is sound. Therefore, the ability of the listener and the art of responding empathetically while forming inquiries that continue interchanges are imperative to conversations with a purpose. As you may deduce, an effective presenter is equally as important as a receptive, absorbent audience. When angelic beings or tarrying immortals show themselves, it is always for a purpose, and the visitation can many times overwhelm the individual who is inexperienced with these things. You can be better prepared when you follow the Lord's guidelines and precepts. Unless you're chosen or prepared from before this life—and even if you are— ministrations will still surprise and leave you speechless and many times without energy to continue your mission until the message is processed and immediately acted upon. With messageurs sent from the Lord to deliver information to you, they are assigned and upon return asked to report on their success in intervening in your life to impart instruction to you on behalf of others to help the Lord's work move forward prior to Jesus Christ's Second Coming, which is coming very soon. Prophets, starting with Joseph Smith in this dispensation of time and currently culminating with Thomas Spencer Monson, speak with Jesus Christ on our behalf constantly to impart wisdom to all mankind or at least those who will listen. When you have an experience where a message is imparted, it may be just for you, a friend, or a family member. To the Lord, the worth of even one soul is great.

There is a difference between the natural man and the spiritual man, for one is an enemy to God and listens to the wrong spirit. You'll need to discern, be baptized by one holding the authority of the Aaronic Priesthood, and receive the gift of the Holy Ghost by the laying on of hands by one having the authority of the Holy Melchizedek Priesthood to be able to complete the baptism and have the constant companionship of the Holy Ghost to attain discernment of Spirits, and even then, there are times other tests will be needed to truly know to whom you are speaking or listening.

On the earth today, there is only one true church, the Church of Jesus Christ of Latter-Day Saints. Opposition will be here until the millennium when Christ will reign, and Satan and his angels will be bound. This opposition is what may make you question the truthfulness of what I tell you until you call the missionaries and are taught correct principles while praying constantly for a testimony of these things which I speak. Until then, you'll remain a natural man with some of the truth. You know, what never ceases to amaze me is how you think you know more than thousands of years of revealed truth through man from God. There's a reason for that, and it's called free agency as your memory of a pre-existence is erased when you receive your mortal body. At some point during the resurrection, you'll be reunited with an immortal body with your Spirit to be judged and placed based on your level of progression in the Gospel of Jesus Christ. Your ultimate goal is to be sealed for time and all eternity in a temple of Our Lord and endure to the end, constantly repenting and remaining pure and clean so you can dwell in the presence of God. Anything short of this will land you in another kingdom, with God in his presence Celestial, below in the Terrestrial, or even further away in the Telestial, and for those sons of perdition who deny the Holy Ghost or commit atrocities such as premeditated murder, Outer Darkness. In Psalms 29:3-5, 7-9, David explains what the voice of The Lord is: "The voice of the LORD is upon the waters: The God of glory thundereth: the LORD is upon many waters. The voice of the LORD is powerful; the voice of the LORD is full of majesty. The voice of the LORD breaketh the cedars; yea, the LORD breaketh the seeds of Lebanon. The voice of the LORD divideth the flames of fire. The voice of the LORD shaketh the wilderness; the LORD shaketh the wilderness of Kadesh. The voice of the LORD maketh the hinds to calve and discovered the forests: and in his temple doth everyone speaks of his glory."

Now, I will share with you two of the most important chapters in Psalms, and they will be repeated as all things must be for effective communication. You usually need to be told three times before you wall act on a message. In Psalms 105, I was unable to eliminate any verse.

In Psalms 105:1-45, you read, "O GIVE thanks unto the LORD; call upon his name; make known his deeds among the people. Sing unto him, sing psalms unto him; talk ye of all his wondrous works. Glory ye in his holy name; let the heart of them rejoice that seek the LORD. Seek the LORD, and his strength: seek his face evermore. Remember his marvelous works that he hath done; his wonders, and the judgments of his mouth; O ye seed of Abraham his servant, ye children of Jacob his chosen. He is the LORD our God: his judgments are in all the earth. He hath remembered his covenant forever, the word which he commanded to a thousand generations. Which covenant he made with Abraham, and his oath unto Isaac; And confirmed the same unto Jacob for a law, and to Israel for an everlasting covenant: Saying, unto thee will I give the land of Canaan, the lot of your inheritance: When they were but a few men in number; yea, very few, and strangers in it. When they went from one nation to another, from one kingdom to another people; He suffered no man to do them wrong: yea, he reproved kings for their sakes; Saying, touch not mine anointed, and do my prophets no harm. Moreover, he called for a famine upon the land: he brakes the whole staff of bread. He sent a man before them, even Joseph, who was sold for a servant: Whose feet they hurt with fetters: he was laid in iron: Until the time that his word came: the word of the LORD tried him. The king sent and loosed him; even the ruler of the people and let him go free. He made him lord of his house, and ruler of all his substance: to bind his princes at pleasure; and teach his senators wisdom. Israel also came into Egypt; and Jacob sojourned in the land of Ham. And he increased his people greatly; and made them stronger than their enemies. He turned their heart to hate his people, to deal subtly with his servants. He sent Moses his servant; and Aaron whom he had chosen. They shewed his signs among them, and wonders in the land of Ham. He sent darkness and made it dark; and they rebelled not against his word. He turned their waters into blood and slew their fish. Their land brought forth frogs in abundance, in the chambers of their kings. He spake, and there came diverse sorts of flies, and lice in all their coasts.

"He gave them hail for rain and flaming fire in their land. He smote their vines also and their fig trees; and brake the trees of their coasts. He spake, and the locusts, and caterpillars, and that without number, and did eat up all the herbs in their land and devoured the fruit of their ground. He smote also the firstborn of their land, and the chief of all their strength. He brought them forth also with silver and gold: and there was not one feeble person among their tribes. Egypt was glad when they departed: for the fear of them fell upon them. He spread a cloud for a covering; and fire to give light in the night. The people asked, and he brought quails, and satisfied them with the bread of heaven. He opened the rock, and the waters gushed out; and they ran in the dry places like a river. For he remembered his holy promise, and Abraham his servant. And he brought forth his people with joy, and his chosen with gladness: And gave them the lands of the heathen: and they inherited the labor of the people; That they might observe his statutes and keep his laws. Praise ye the LORD." Please, read this, Psalms 105, three times as this is part of the reason that Lehi asked Nephi to go get the plates from Laban in Jerusalem, which is now translated as The Book of Mormon.

In Psalms 106: 1-48, David continues some of the most important review of history for us today, which is integrally laced with Genesis and Exodus in the Bible and continues a message from Psalms 105 when David explains, "PRAISE ye the LORD. O give thanks unto the LORD; for he is good: for his mercy endureth forever. Who can utter the mighty acts of the LORD? Who can shew forth all his praise? Blessed are they that keep judgment, and he that doeth righteousness at all times. Remember me, O LORD, with the favor that thou bearest unto thy people: O visit me with thy salvation; That I may see the good of thy chosen, that I may rejoice in the gladness of thy nation, that I may glory with thine inheritance. We have sinned with our fathers, we have committed iniquity, we have done wickedly. Our fathers understood not thy wonders in Egypt; they remember not the multitude of thy mercies; but provoked him at the sea, even at the Red Sea. Nevertheless, he saved them for his names sake, that he might make his mighty power to be known. He rebuked the Red Sea also, and it was dried up: so, he led them through the depths, as through the wilderness. And he saved them from the hand of him that hated them and redeemed them from the hand of the enemy. And the waters covered their enemies: there was not one of them left. Then believed they his words; they sang his praise. They soon forgat his works; they waited not for his counsel: But lusted exceedingly in the wilderness, and tempted God in the desert. And he gave them their request; but sent leanness into their soul. They envied Moses also in the camp, and Aaron the saint of the LORD. The earth opened and swallowed up Dathan and covered the company of Abiram. And a fire was kindled in their company; the flame burned up the wicked. They made a calf in Horeb and worshipped the molten image. Thus, they changed their glory into the similitude of an ox that eateth grass. They forgat God their saviour, which had done great things in Egypt; Wondrous works in the land of Ham, and terrible things by the Red Sea. Therefore, he said that he would destroy them, had not Moses his chosen stood before him in the breach, to turn away his wrath, lest he should destroy them. Yea, they despised the pleasant land, they believed not his word: But murmured in their tents and hearkened not unto the voice of the LORD. Therefore, he lifted up his hand against them, to overthrow them in the wilderness: To overthrow their seed also among the nations, and to scatter them in the lands. They joined themselves also unto Baal-peor and ate the sacrifices of the dead. Thus, they provoked him to anger with their inventions: and the plague brake in upon them. Then stood up Phinehas, and executed judgment: and so, the plague was stayed. And that was counted unto him for righteousness unto all generations for evermore. They angered him also at the waters of strife, so that it went ill with Moses for their sakes: Because they provoked his spirit, so that he spake unadvisedly with his lips. They did not destroy the nations, concerning whom the LORD commanded them: But were mingled among the heathen, and learned their works. And they served their idols: which were a snare unto them. Yea, they sacrificed their sons and their daughters unto devils, and shed innocent blood, even the blood of their sons and their daughters, whom they sacrificed unto the idols of Canaan: and the land was polluted with blood. Thus, were they defiled with their own works, and went a whoring with their own inventions. Therefore, was the wrath of the LORD kindled against his people, insomuch that he abhorred his own inheritance. And he gave them into the hand of the heathen; and they that hated them ruled over them. Their enemies also oppressed them, and they were brought into subjection under their hand. Many times, did he deliver them; but they provoked him with their counsel, and were brought low for their iniquity. Nevertheless, he regarded their affliction, when he heard their cry: And he remembered for them his covenant and repented according to the multitude of his mercies. He made them also be pitied of all those that carried them captives. Save us, O LORD our God, and gather us from among the heathen, to give thanks unto thy holy name, and to triumph in thy praise. Blessed be the LORD God of Israel from everlasting to everlasting: and let all the people say, Amen. Praise ye the LORD." There's a reason why the word remember is used 118 times in the Book of Mormon. These same acts of forgetfulness will and do reap similar rewards today in parallel situations.

Once you have advanced and learned the process of delivery of messages and those that deliver in obedience returning to the sender to report, you will become more receptive and be a spirit reborn.

Regardless of how your message is received, you will be blessed through conversion and become a father figure to others. In Doctrine and Covenants section 62, verse 3, Joseph received this revelation from the Lord after meeting brethren going to teach: "Nevertheless, ye are blessed, for the testimony which ye have borne is recorded in heaven for the angels to look upon; and they rejoice over you, and your sins are forgiven you." You also must inquire of the Lord on a daily basis as to his wishes and commandments on your behalf. A king trusted and asked Ammon to inquire of the Lord what the king's people should do, and he would do it.

In Alma 27:11-14, this is an example for you: "And it came to pass that Ammon went and I inquired of the Lord, and the Lord said unto him: Get this people out of this land, that they perish not: for Satan has great hold on the hearts of the Amalekites, who do stir up the Lamanites to anger against their brethren to slay them; therefore, get thee out of this land; and blessed are this people in this generation, for I will preserve them. And now it came to pass that Ammon went and told the king all the words which the Lord had said unto him. And they gathered together all their people, yea, all the people of the Lord, and did gather together all their flocks and herds, and departed out of the land, and came into the wilderness which divided the land of Nephi from the land of Zarahemla and came over near the borders of the land." If those pioneers in Haun's Mill had heeded the counsel of Joseph Smith, the prophet, their fate would have been different, and many lives would have been spared. The slaughter that took place in Missouri is a similitude, and Joseph attempted to intervene with counsel unheeded.

You see the connection between inquiry, answer, and action, don't you? If you don't believe in inquiry, or prayer as we call it, then your life will not be open to help when you need it, and you'll constantly be a victim of "circumstance." Once baptized and with the constant companionship of the Holy Ghost, you will be able to feel promptings, and when acted upon, these can save your life and help you avoid many hardships. The key, then, is to put off the natural man who teaches you not to pray. All through the scriptures, fathers teach their children to pray and to seek guidance. If you're like me and never prayed with your father, then start teaching your children how to pray. The missionaries from the Church of Jesus Christ of Latter-Day Saints will be happy to help you learn the proper way to pray and to not use vain repetition. Prayer can be constant. I find myself opening prayers and talking with the Lord for an hour sometimes, and I pray with my children morning and night and in gratitude for meals or occasions and also for the local and general leaders of the church and for the missionaries' protection. Worthiness through constant repentance to remain spotless before the Lord is most important, and I believe prayer is second. You must pray to know the truthfulness of a message. You pray by addressing Heavenly Father and saying, "I'm grateful for…" and then saying," I ask thee for…" and closing in the name of Jesus Christ, Amen. Have you ever prayed and waited for an answer? Or do you hastily offer up a prayer and rush off without allowing the Savior of all mankind to respond? Remember, a prayer has a sender and a receiver, and a conversation alternate between the two. I would challenge you to commune with Jesus Christ when you pray. By listening are the greatest lessons and messages imparted. Many times, the Lord will impress things on you hadn't even thought to pray about once He knows you're LISTENING and that you're likely to ACT upon His counsel. Opposition to prayer will be constant as the adversary places earthly demands over the keeping of commandments and sacred covenants. When you get caught without your armor on or become evil, as it says in Psalms 52:5, "God shall likewise destroy thee forever, he shall take thee away, and pluck thee out of thy dwelling place, and root thee out of the land of the living. Selah. Like David, when praying you should use thee, thine, thou, thy and not address deity in a personal salutation.

As it states in Jacob 4:8, "Behold, great and marvelous are the works of the Lord. How unsearchable are the depths of the mysteries of him; and it is impossible that man should find out all his ways. And no man knoweth of his ways save it be revealed unto him; wherefore, brethren, despise not the revelations of God." The Lord loves and forgives all men, but He only talks to those who know how to hear His voice and take heed.

In Psalms 108:6, David pleads, "That thy beloved may be delivered: save with thy right hand and answer me." Hymns are prayers set to music and have a penetrating effect on our souls as music from the Mormon Tabernacle Choir has for decades. A psalm is a song, just as a hymn, and for many, a message can come while listening to a hymn or a message from the opposition avoided while humming or singing a favorite hymn. In Psalms 54:2, David pleads, "Hear my prayer, O God; give ear to the words of my mouth." And in Psalms 55:17, David adds, "Evening, and morning, and at noon will I pray, and cry aloud: and he shall hear my voice." David asks the lord to hear his voice in Psalms 5:1-7: "GIVE ear to my words, O LORD, consider my meditation. Hearken unto the voice of my cry, my King, and my God: for unto thee will I pray. My voice shalt thou hear in the morning, O LORD; in the morning will I direct my prayer unto thee and will look up. For thou art not a God that hath pleasure in wickedness: neither shall evil dwell with thee. The foolish shall not stand in thy sight: thou hatest all workers of iniquity. Thou shalt destroy them that speak leasing: the LORD will abhor the bloody and deceitful man. But as for me, I will come into thy house in the multitude of thy mercy: and in thy fear will I worship toward thy holy temple." It is important to be in the world but not of the world. Daily prayer and meditation are important for you to open the channel the Lord's on. David, whose line produced the Savior, temporally, even though we know His Father is Eloheim, the Eternal Father, constantly sought an open line of communication.

In Psalms 104:33-34, he announces, "I will sing unto the LORD as long as I live: I will sing praise to my God while I have my being. My meditation of him shall be sweet: I will be glad in the LORD." The Lord is not a respecter of persons. David is a king; however, in Psalms

102:17, David explains, "He will regard the prayer of the destitute, and not despise their prayer." You must not be a hypocrite who speaks one thing and does another or, in the earthly sense, praises Jesus Christ on Sunday and lies, cheats, and steals from anyone on the other six days of the week—in other words, growing closer to Him with your lips but denying His power and authority by not living His commandments and progressing in His Restored Gospel. David pleads again to the Lord in Psalms 28:2-3, "Hear the voice of my supplications, when I cry unto thee, when I lift up my hands toward thy holy oracle. Draw me not away with the wicked, and with the workers of iniquity, which speak peace to their neighbors, but mischief is in their hearts."

David thirsts for God when he says in Psalms 63:6, "When I remember thee upon my bed, and meditate on thee in the night watches." And Psalms 86:6: "Give ear, O LORD, unto my prayer; and attend to the voice of my supplications."

"David implores God for mercy and is saved from the lowest hell," is the heading of Psalms 86. Obviously, David has sinned against the greater light and is seeking forgiveness for his mortal weakness and lack of judgment.

When you look at the word in my title, "Messageur," you may think of a massage therapist or something French like the word voyageur. In both cases you might be right. I look at it as a common word, "message," with an acronym of sound and meaning, "urs." The message is yours. The Prophet, Thomas S. Monson, receives as a prophet, seer, and revelator messages for the whole world and every person in the world, member or not, who may find themselves within earshot of his message or gain it from a faithful servant secondhand. As far as you're (ur) concerned, personal revelation and the truthfulness of wires from the Lord whether you receive them or not, are for you and your family or those whom you serve. The channel must be on, and you must be listening without distraction. Many times, I have sought the Lord's counsel on matters and received instruction, and other times I've been suddenly interrupted when I least expected and asked by the Lord to go and help someone over whom I was a steward, like a shepherd and his sheep.

Moroni was a great leader over the Nephite armies, and when confused about the Lamanites' strategy, he turned to Alma to seek direction from the Lord. In Alma 43:23-24, it states, "But it came to pass, as soon as they had departed into the wilderness Moroni sent spies into the wilderness to watch their camp; and Moroni, also, knowing of the prophesies of Alma, sent certain men unto him, desiring him that he should inquire of the Lord whither the armies of the Nephites should go to defend themselves against the Lamanites. And it came to pass that the word of the Lord came unto Alma, and Alma informed the messengers of Moroni, that the armies of the Lamanites were marching round about in the wilderness, that they might come over into the land of Manti, that they might commence an attack upon the weaker part of the people. And those messengers went and delivered the message unto Moroni." The prophet is the mouthpiece of God, and Moroni knew who to ask and was able to strategize based on information that was not known until he inquired of Alma, who wasn't even near the fighting, whom the Lord had chosen to be the medium for the message.

I was in a health food restaurant in Springville, Utah, having some pumpkin soup and a shot of wheatgrass along with a shot of ginger when two men walked up to my table and proceeded to tell me without words about my life, and I asked who they were. The first said, "I am James," and pointing to the other, he said, "He is John." I immediately asked if they were the brothers of thunder and the sons of Zebedee. They turned and walked away as I was in amazement and asked, "Where is Peter?" These men, John the beloved and James, had come to see me. They looked like they were in their eighties, and yet they had the muscular structure and erectness of twenty-year-old athletes. I'll never forget that experience. These men like the three Nephites tarry on the earth still today, and James and John along with Peter, the senior Apostle, were responsible for restoring and conferring the Melchizedek Priesthood to Joseph Smith and Oliver Cowdery on the banks of the Susquehanna River in Harmony, Pennsylvania. Don't ask me how I knew who these sacred visitors were; I just knew. This may never happen to you, and I'm still not sure why it happened to me except Jesus Christ must have had a message for me, and he sent holy messengers to prepare me to help his ministers in the future. I look forward to the next time I meet them.

There are two schools of thought on this sphere, and they are the one that listens and acts on worldly noise and the one that listens and acts on meditative promptings and impressions from the divine source. Moderation in all things would suggest that filtration and discernment is necessary, and again this comes from the Holy Ghost. Alma, when talking to his son, Helaman, expounds in Alma 37:32-47, "And now; my son, remember the words which I have spoken unto you; trust not those secret plans unto this people, but teach them an everlasting hatred against sin and iniquity. Preach unto them repentance, and faith on the Lord Jesus Christ; teach them to humble themselves and to be meek and lowly in heart; teach them to withstand every temptation of the devil, with their faith on the Lord Jesus Christ. Teach them to never be weary of good works, but to be meek and lowly in heart; for such shall find rest to their souls. O, remember, my son, and learn wisdom in thy youth; yea, learn in thy youth to keep the commandments of God. Yea, and cry unto God for all thy support; yea, let all thy doings be unto the Lord, and whithersoever thou goest let it be in the Lord; yea, let all thy thoughts be directed unto the Lord; yea, let thy affections of thy heart be placed upon the Lord forever. Counsel with the Lord in all thy doings, and he will direct thee for good; yea, when thou liest down at night lie down unto the Lord, that he may watch over you in your sleep; and when thou risest in the morning let thy heart be full of thanks unto God; and if ye do these things, ye shall be lifted up at the last day. And now, my son, I have somewhat to say concerning the thing which our fathers call a ball, or director—or our fathers called it Liahona, which is, being interpreted, a compass; and the Lord prepared it."

You see, this compass will only work upon principles of righteousness, and as soon as the possessor uses unrighteous domain or adversarial force on the Lord's anointed, the Liahona will cease to give direction and leave the perpetrators to their own demise.

And in Alma verses 39-47, you read, "And behold, there cannot any man work after the manner of so curious a workmanship. And behold, it was prepared to show unto our fathers the course which they should travel in the wilderness. And it did work for them according to their faith in God; therefore, if they had faith to believe that God could cause that those spindles should point the way that they should go, behold, it was done; therefore, they had this miracle, and also many other miracles wrought by the power of God, day by day. Nevertheless, because those miracles were worked by small means it did show unto them marvelous works. They were slothful and forgot to exercise their faith and diligence and those marvelous works ceased, and they did not progress in their journey; Therefore, they tarried in the wilderness, or did not travel a direct course, and were afflicted with hunger and thirst, because of their transgressions. And now, my son, I would that ye should understand that these things are not without a shadow; for as our fathers were slothful to give heed unto this compass (now these things were temporal) they did not prosper; even so it is with things which are spiritual. For behold, it is as easy to give heed to the word of Christ, which will point to you a straight course to eternal bliss, as it was for our fathers to give heed to this compass, which would point unto them a straight course to the promised land. And now I say, is there not a type in this thing? For just as surely as the director did bring our fathers, by following its course, to the promised land, shall the words of Christ, if we follow their course, carry us beyond this vale of sorrow into a far better land of promise. O my son, do not let us be slothful because of the easiness of the way; for so was it with our fathers; for so was it prepared for them, that if they would look they might live; even so it is with us. The way is prepared, and if we will look we may live forever. And now, my son, see that ye take care of these sacred things, yea, see that you look to God and live. Go unto this people and declare the word and be sober. My son, farewell." Please, heed the Lord Jesus Christ's warning as I witness to you the truthfulness of these scriptures and the entirety of the Book of Mormon. You have the truth; now do something with it, besides asking the ignorant if you should read it.

This message IS URS, and I haven't wasted my time inviting you to read it, have I? Am I a messageur?

In Psalms 105:1-45, you read, "O GIVE thanks unto the LORD; call upon his name; make known his deeds among the people. Sing unto him, sing psalms unto him; talk ye of all his wondrous works. Glory ye in his holy name; let the heart of them rejoice that seek the LORD. Seek the LORD, and his strength: seek his face evermore. Remember his marvelous works that he hath done; his wonders, and the judgments of his mouth; O ye seed of Abraham his servant, ye children of Jacob his chosen. He is the LORD our God: his judgments are in all the earth. He hath remembered his covenant forever, the word which he commanded to a thousand generations. Which covenant he made with Abraham, and his oath unto Isaac; And confirmed the same unto Jacob for a law, and to Israel for an everlasting covenant: Saying, Unto thee will I give the land of Canaan, the lot of your inheritance: When they were but a few men in number; yea, very few, and strangers in it when they went from one nation to another, from one kingdom to another people; He suffered no man to do them wrong: yea, he reproved kings for their sakes; Saying, touch not mine anointed, and do my prophets no harm. Moreover, he called for a famine upon the land: he brake the whole staff of bread. He sent a man before them, even Joseph, who was sold for a servant: Whose feet they hurt with fetters: he was laid in iron: Until the time that his word came: the word of the LORD tried him. The king sent and loosed him; even the ruler of the people and let him go free. He made him lord of his house, and ruler of all his substance: to bind his princes at pleasure; and teach his senators wisdom. Israel also came into Egypt; and Jacob sojourned in the land of Ham. And he increased his people greatly; and made them stronger than their enemies. He turned their heart to hate his people, to deal subtly with his servants. He sent Moses his servant; and Aaron whom he had chosen. They shewed his signs among them, and wonders in the land of Ham. He sent darkness and made it dark; and they rebelled not against his word. He turned their waters into blood and slew their fish. Their land brought forth frogs in abundance, in the chambers of their kings. He spake, and there came diverse sorts of flies, and lice in all their coasts.

"He gave them hail for rain and flaming fire in their land. He smote their vines also and their fig trees; and brake the trees of their coasts. He spake, and the locusts, and caterpillars, and that without number, and did eat up all the herbs in their land and devoured the fruit of their ground. He smote also the firstborn of their land, and the chief of all their strength. He brought them forth also with silver and gold: and there was not one feeble person among their tribes. Egypt was glad when they departed: for the fear of them fell upon them. He spread a cloud for a covering; and fire to give light in the night. The people asked, and he brought quails, and satisfied them with the bread of heaven. He opened the rock, and the waters gushed out; and they ran in the dry places like a river. For he remembered his holy promise, and Abraham his servant and he brought forth his people with joy, and his chosen with gladness: And gave them the lands of the heathen: and they inherited the labour of the people; That they might observe his statutes and keep his laws. Praise ye the LORD."

Please, read this, Psalms 105, three times as this is part of the reason that Lehi asked Nephi to go get the plates from Laban in Jerusalem which is now translated as. As you see, unlike *Howning Your Sphere*, where the heart of the work centered around Job as an example and a memoir of experiential and spiritual evolving of me, the author, *The Psalm of the Messageur* is helping you as a student who is teachable, through obedience and experimentation upon the words and songs of great men throughout the standard works of Christ's gospel, to mature and take heed of the warnings by being exposed to another, more immediate eternal perspective. You've gotten some milk, and now it's time for some meat.

When you bear with me on a journey already revealed, my hope is that you realize that I am only a vessel to expose you to knowledge not created by me but by beings beyond the veil. I promise your awareness has already increased, and when you're ready as the student, the Teacher will appear, as long as you continue to progress with the missionary discussions from the Church of Latter-Day Saints. For those of you who have already joined the church or have been members for years or even generations, I welcome you to take this journey with me and to maintain a steady diet of temple attendance, genealogy work, and daily prayer and scripture study along with fellowship and full activity, while helping others to hold to the rod by your example along the way. You must continuously read: The Book of Mormon, the Old and New Testaments, the Doctrine and Covenants, and the Pearl of Great Price, and share them with your children and relatives along with friends and acquaintances. A pair of elders (missionaries), as they are called, challenged me at our correlation meeting this week to share a Book of Mormon with someone this week and gave me a copy. Since this book changed my life, it behooveth me to share with others the peace, joy, and happiness that will be imparted to you when you read this book along with being taught by the missionaries. I know that the Lord will help me as I prayerfully seek an individual through inspiration and prompting to whom to give this book, with my testimony of its truthfulness written inside and my phone number when they want to know more.

So if the scriptures confuse you or make you feel like the message is disjointed, obedience to the challenges I propose in the trilogy will open your eyes and allow understanding, and every fiber of your being will know that Jesus is the Christ and that the Gospels are true and with the Book of Mormon, many lost truths are restored with a second witness of the divinity of Christ and his mission, which is soon to apex with his second coming.

In Psalms 1:19 BETH: 9-16, you read, "Wherewithal shall a young man cleanse his way? by taking heed thereto according to thy word. With my whole heart have I sought thee: O let me not wander from thy commandments. Thy word have I hid in mine heart, that I might not sin against thee. Blessed art thou O LORD: teach me thy statutes. With my lips have I declared all the judgments of thy mouth. I have rejoiced in the way of thy testimonies, as much as in all riches. I will meditate in thy precepts and have respect unto thy ways. I will delight myself in thy statutes: I will not forget thy word."

Now you understand what has happened to me and it will happen to you if you let it; first you must receive the truth, be faithful unto baptism by one holding the same authority as John the Baptist and endure to the end. I'm still a work in progress. Come unto Christ, and we'll share this journey together.

Psalm 43:3-4 exclaims, "O send out thy light and thy truth: let them lead me; let them bring me unto thy holy hill, and to thy tabernacles. Then will I go unto the altar of God, unto God my exceeding joy: yea, upon the harp will I praise thee, O God my God." This place is the temple of our Lord, and you may enter after one year of membership and worthiness. You will read Psalms 105 again, this time in a silent state of meditation and breathing and think about the way you feel. This is the Holy Ghost, and you must act upon the promptings you feel as the passage is narrow, and the time fleeting for you to accept this message and seek progression. Let me share a few more scriptures on the subject, and as you have read Psalms 105 in previous pages, this will be preparatory for your next quantum leap of faith to seek baptism into the fold.

Psalms 44:1 states, "We have heard with our ears, O God, our fathers have told us, what work thou didst in their days, in the times of old." The message is the same today. By studying that which has occurred in the past, we may tell the future based on doing the same thing over and over again and expecting a different outcome. When you realize we're in a compulsive cycle of repentance, prosperity, pride, sinfulness, humility, and repentance again by studying thousands of years of documented suffering through action and resulting consequence, you will realize the grander plan of the overseer. Until then you are "earth people" and will cease to see beyond the physical reality that we all struggle with daily pursuit of happiness in material possessions instead of the prize that goes beyond this existence into the next. If this doesn't intrigue you, then put this book down and pray. You may wonder, "Why the redundancy of reading Psalms 105 so many times?" If you are, read it again and again and again. Three times will work!

Please, read this, Psalms 105, three times as this is part of the reason that Lehi asked Nephi to go get the plates from Laban in Jerusalem, which is now translated as Prophets, and those with wisdom to impart from on high have been on the earth during the Old Testament before Christ foretelling of His coming. During the New Testament, Christ was here, and after His ascension to the Father, His Apostles remained on the North and South American continents. As recorded in the Book of Mormon, the last presence of a prophet was 400 A.D., when the sacred records were sealed and hidden. So, until Joseph Smith came forth, there was a time of darkness where no prophet who spoke with God was available to men. For over fourteen hundred years, messages from deity to man for the entire race world-wide ceased. I am grateful for the restored priesthood and a prophet, seer, and revelator being with us today, the only man who communes with Jehovah on our behalf, even Thomas Spencer Monson. He is the president of the Church of Jesus Christ of Latter-Day Saints and my favorite General Authority. There are witnesses in all forms when the Lord sees fit to impart messages for specific individuals to accomplish His desires among the children of men. For instance, John the Beloved walks the Earth today as an immortal being. The three Nephites who requested to tarry rather than join Christ on the other side remain among us as immortal beings. Many came forth, as it states in Philippians and Ephesians, simultaneously resurrected with the Savior when he walked out from the sepulcher, and they remain some of the three hundred souls with us today. You may or may not be aware of them even if you've met, unless you have discernment and the Gift of the Holy Ghost and, most importantly, the Lord wants you to see and know so as to accomplish His work or to further such work in this realm. As you will find in Psalms 113:6, "Who humbleth himself to behold the things that are in heaven, and in the earth!" You cannot buy or control these gifts; you must receive them through a series of obedient converted time periods and only exercise them for the Lord's purpose and with meekness and submission. In a Messianic Psalms 89:48, Maschil of Ethan the Ezrahite asks in song of David's seed, which includes Jesus

Christ, "What man is he that liveth, and shall not see death? Shall he deliver his soul from the hand of the grave? Selah."

Angels have always been on the Lord's errand and have often been used to relay messages to the children of men. Psalms 104:4 explains what happened to me as a not-yet member in Kensington, Maryland, at the D.C. temple while walking up the hill after seeing the light display and multi-cultural Christmas trees, "Who maketh His angel's spirits," and as it states in the footnote 4a, "OR the winds his messengers," when I was frozen on the sidewalk by an unseen force and had vortexes of wind alternately coming towards me from the left full of leaves that fell as the wind passed through me with a message: "Let Satan out, and let me in," passing from the right and then the left, again repeating the exact same words. As I looked to the golden statue of Moroni, I knew my life had been altered in that moment like never before.

Psalms 34:7 explains, "The angel of the LORD encampeth round about them that fear him, and delivereth them." David exhorts the saints to bless the LORD in Psalms 103:20-22: "Bless the LORD, ye his angels, that excel in strength, that do his commandments, hearkening unto the voice of his word. Bless ye the LORD, all ye his hosts; ye ministers of his, that do his pleasure. Bless the LORD, all his works in all places of his dominion: bless the LORD, O my soul." When you are on the Lord's errand, you are blessed to be as an angel among men to share his restored message and partake of the eternal blessings that caused many to want to remain in an earth stained by sin and transgression to continue the work of the Savior until he comes again, when we will all be resurrected and judged after one thousand years, a millennial reign in the absence of Satan and his angels, when the mediator will complete the work of the entire human race, sealing us all to each other and completing this earthly mission so that we can go forth and do the same for future inhabitants of this planet and others.

I feel as Alma to humble myself as I share my conversion experiences with you inside and outside the church. Alma 38:6-9 explains to his son, Shiblon, how I feel: "Now, my son, I would not that ye should think that I know these things of myself, but it is the Spirit of God which is in me which maketh these things known unto me; for if I had not been born of God I should not have known these things. But behold, the Lord in his great mercy sent his angel to declare unto me that I must stop the work of destruction among his people; yea, and I have seen an angel face to face, and he spake with me, and his voice was as thunder, and it shook the whole earth. And it came to pass that I was three days and three nights in the most bitter pain of anguish and soul; and never until I did cry out unto the lord Jesus Christ for mercy, did I receive a remission of my sins. But behold, I did cry unto him and I did find peace to my soul."

I feel like Saul of Tarsus on the road to Damascus when the Lord asked him, "Why persecutest thou me?" Saul became Paul the Apostle and is a Benjamite, or of the Tribe of Benjamin in house of Israel, who was Jacob. I also am a Benjamite, and as Israel blessed each son with unique gifts, I feel that due to my lineage from my patriarchal blessing that I, too, have inherited the ability to require much to turn my direction to the straight and narrow path. I also have to remember the counsel in Alma 38:10-12, which warns Shiblon, "And now, as ye have begun to teach the word even so I would that ye should continue to teach; and I would that ye would be diligent and temperate in all things. See that ye are not lifted up unto pride; yea, see that ye do not boast in your *aun* wisdom, nor of your much strength. Use boldness, but not over-bearance; and also, that ye bridle all your passions, that ye may be filled with love; see that ye refrain from idleness." There was a time when I felt idle and devastated with loss. I've overcome this through the Lord Jesus Christ and many messageurs along the journey's path.

David pleads in Psalms 25:4, "Shew me thy ways, O LORD; teach me thy paths." On a sacred day for me, I chose to go on the Appalachian Trail for an experience like Joseph Smith had in the sacred grove, and when tapped on the shoulder while my guard dogs lay there as if no one was there, I had a conversation with a guy in military fatigues, which is what I was wearing, up on this cliff where the trees were deformed and dwarfed as a result of harsh climate and elevation. We talked about the Savior Jesus Christ, and then I followed a path of white stones that transported and translated me to another dimension where I traveled three miles without walking. When I realized I was home, I turned around and my dogs that always followed me religiously were nowhere to be seen. I saw an altar of white stones and realized that either I had done this before or someone else had. I later met the gentleman who worked in an eighty-story underground FEMA complex for the President and his cabinet in case of a nuclear strike on D. C., and he didn't remember anything about our meeting on the cliff, and he also spoke in a different voice and accent. The Lord had used him as a messageur and had an angel step into his body to lead me to the experience I had. There was a lot more that happened that day, and as you'll recall, I wrote about it in *Howning Your Sphere*. Psalms 102:6, which reminds me of Pine Knoll Shores in North Carolina, states, "I am like a pelican of the wilderness: I am like an owl of the desert." In footnote 6a, pelican means "walking with God." I try to do that daily through studying scripture, magnifying my responsibilities in the church, and praying meditatively.

My experience in Virginia Beach defies earthly logic. As I was driving down towards Oceana in my old '72 F-250 by myself, someone unseen in my pickup truck told me three times to "go in there." I was dumbfounded as I looked and beheld what looked like a large church building, and as I recognized the experience to be of God, I hearkened unto the command and went inside the church and met a bishop and missionaries of the

LDS persuasion. I relayed to them what had happened, and they called me "golden," moved me into a room, and began to teach me. These were Elders Davis and Peterson who eventually were disappointed weeks later to find I had to clear up a legal issue before I could be baptized. I knew this was the right thing to do after having read the Book of Mormon in seven days and having gained a testimony of the truthfulness of the missionaries' teachings. You can see patterns of repetition and the three-time significance throughout the scriptures once you study them and they become, as Alma said, "delicious" to you.

Psalms 115:9-11 uses the phrase, "Trust in the LORD" three times. My experience has been that the Lord gets your attention the first time, helps you realize you're not audibly doing this yourself the second time and, ultimately convinces you to ACT on the message the third time. Like Joseph Smith's first vision, which, by the way, is either totally true and all that comes from it or totally false, Moroni visited him three times in the night and rehearsed the same message in its entirety exactly using the same words. Do you see a habit forming?

Psalms 34:18 explains what your state of mind must be to receive messages and also correlates to Moroni 10:3-5, when you are informed, "The Lord is nigh unto them that are of a broken heart; and saveth such as be of a contrite spirit. Peter, James, and John came to Joseph Smith and Oliver Cowdery on the banks of the Susquehanna River in Harmony, Pennsylvania, to confer the Priesthood of God that left the earth when the last Apostle died to both men and to restore the ability of the sealing power once again to the earth through Elijah in the Kirtland temple while all keys were restored, including the keys of the gathering from Moses who appeared also in Kirtland temple. If I'm getting too heavy for you, take a breath and let your analytical guard down, and learn to ponder and lose yourself between the lines. This is where true understanding is realized. John the Baptist appeared to Joseph Smith and

Oliver Cowdery when they inquired of the Lord concerning baptism. The keys of the kingdom are restored again, and Elijah has turned the hearts of the children to the fathers through genealogy work.

It is with much difficulty that I overcome current circumstances to sit here and compose this life-changing prose, and only if my perspective is redirected, the sacrifice to bring this information to you is worth it. When my first daughter Elizabeth came into my living room in Independence, Missouri, and in perfect vernacular told me that she had seen me in the temple, I asked if she spoke of the photo album I was looking at.

She said, "No, Daddy, I saw you on the stairs."

I immediately and instantly recalled the event in the D.C. temple that she was reminding me of. A full-grown woman appeared on the stairs leading to the Holy of Holies outside of the sealing rooms, and I caught a glimpse of her looking at me. When she realized I could see her, she turned and went up the stairs and vanished into thin air. My daughter had visited me before her birth as an adult spirit in the temple and was reminding me of the experience as a two-year-old who, up until that point, couldn't put a sentence together and had trouble pronouncing the simplest words. I share this because I want you to know of the sacred nature of the temples and challenge you to do all that you can to hold a temple recommend and enter the house of the Lord to commune with your ancestors, to be sealed for time and all eternity to your living family, and to remain worthy to visit and make sacred covenants and learn the process of making your way to the Celestial Kingdom where your Heavenly Father, Eloheim, and His Son, Jesus Christ, live, along with all who have made their calling in election made sure by enduring to the end living Christ's example. Children remember the pre-existence until the world takes over, and we seem to grow further and further from any recollection as we age; then life goes full circle as we ponder our terminal physical existence and begin to wonder what the purpose of life is.

In Psalms 8:2, a Messianic Psalm of David, you learn, "Out of the mouth of babes and sucklings hast thou ordained strength because of thine enemies, that thou mightest still the enemy and the avenger." In footnote 2a, "babes" means "children." So, many times as the first shall be last and the last shall be first, you'll find that seemingly younger and ignorant children may know the things that we spend our whole life suffering through trials and tribulations to find out. In other words, the most important things in this life are easily accessible when you know where to find them, or even more importantly, when you're ready to learn them, and implement the knowledge into your ACTSYS (action system from *Howning Your Sphere*).

There is a type of message that the greatest messageur, the Holy Ghost, has brought me repeatedly, and it's always in the same format even though the content varies. In Psalms 18:2-4, a Messianic Psalm, a message important enough to repeat four times is given as follows, "O GIVE thanks unto the LORD; for He is good: because his mercy endureth forever. Let Israel now say, that his mercy endureth forever. Let the house of Aaron now say, that his mercy endureth forever. Let them now that fear the LORD say, that His mercy endureth forever." It's written four times, all for the same people, it seems; however just so you know, we have more than half of our church members who don't go or participate, and it was no different in David's time, even if it was a way of life. In the residence Marriot in Bethesda, Maryland, after receiving the ultimate sealing covenants of temple marriage, I was reading Lectures on Faith by Joseph Smith, and after completing a section of one brother who begat, who begat, who begat, not understanding why a list needed to be made from Adam through all dispensations of time to Joseph Smith's last dispensation, I knelt to pray. I asked, "What wilt thou have me to do for thee?"

Just then, in the darkness of our room I heard a man telling me, "Go to Missouri, go to Missouri, go to Missouri."

I immediately knew that we had to go, but I didn't know how. We were struggling financially, and I had a construction company in Virginia, and a lease on our house in Harper's Ferry, West Virginia, along with vehicles with mechanical problems. I didn't know how, but the Lord did. We received a call from Korea from my wife's aunt requesting me to go look at a house in Winchester, Virginia, to renovate. We ended up receiving enough to tie up loose ends even after many sabotage attempts by those close to us, and we left. Psalms 107, verses 8, 15 ,21, and 34 all say the exact same words: "Oh that men would praise the LORD for his goodness, and for his wonderful works to the children of men!" Again, the Lord doesn't waste his breath. Repetition is necessary; daily prayer and scripture study are necessary; dedication and ACTS in unison are necessary to keep at the forefront of your conscience an indelible impression significant enough to derail the train going in the other direction seeking to thwart your awareness.

Laveda, a lady in Missouri whom I was assigned to home teach, *was* less active for years. The missionaries and I pronounced a blessing on her which stated that if she chose to not work on Sundays and if she instead attended to her family's spiritual needs and came to the three-hour block of meetings every Sunday, her income would be replaced. Two months went by, and I was sitting down to a nice medium-rare Delmonico Steak dinner complete with the trimmings when a voice said, "Go to the stake center, go to the stake center, go to the stake center."

I got up and went to the stake center about three miles away. It only took a few minutes. I walked into the church building we call the stake center, where the center of many wards is overseen. I noticed a baptism going on, so I sat down to wait for an impression or prompting, anything to explain why I had been called away from my dinner. Just in that moment, I felt like I needed to get up and further look for the Lord's purpose in all this. As I went into the hallway I saw Ifo, my Hawaiian friend, and asked if he needed me for anything and he said, "No, why do you ask?"

I moved on without an explanation and turned the corner and saw the bishop's door ope. Feeling impressed to go in, I asked, "Bishop, do you need me for anything?"

He said, "No, why?"

I started to explain when the high priest group leader rushed in a panic and said that Laveda had fallen at work and broken her hip. I failed to mention that we had just experienced a bad winter ice storm, and everything was covered. At the time, I had a four-wheel-drive Expedition and was able to transport her after she was home to her surgeon in Kansas, even though we still didn't top forty miles an hour on the interstate. If you believe that these things are coincidental or that I'm schizophrenic, there may be no hope of bringing you to awareness at this time. If you find yourself trying to intellectualize an explanation for how this could happen, or if you're pondering the possibility, maybe you're ready. If you feel elation and are reminded of similar experiences in your life, or if you feel that this is possible, congratulations. Either you're a member, or you should be. Read the Book of Mormon, contact the missionaries, be baptized, and have your family sealed together for time and all eternity or get married in the temple. Just take that first step, that leap of faith, and when you arrive, don't thank me—thank Jesus Christ for helping us progress towards exaltation in the life to come.

I'll never forget President McGill during my conversion process when he asked me how I felt about being denied baptism. I told him I'd found the true church, and I would pay tithing whether a member or not, and that no matter how long it took, like Francenso De Francheska, I would do what it took to be baptized; and I did. Later, after leaving Virginia

Beach without being baptized to the disappointment of Elders Davis and Peterson, the first from California and the second from Illinois, I traveled to Loudoun County, Virginia, to be with my sister, brother-in-law, and their children, where we all lived in a converted chicken coop until Steve and I were able to lease six acres and a sizable house on the top of a mountain on the Appalachian Trail. There I met Elders Harrison and Barnhill, who ultimately became the beneficiaries, along with me, of the convert baptism of Michael E. Durgin. During the interview process with then-Mission President Hamula, of the D.C. Mission South, who is now in the Seventy, I shared my story of the dark side and how I'd managed to follow promptings from unseen beings to be in his office to interview for baptism.

He exclaimed after hearing of the carnage, "Brother Durgin, you must have been real valiant in the pre-existence to have gone through what you have and be sitting here now in my office." We talked of family and of my talents as a general contractor, and he asked if I might build him a house in Mesa, Arizona, after he was released. I recently emailed him at an address I found online to ask President Monson about a sealing clearance for me to take my current wife to the Boston temple to be sealed, and I heard nothing back. Oh well, that's neither here nor there. These things take time.

President Thomas Spencer Monson is the prophet on the Earth today, and I've always loved his inspirational talks with poetry and personally journal-led experiences throughout along with tonality shifts and resonation that move many times to tears as he speaks of his lengthy selfless service as a young bishop. President Monson, I love you and sustain you as prophet, seer, and revelator. Once, while at the Saint Louis temple dedication, I sat three floors down from President Monson during a dedicatory session and looked at him on the television screen provided for those not in the same room or floor with him. I looked at him and thought how wonderful it would be to meet him face to face, and at that moment, he stopped as we connected telekinetically and stared into the camera and said, "I wish I could meet all of you face to face." That was a special moment for me as I knew he could hear my thoughts—no coincidence, you think? The Lord hears you when you pray, especially with a contrite spirit and broken heart. This is why the Book of Mormon prophet, Moroni, challenges its readers to ponder the message and ask Heavenly Father, in the name of Jesus Christ, if it is not true, and the truth shall be manifest unto you by the power of the Holy Ghost. Remember, the Book of Mormon is translated by the gift of God and using the Urim and Thummim to translate from reformed Egyptian and ancient Hebrew. This is why the words, if it is not true, mean to see if it is true. If you haven't read the Book of Mormon or listened to the missionaries of the Church of Jesus Christ of Latter-Day Saints yet, DO IT NOW with real intent! Many of your loved ones, past and present, are depending on you.

I still recall being at my dinner table in Independence, Missouri, and hearing the familiar voice three times, just as in the past messages. This time, the Spirit directed me to go to the Salt Lake temple as the Lord had a message for me. This was twelve hundred miles, and the first time we tried to go, the motor blew in my Explorer. The second time we went was in my Expedition with luggage on the roof, my entire family, and two children from another family to drop off with their Mom for the summer. We hit a storm with golf-ball-sized hail on the Nebraska-Wyoming border that dented my SUV mercilessly. We made it through this time, and we went to the temple, my wife and I, and through sentinels who knew we were coming, we were directed to the room and given the message. The Lord said, "You are a high priest in Heaven." Like what President Hamula said to me about being valiant in the pre-existence, this reinforced that statement, and I have yet to be called to a high priest position on Earth. Being an elder and holder of the Holy Melchizedek Priesthood is a privilege and an honor that I hold sacred, and being sealed by the authority of the Priesthood for time and all eternity to my wife and my children is also quite an accomplishment and a feat that I'm certain would not have occurred had I not been visited many times by the Lord and his Spirit and given guidance and direction to keep me on the straight and narrow path. I can only hope that my sitting here and punching my life out on this computer for you will make a difference for generations to come as the Lord has beckoned and nudged me forward in this trilogy.

Jim, the owner of a cab company and a leader in the church in Virginia, asked me while I was working on his house with my brother-in-law Steve, "Mike, if you knew there was a church on the Earth today that Jesus Christ himself was the head of, would you want to be a member of it?"

I responded, "Well, yeah, Jim, that's a no-brainer."

Jim was a messageur who broke the ice and another who planted a seed that made me think for a moment about things I'd never considered before. Thank you, Jim. I'll never forget your bold question that helped me to join this church and bless the living and the dead in my ancestry along with my family in the future. Elder Harrison taught me how to tie a double Windsor on my necktie at the tender age of thirty-four the day of my baptism. Small things mean a lot.

Then there's the story of Ray, one of my air conditioning service technicians who was investigating the church. At the time I was running a fast-growing service company out of my home, which many times caused the sanctity of my home to be violated by unwanted beings, both living and not in bodies. This one day, things were unusually stressed in my home, and my little children were having accidents left and right, and as we do in the church, I felt impressed to rededicate our home and cast the evil out. Using the authority of the priesthood, I cast out devils, and the front door opened and slammed by itself, and you could feel the air change. I had invited Ray over for dinner. Even though Ray's habits and lifestyle were very foul and left much to be desired, I felt he earnestly deserved a chance to hear the Gospel of Jesus Christ. He was approaching my front step and came towards the door when suddenly he did a gainer back flip fifteen feet in the air and landed out in the yard about twenty feet away. If I wouldn't have seen it with my own eyes, I wouldn't have believed it either. It was as if a force field rejected him and threw him away from the house. When I went outside, he was confused and dazed and asked, "What happened? I must have fallen?"

I tried to explain that I had blessed the house and asked that the Spirit circumnavigate the house and shun all evil from it. Of course, he didn't get it, and maybe you don't either. Suffice it to say, the things we speak of and the Priesthood of God is real and has been restored to the Earth to bless the human race prior to Christ's Second Coming. In Doctrine and Covenants 50:12-24, you learn, "Now, when a man reasoned he is understood of man, because he reasoned as a man; even so will I, the Lord, reason with you that you may understand. Wherefore, I the Lord ask you this question—unto what were ye ordained?" Footnote 13a for "ordained" is "TG Priesthood, Ordination." "To preach my gospel by the Spirit, even the Comforter which was sent forth to teach the truth. And then received ye spirits which ye could not understand, and received them to be of God; and in this are ye justified? Behold ye shall answer this question yourselves; Nevertheless, I will be merciful unto you; he that is weak among you hereafter shall be made strong.

"Verily I say unto you, he that is ordained of me and sent forth to preach the word of truth by the Comforter, in the Spirit of truth, doth he preach it by the Spirit of truth or some other way? And if it be by some other way it is not of God. And again, he that receiveth the word of truth, doth he receives it by the Spirit of truth or some other way? If it be some other way it is not of God. Therefore, why is it that ye cannot understand and know, that he that receiveth the word by the Spirit of truth receiveth it as it is preached by the Spirit of truth? Wherefore, he that preacheth and he that receiveth, understand one another, and both are edified and rejoice together. And that which doth not edify is not of God and is darkness. That which is of God is light; and he that receiveth light, and continueth in God, receiveth more light; and that light growth brighter and brighter until the perfect day." Where two are gathered in Christ's name, the Holy Ghost will be present, and the exchange will be fruitful and bless both the teacher and the pupil, for the message will edify both.

The experience I had with the white stones and the new name was a result of purpose, faith, and an ACTSYS that took me to that ridge and allowed me to pass into a state of being I had yet to ever realize, allowing me to see through the veil and feel the honor of my calling in election being made sure as long as I remained on the path to eternal life and continued to seek the guidance that white stones of experience and wisdom provide. For you, I have no idea what your experiences will be like, but it will be fun to find out. Psalms 104:10 sums up the nature of our souls being harrowed up in a perfect way similar to that day on the Appalachian Trail on that ridge of extreme weather deformed trees: "He sendeth the springs into the valleys, which run among the hills." The spring I drank from that day before I heard the mountain lion capture the turkey allowed me to see a dimension all around us that only relaxation and an eye single in purpose will allow. The spring I speak of is eternal life, and once you've drank from it, you will never thirst again spiritually. Psalms 119GIMEL:18 explains how I felt before I left my house that day: "Open thou mine eyes, that I may behold wondrous things out of thy law." Psalms 119DALETH:27 is the purpose of this work: "Make me to understand the way of thy precepts: so, shall I talk of thy wondrous works." I am grateful that I have lived to share the experiences of my life with you; I only ask one thing in return. Go and do the same.

As I seek to differentiate between my personal revelations for myself and eventually for my family and the revelations that the Prophet receives, I'd like to clear one thing with you; I do not receive revelation for you or another's family unless the Lord calls me to be a judge in Israel or a bishop, and then and only then can I receive counsel and inspiration for those over whom I am a steward. My experiences are exactly that. For that reason, I need only share them with you as my truth, and beyond that validation is unnecessary. The Prophet holds all priesthood keys, and if you'd like to know what he feels, you should do what he says, be obedient, listen to your bishop, and attend faithfully your meetings, classes, and general conference in October and April. Listen and do the things you are told and avoid the things that would plague you according to the words of general authorities of the church, appointed as your seers and revelators at this time. The greatest messageur is the Savior, Jesus Christ and his servants are his voice to us. Pay attention and give heed to their warnings, counsel, and advice. When there was no prophet on the Earth, Maschil of Asaph says, in Psalms 74:9-11, "We see not our signs: there is no more any prophet: neither is there among us any that knoweth how long. O God, how long shall the adversary reproach? Shall the enemy blaspheme thy name forever? Why withdrawest thou thy hand, even thy right hand? pluck it out of thy bosom." Obviously, a prophet is important to man in general. First, you must gain a testimony of the prophet and his importance. Then Psalms 89:15 reveals, "Blessed is the people that know the joyful sound: they shall walk, O LORD, in the light of thy countenance." Psalms 119GIMEL: 19 reads, "I am a stranger in the earth: hide not thy commandments from me." In footnote 19a, "stranger" means HEB "sojourner," i.e., not of this world. I am now a stranger, will you come with me to a familiar place?

I've often felt that I needed rescue from this place and have found many willing to throw me a rope and pull me to higher ground where a new perspective and awareness existed that up to that point of surrender I was unaware of completely. First, again, and one more time, read Psalms 105 in its entirety, which will be preparatory for my rope analogy to follow. Every time I read the same scripture, not only can I not remember what it meant to me before, but it inevitably takes on new meaning based on circumstance and wisdom of progression.

I snuck that communication excerpt in there before Psalms 105 with purpose. Did it seem totally different this time? If so, I accomplished my objective. If not, you still have some work to do. Remember, the student must be ready before the teacher will appear. I could be standing right in front of you right now, and you wouldn't even know that I had a message for you unless you were receptive and openly prepared. Then if you alleviate noise and focus on me, the visitor, I could impart what you seek but not until then.

The Lord works in much the same way. John the Beloved or the three Nephites could walk up to you today, and if you were too busy to discern, they would move on unnoticed by you.

A rope is quite a complex creation that has many functions, and the proper knowledge in knot-tying can provide help and assistance that without a rope would be impossible. Let's look at a rope and compare it to a single strand of sewing thread. Cordage, the stringy strands that comprise the makeup of a strong rope, are very thin and not as strong as thread. When the cordage is twisted together, strands of greater thickness are created that, when woven, will become a rope that, with one's hand and some knowledge of the "bowline" knot, can retrieve a victim from a cliff without slipping and cutting off circulation, potentially harming the victim. Now, if you don't have a rope and you've never learned the knot, then the victim will probably perish unless you go find an experienced rescue crew with the ropes and the knowledge. The rope started with a single strand of cordage that would hold little weight and grew into a rope that, when used by the proper person, will save a life. This is the rope that I'm throwing you with this trilogy. You must grab the rope and tie it around yourself and receive instruction on how to secure yourself and allow the rescue to take place. Only you know how long you'll last on the cliff without any help. Depending on darkness, elevation, and your preparedness, nights can be very lonely when isolated from those you love, and helplessness can set in. Usually when you've reached the end of your rope, the Savior's hand is there to catch you and comfort you and show you the way to safety. I can grab a rope with one hand and tie the knot around my waist in thirteen seconds. That takes practice; also, faith is required to let go of the cliff you're clinging to and trust the rope and the rescuer to do what they do best. In one of my favorite movies, the main character stands over a bottomless chasm looking across the abyss at the cave that holds the holy grail for which his father spent his lifetime searching. At that moment while he's helpless to cross, his father's voice in his memory gives him the clue that if he steps into the canyon there will appear out of invisibility a way. Having faith in his father, he steps out over the bottomless chasm, and a stepping stone appears. In amazement, he realizes that the invisible stones were there all along. He grabs a handful of sand and throws it in the direction in front of him, which reveals a path of similar stones that will allow him to cross and claim a prize that only he was allowed to claim. I extend an invitation from the Lord for you to take that leap of faith and to be baptized and find the path that you were on prior to this life that you lost sight of upon physical birth and that you must find again to find your way back from whence you came, this time improved through mortal probation.

Hopefully, the rope analogy didn't throw you for a loop. Doctrine and Covenants 123:12-17 states plainly the dilemma, "For there are many yet on the earth among all sects, parties, and denominations, who are blinded by the subtle craftiness of men, whereby they lie in wait to deceive, and who are only kept from the truth because they know not where to find it— Therefore, that we should waste and wear out our lives in bringing to light all the hidden things of darkness, wherein we know them; and they are truly manifest from heaven— THESE SHOULD THEN BE ATTENDED TO WITH GREAT EARNESTNESS. Let no man count them as small things; for there is much which lieth in futurity, pertaining to the saints, which depends upon these things. You know, brethren, that a very large ship is benefited very much by a very small helm in the time of a storm, by being kept workways with the wind and the waves. Therefore, dearly beloved brethren, let us cheerfully do all things that lie in our power; and then may we stand still, with the utmost assurance, to see the salvation of God, and for his arm to be revealed."

Do you believe that you're worth my time writing this to help you to the light? If so, then ACT accordingly; put this book down, and call the missionaries. If you're already a member and have a temple recommend and hold the priesthood, pick up the phone and check in with your home-teaching or visiting-teaching assignments. Sign up for genealogy classes or set a date each month to go to the temple. Cheerfully progress, and all my words will have meaning for you as I learned from others and the Holy Spirit of truth and promise.

There are two Josephs that in different times in history brought to pass very important tasks for the Lord, and one thousands of years before told of the other to come. Without them, I wouldn't be imparting from their works and my experience in the way I am. One was Joseph, son of Israel who was sold into Egypt by his brothers; the other by the same first name was Joseph Smith, the first Prophet of the Last Dispensation of time. The first is mentioned in Psalms 105:17-45: "He sent a man before them, even Joseph, who was sold for a servant: Whose feet they hurt with fetters: he was laid in iron: Until the time that his word came: the word of the LORD tried him. The king sent and loosed him; even the ruler of the people and let him go free. He made him lord of his house, and ruler of all his substance: To bind his princes at his pleasure; and teach his senators wisdom. Israel also came into Egypt; and Jacob sojourned in the land of Ham. And he increased his people greatly; and made them stronger than their enemies. He turned their heart to hate his people, to deal subtly with his servants. He sent Moses his servant; and Aaron whom he had chosen. They shewed his signs among them, and wonders in the land of Ham. He sent darkness and made it dark; and they rebelled not against his word. He turned their waters into blood and slew their fish. Their land brought forth frogs in abundance, in the chambers of their kings. He spake, and there came divers sorts of flies, and lice in their coasts. He gave them hail for rain and flaming fire in their land. He smote their vines also and their fig trees; and brake the trees of their coasts. He spake, and the locusts came, and caterpillars, and that without number, and did eat up all the herbs in their land and devoured the fruit of their ground. He smote also the firstborn of their land, the chief of all their strength. He brought them forth also with silver and gold: and there was not one feeble person among their tribes. Egypt was glad when they departed: for the fear of them fell upon them. He spread a cloud for covering; and fire to give light in the night. The people asked, and he brought quails, and satisfied them with the bread of heaven. He opened the rock and the waters gushed out; they ran in the dry places like a river. For he remembered his holy promise, and Abraham his servant. And he brought forth his people with joy, and his chosen with gladness: And gave them the lands of the heathen: and they inherited the labor of the people; that they might observe his statutes and keep his laws. Praise ye the LORD."

Without the scriptures, you would have to go through the same things; what am I saying? You have the scriptures, and ye wrest them or worse yet know not of their existence or the wisdom and guidance therein. Read the scriptures of the Old Testament and the New Testament and combine them with the restored testament of Jesus Christ, a second witness from the Americas, the Book of Mormon, Doctrine and Covenants, and the Pearl of Great Price, which contains the writings of Moses and Abraham and pays great heed to their counsel.

Joseph Smith's First Vision, the restoration of the priesthood, and revelation pertaining to the organization and government of Christ's church on the earth today make the second Joseph even more important to us than the first. Joseph Smith saw Jesus Christ and Heavenly Father in the sacred grove in New York. He also was visited and taught by John the Baptist, John the Beloved, Elijah, Elias, Moses, Peter, James, John, and Moroni the angel. All the keys of the kingdom were bestowed on him as the medium for the restoration of all things as a prophet, seer, and revelator. Those keys are held by each successive Prophet and are bestowed upon Thomas Spencer Monson as the current Prophet on the Earth today.

President Gordon Bittner Hinckley was the Prophet of the church when I joined and for the first fourteen years in the church. During his tenure, more temples were built than in any prophet's period of leadership. President Hinckley died while I was composing the first book of this trilogy, and I have no doubt that he is reunited with Marjorie Pay Hinckley, his wife, on the other side of the veil. Brigham Young was the prophet who waited the longest after the martyrdom of the Prophet Joseph Smith and his brother, the patriarch of the church,

Hyrum Smith at the Carthage Jail. Brigham Young would not live to see the completion of the Salt Lake temple as it was dedicated by Wilford Woodruff. Brigham Young and his cousin Elizabeth Haven Young, who later married Israel Barlow and became my children's fourth great-grandmother, came from Menden, New York, and were later called the Menden, New York, Mormons. Psalms 118:22 proclaims, "The stone which the builders refused is become the headstone of the corner."

The people of Christ rejected Him and didn't realize that He is the rock of your salvation. Many today reject the Prophet and the true Gospel the same way while professing being "saved" as an excuse for turning a blind eye to the restored truth and its inherent eternal blessings found in making eternal covenants in the Temples of our Lord. What say ye? The Urim and the Thummim are seer stones that allowed Joseph Smith to hear God's translation of the ancient Hebrew and reformed Egyptian text found in the Book of Mormon. The Freemasons have gone to great lengths along with the Templars to hide and to find the "philosopher's stone" that would allow men to talk with God. I wonder if there's any relation as Lehi felt it important enough for his sons to risk their lives to retrieve the records and these sacred articles for future generations. In a little over two months, what took almost a century to do with scholars—the translation of the Bible—was accomplished by a young man with a fifth-grade education. The Book of Mormon was first published, five thousand copies, by the Grandin Printing Company and is available today for you to read AND TO FIND AS I DID OF ITS TRUTH AND ENTER IN TO THE ONLY TRUE CHURCH ON THE FACE OF THE EARTH THROUGH THE WATERS OF BAPTISM.

You've probably noticed that included in this second of three works are many more scriptures than in the previous first of my published works. The scriptures should be delicious to you by now, and if not,

I pray that you will delve prayerfully into these books of ancient and current significance. If your only exposure thus far has been within these pages, then I consider it a privilege to have been a guide to the portal of eternal life and exaltation. However, I am not the teacher from whom you seek forgiveness; He died on the cross and was resurrected for you and for me, and you will gain entrance into His Kingdom and rest through the waters of baptism only done by one who has the authority as John the Baptist did to baptize Jesus Christ. Then and only then are your sins forgiven and your journey begun to help others in your past and your future to do as you have done. Psalms 32: 1,2, and 5 clarify this by describing the process: "BLESSED is he whose transgression is forgiven, whose sin is covered. Blessed is the man unto whom the LORD imputeth not iniquity, and in whose spirit, there is no guile. I acknowledged my sin unto thee, and my iniquity have I not hid. I said, I will confess my transgressions unto the LORD; and thou forgavest the iniquity of my sin. Selah."

You will want to do as I have done and become unspotted form the sins of this world and afterward partake of the sacrament regularly to remain such as we all continue to sin daily. After David went to Bathsheba, he pleads in Psalms l: 10 and 17 "Create in me a clean heart, O God; and renew a right spirit within me." David had fornicated and committed adultery, and even though he was king, his soul ached to be back in the graces of the Lord. Forgiveness is a cleansing that restores the channel of communication with the Holy Ghost. Psalms 103:17-19 is a Psalm of David: "But the mercy of the LORD is from everlasting to everlasting upon them that fear him, and his righteousness unto children's children; To such as keep his covenant, and to those that remember his commandments to do them. The LORD hath prepared his throne in the heavens; and his kingdom ruleth over all." Jesus Christ has commanded, "Do even as I do." If you are not yet baptized into the Church of Jesus

Christ of Latter-Day Saints, do you believe Christ's commandment and example is for you?

The day I went from an Aaronic Priesthood holder to having conferred upon me the Melchizedek Priesthood was a great day. I remember my brother-in-law and members of the bishopric in Hamilton Ward laying their hands upon my head and performing the ordinance. As I listened, I had a song come into my mind that stated, "Mama, Mama, I'm coming home." I felt like I had accomplished a rite of passage with this sacred privilege of being able to bless others using the authority of God for his purpose here on Earth. Peter, James, and John, the apostles, personally, as resurrected beings, appeared to Joseph Smith and Oliver Cowdery to bestow and restore this sacred priesthood to the Earth for the use of man preparatory for the Second Coming of Christ, never to be taken from man again. Psalms 132:9 exclaims, "Let thy priests be clothed with righteousness; and let thy saints shout for joy." Indeed, this is what I felt the day of my ordination, to shout for joy! Psalms 110:4 states, "The LORD hath sworn, and will not repent, Thou art a priest for ever after the order of Melchizedek." There is validation of the truthfulness of the restored Gospel of Jesus Christ and the authority to act on His behalf and in His name utilizing His Priesthood of old.

My experiences leading up to these great bestowals were many, and I'd like to share with you some brushes with death and guardians that I've encountered along with messages from beyond the veil. Some were interventions and other warnings and advice from friends and family from the post-mortal existence. If you have not had similar things happen, just understand that occurrences of this sort are only necessary for those of us who have faith in and a reason for such manifestations. During the birth of Isaiah, who was my only child born full-term (actually, ten days late), I thought that my wife would be able to deliver naturally without medication. I don't know what I was thinking, except that my ignorance and lack of understanding of my wife's epilepsy, which led to her death six years later, must have been absent from the forefront of my mind in a Utopian, homeopathic misperception. The extreme pain and labor eventually gave way to the use of Pitocin, a drug drip used to accelerate dilation. While this confusion and labor gave way to panic on my part, Paula started talking to her dead grandfather, Grandpa Lisonbie, asking him where I was, and I kept trying to butt in and say, "I'm right here." During travail, and in a state of pain, she had been visited by her dead grandpa, whom I could not see, and I feel he accompanied Isaiah into this life. There is no doubt that he was there, and even though my discernment at the time was blocked by circumstance, the Lord's will of seeing him was done. He comforted her as her guardian angel. Even though we never met, Paula had been closest to him before he died, and he was there in spirit.

Psalms 78 reminds me of another repetition of Psalms 105; please read it as I will not put it again as you have been exposed to Psalms 105 four times and that is sufficient. As far as Grandpa Lisonbie coming during Isaiah's birth, I will share Psalms 78:6-7, which states how I felt after having been third party during a sacred labor experience with my first son and his deceased great grandfather: "That the generation to come might know them, even the children which should be born; who should arise and declare them to their children: That they might set their hope in God, and not forget the works of God, but keep his commandments: And might not be as their fathers, a stubborn and rebellious generation; a generation that set not their heart aright, and whose spirit was not steadfast with God."

All of the children's deliveries were difficult and traumatic because of Paula's epilepsy. Her father, Paul, had told me that she wouldn't be able to have children on our way to the temple that day we were married, accompanied by a brother-in-law who I found out later was a multiple adulterer who lied his way into the temple. Isaiah is extremely creative and looks more like the Barlow side of the family. Isaiah Michael Durgin was born on August 22, 1997 and has been my only son of birth as I also claim my nephew who we had custody of for eight years as a son of inheritance. Jesse helped us immensely and we him. I'll not forget him in my will or for the rest of his life as I hope he'll be serving a mission one year before Isaiah goes on his.

Elizabeth Haven was born on September 24, 1998, the same day in September as my sister, Sharon, and named after her fourth-great-grandmother, Israel Barlow's wife and Brigham Young's cousin. Elizabeth was breach and had to be taken and induced three weeks before her due date. She was breach and required an internal aversion so as to avoid a Caesarian section. This means they oiled Paula's belly and turned the baby 180 degrees, so the head was down and then used a crochet-like hook to break the sack of amniotic fluid and then used Pitocin to speed dilation. She was delivered healthy and became our first daughter, and Isaiah nicknamed her "Sissy" or "Abilabet" because he was too young to pronounce her name. Elizabeth is musically inclined and is also athletic. They were very close, and I wonder now how that could have been as they are now almost thirteen and fourteen and seem incompatible.

Naomi Isabel was born January 25, 2000, the new millennial baby. What a way to ring in the new millennium. She was also breach and required an internal aversion, the unique thing being that each contraction made her heartbeat stop. We didn't know until her accelerated birth which was almost precipitous in nature, meaning fast, as Paula felt like she needed to use the bathroom, and the nurse came in and asked where she was. I told her she had needed to use the bathroom, and the nurse said, "What?" She ran in the bathroom, and Paula was already crowned. The problem that caused Naomi's heart to stop was caused by the umbilical cord being wrapped around her neck from being turned and rotated during the internal aversion. Fortunately, both she and my wife were okay. Elizabeth would later, when she could talk, nickname Naomi "Noni Bell," and that still is used on occasion. Naomi got the tongue thrust inherited from my dad and is very athletic.

Rebekah Loreine Yvonne was born on April 16, 2001, and she was six weeks early and also breach. This time after the aversion and the sac puncture, Rebekah turned 180 inside the uterus and caused an emergency C-section, which I personally witnessed even though the doctors said I shouldn't be in there. I gave Paula a priesthood blessing on the way to the emergency room. The uterus was on Paula's chest as they couldn't get Rebekah out without a T-cut and much difficulty. She came out blue, and Paula's vitals took a nose dive. It seemed like forever before the doctors were able to get Rebekah to cry. They handed her to me, so they could work on Paula. We almost lost both of them. Rebekah is the image of her mother, who is now dead, with the freckles and the big blue eyes. Naomi also got Paula's large blue eyes. Isaiah and Elizabeth got the dark brown eyes from the Lisonbie side of the family. Naomi nicknamed her "Beka."

Today, after an extremely difficult life and subsequent divorce from an abusive second wife, I have found a perfect wife to finish raising my children, a nurturer, Dana. She and I hope to have at least one child of our own, the Lord willing. We are currently in Caribou, Maine, struggling financially as I look to renew intellectual possibilities left unfinished from the life left behind. I am practicing what I preach as I have been working and changing and accommodating things that in the past would have devastated me. The best is yet to come as I turned fifty and a new life has begun. I'm grateful for the journey thus far; I'm sorry and ask the forgiveness of all I have harmed in any way during my grieving process, and I forgive and forget all wrongs done to me by those who I'm certain did the best they could with what they had. I forgive myself and completely and lovingly accept myself and my shortcomings and seek understanding from the poor souls who bore with me through my trials and tribulations. Like Jesus Christ, Job, Joseph Smith, and (I believe) all who chose Christ's plan to receive a body, I have suffered. However, I live on to tell you and others that there is a better way, and for this reason I have dedicated myself to the work of bringing souls unto Christ through my example, most of the time, and through my writing.

I will not review the specifics of Paula's death as I have already iterated this in *Howning Your Sphere.* She visited me in a dream after I dedicated her grave to call her forth in the resurrection. She said that I would have to forget her so as to move on and find another wife and mother for the children. Much of her memory is gone as I have heeded her counsel from that dream. I still remember the wake with all her family there in a circle. She had said it would take a death to bring everyone together again; little did she know it would be hers. I saw her outside the circle walking around and stopping at each person. She was there, and her prophesy was fulfilled. Psalms 69:20 sums up my feelings: "Reproach hath broken my heart; and I am full of heaviness: and I looked for some to take pity, but there was none; and for comforters, but I found none."

The next visitor also came in a dream before I was a member of the church and was pondering those that I had known before who had died as I was getting ready to sleep. Scotty, whom I hadn't thought of since my freshman year in college, ten years later, came to mind. Have you ever wondered where your dead friends and relatives are? It seems like such a waste; only the good die young. Well, I'm here to witness that when you die, you live, you live, YOU LIVE!

Psalms 87:7 explains that in Zion, "As well the singers as the players on instruments shall be there: all my springs are in thee." Spring is footnoted 7a OR sources; i.e., of joy, happiness, etc. Scotty was the best athlete in my high school and was a year ahead of me. I always looked up to him as I would see him running bow-legged with his knee-high socks. He always outworked his opponents and was equally talented at everything he did. When I learned of his death, I couldn't believe it. He had fallen out of Carol's convertible when she went around a turn as he was sitting with his rear end on the trunk out of the car with his feet on the seat. His neck was broken, and he died instantly. This particular evening, I was thinking about him and what a waste it was as he was at Keene State University at the time. We weren't close; heck, we only knew each other from sports, and I heard his Dad was real mean, like mine had been. This night I went to sleep, and Scotty visited me as I had a vivid recollection of the dream when I awoke. Have you ever had a visitor in your dream and shrugged it off? Scotty told me he was okay and said to tell everyone that he was fine where he was in the after-life. He had a gift with children. They always flocked to him, even the toddlers. I always wondered why and thought that was so cool. I've since measured my spiritual level by the way children are around me. When I told his brother, Kim, at the bar he worked at that Scotty had asked me to tell him he was okay in a dream, Kim basically blew me off. He totally wasn't ready to hear that information that way, especially coming from someone he'd hardly known who had been away for years. I share this with you for one reason: because I love you, and I want you to know that vivid dream recollection is a form of message from the part of you that cannot be reached while you are awake and being a human doing instead of a human being. Yes, Scotty was a MESSAGEUR from the other side preparing me to hear the Gospel of Jesus Christ. Awareness comes in many forms and only to those sensitive enough to discern. The gift of the Holy Ghost is necessary to continually be aware of things not seen by others who lack spiritual discernment.

The next experiences I will share with you happened eight years apart and almost cost me my life in similar circumstances as both happened in water, one involuntary and accidental and another voluntary and almost tragic, both cases spurred by ignorance.

The first incident happened in Japan and was explained to you during the fictional autobiographical introduction in *Howning Your Sphere*. As a two-year-old I went fishing with my family to a lake in Japan. I had gone down to the water to watch my Dad fish when I spotted a goldfish. I just knew I could catch it, so I lunged for it and fell in the water. I don't remember this; however, somehow no one noticed that I had fallen in. My mother yelled to Dad to see if I was with him, and he said no. My mom panicked, and my dad looked behind him and saw some movement and bubbles coming up from the lake near the shore. Then he saw me and dove in and pulled me out. I guess it wasn't my time to go. The second experience was at a man-made lake in West Virginia called Rippling Waters. I had grown to love the water and still do today as a very strong swimmer. This time, my parents had bought me some new flippers. They allowed me to swim twice as fast and further than I could barefooted. I just knew I could swim out to the middle of the lake and touch the bottom, which someone had said was twenty-six feet deep. I didn't tell anyone as I had many times swam back and forth across the lake to get to the slides and the diving boards, one of which was a high dive. I went out to the middle, took a quick breath, and swam towards the bottom. It was so cool on the way down, AND THE WATER GOT COLDER THE DEEPER I WENT. I looked around and saw the bottom and touched it. Then, I turned to start up and realized I had no air left. I frantically swam towards the surface trying not to breathe, and just when I thought it was over, I burst through the surface and gasped for air. I'll never forget almost drowning. I had never been that deep before or since, and I didn't realize the pressure on your chest or the effect of temperature and the lack of light when that deep. I also should have kicked off the bottom stronger. I did so many things wrong and still managed to resurface. This is how I came to the knowledge of the church. I was drowning in my own self-created misery and consequential guilt, and I just knew there had to be more to this existence than what I was suffering through. When reproach broke David's heart, he wrote in Psalms 69:2 and 14, "I sink in deep mire, where there is no standing: I am come into deep waters, where the floods overflow me," AND "Deliver me out of the mire, and let me not sink: let me be delivered from them that hate me, and out of the deep waters." The Lord listens and waits for our submission and humility to be sufficient before the miracle happens and the teachers begin to appear and continue to do so until the student again closes the book on him- or herself. Then, the Lord waits again for another opportunity to get your attention again. Unfortunately, usually like for Job, many traumas precede the blessings.

Proverbs 3:1-14 says, "My son, forget not my law; but let thine heart keep my commandments: For length of days, and long life, and peace, shall they add to thee. Let not mercy and truth forsake thee: bind them about thy neck; write them upon the table of thine heart: So shalt thou find favour and good understanding in the sight of God and man. Trust in the LORD with all thine heart; and lean not unto thine own understanding. In all thy ways acknowledge him, and he shall direct thy paths. Be not wise in thine own eyes: fear the LORD and depart from evil. It shall be health to thy navel, and marrow to thy bones. Honour the LORD with thy substance, and with the first fruits of all thine increase: So, shall thy barns be filled with plenty, and thy presses shall burst out with new wine. My son despises not the chastening of the LORD; neither be weary of his correction: For whom the LORD loveth he correcteth; even as a father the son in whom he delighted. Happy is the man that findeth wisdom, and the man that getteth understanding. For the merchandise of it is better than the merchandise of silver, and the gain thereof than fine gold."

My hope is that you, the reader, will avert tragedies that happen to those in the world, and whether by accident or knowingly, with purpose. Sin carries a penalty. Until you find your direction and learn to look to the Lord as Lehi looked to the Liahona for direction, your compass will spin and lead you astray. Don't find yourself wrapped around a four-foot-diameter American Elm, your spirit looking at the poor fool dismembered in the car feeling grateful it wasn't you, only to find that it *is* you. I've put the Lord through a lot to help me gain exaltation. My prayer is that my books will aid you in your search for true meaning in this life and the life to come. My car accident was life-changing. However, after a short while and a miraculous recovery, I went back again for another taste of the "good life" and continued to suffer for two more years. I promised the Lord that if I could walk out of the hospital, that I wouldn't do drugs and alcohol again. I LIED!

How about you? Is there something that you do that doesn't feel right, but everyone around you does it, so you'll probably never give it up? Try changing people, places, and things. If you find you still need it, then you know you're addicted to the behavior. Talk to the missionaries and get a priesthood blessing and ask about "The Lord Did Free Me from Bondage" recovery program. Sometimes, it's better to leave the old crowd and lifestyle alone and find new people to be with better standards. You may think that by giving up bad and immoral habits, you're giving up your freedom, but actually the habits themselves are what create the real bondage and disallow your spirit from being aware of the many MESSAGEURS who cross your path. Let me share some more scriptures with you from Psalms.

After my accident, I was like this in Psalms 22:14: "I am poured out like water, and all my bones are out of joint: my heart is like wax; it is melted in the midst of my bowels." And when my spirit reentered my body and I lay in that hospital for six months in traction, longing for fresh air and to walk again, I was like this in Psalms 56:13: "For thou hast delivered my soul from death: wilt not thou deliver my feet from falling, that I may walk before God in the light of the living? I longed to be out of this bed I was imprisoned in due to my own mistake. Then there's Psalms 51:7-15, in which David pleads as I did: "Purge me with hyssop, and I shall be clean: wash me and I shall be whiter than snow. Make me hear joy and gladness; that the bones which thou hast broken may rejoice. Hide thy face from my sins and blot out all mine iniquities. Create in me a clean heart, O God; and renew a right spirit within me. Cast me not away from thy presence; and take not thy holy spirit from me. Restore unto me the joy of thy salvation; and uphold me with thy free spirit. Then will I teach transgressors thy ways: and sinners shall be converted unto thee. Deliver me from blood guiltiness, O God, thou God of my salvation: and my tongue shall sing aloud of thy righteousness. O LORD open thou my lips; and my mouth shall shew forth thy praise."

When you are forgiven of your sins through baptism, it behooveth you to warn others. Psalms 69:12 states, "They that sit in the gate speak against me; and I was the song of the drunkards." On your own, go to Job 30:9. I would hope you have a set of scriptures by now. If not, ask the missionaries for the scriptures. This scripture also applies to my being stabbed three times and disarming the perpetrator and escaping. In Psalms 27:5-7, David explains, "For in the time of trouble he shall hide me in his pavilion. In the secret of his tabernacle shall he hide me; he shall set me up upon a rock. And now shall mine head be lifted up above mine enemies round about me: therefore, will I offer in his tabernacle sacrifices of joy; I will sing, yea, I will sing praises unto the LORD. Hear, O LORD, when I cry with my voice: have mercy also upon me and answer me."

One of the most devastating and eye-opening experiences of my life started one night with a fight. My co-owner of a townhouse had been disowned by his father for embezzling an insurance agency to buy his Trans Am and was behind on his financial commitments to me. Because I was arrogant, I had taken the upstairs while he finished the downstairs. I had lived with his cousin for a year, and she was from Ireland. Mostly, I was making great money and drinking and drugging quite heavily at the time. I had some big parties and probably was a little irrational at the time. I don't remember what started the argument, but he pushed me, and I went backwards and rolled down the stairs. When I got up to retaliate, I was confused and hit him a couple times and got tired. He grabbed me by the hair, and my girlfriend, his cousin, was standing there along with my friend Barry. I told Barry to get him off me, and he hit him several times until he let go. Much confusion happened, and Barry felt like he needed to leave right away, and he did as Stephanie gave him a ride. I was by myself in my room trying to figure out what had just happened when there was a knock on my bedroom door. I opened the door and Jim said, "It's just you and me now!" He began slashing at me with this twelve-inch-long survival knife that I would see him sharpening every time I went into the basement where he and his girlfriend from New York stayed. I turned in a Kung Fu position to take my body away as he lunged toward me and slashed at my neck. Instinctively, I put up my left arm to stop the deadly attempt, and the knife landed on my left wrist, spraying the wall with blood. I didn't feel pain; my adrenalin kicked in as he stabbed towards my stomach after a circular flurry of attempts to kill me landed in my sweat pants and loose shirt. I grabbed the knife by the blade when he went for my abdomen, held it above his head, drove him back with my height advantage over the water bed, hit him with all my force with a left cross that turned his head, and forced him to release his grip on the knife. I turned and ran to the neighbor who was the head of the board in the townhouse development and told her to call the police and that Jim might be coming. I sat in terror as I realized that when I had grabbed the blade, I had cut myself severely in the upper thigh, and at this point I was holding my wrist to keep it from feather painting her walls.

The ambulance came, and I told the police what had happened, and the state of Virginia took the case and put him in prison for malicious wounding. We sold the house, and things were never the same with Stephanie and me. This was a low point in my life as I felt violated. My life had flashed before my eyes, and the court continuances and Jim's father's offer of money in return for dropping the charges led me not even to be in court the day that Jim was convicted. I was in no condition to be in public anyway as I had wasted little time in sending the proceeds from the townhouse sale on that which does not satisfy. Have you ever had traumatic experiences and blamed everyone but yourself? I played a role in my demise, even though it is not entirely my own, like Job.

David, even though a king, made grave errors, and his errors became Psalms for you to read as he sought to reconnect to the Lord. You must see the parallel between those who have gone before you and the consequences of your behavior before it happens. The scriptures are experiences that happened that the Lord asked men to document for future generations. My life has been full of experiences that should help others avoid misery and suffering. Why wouldn't I help you by writing them down? These events in my life do not make me proud; in fact, it's very difficult for me to reveal them. However difficult it must have been for David to write about his transgressions, if he had not, you and I would not know of the intense torment of our souls that takes place when we are separated from Jesus Christ because of our own choices.

Understand that I do not wish to glorify the horrible choices that I made in the past. I simply want to implore you to seek higher ground sooner than I did by learning from my mistakes and David's so as to avert history repeating itself again. You may be a three-bricks-in-the-face person like me who needs to suffer before being compelled to be humble and to seek the Lord and His Spirit for guidance and protection. I only pray that my words of truth will inspire others to find their way to what I'm sharing with you right now. There is more to this life than what meets the eye, and you'll never see it unless you walk the path I am now on and endure to the end, blessing all who are around you with the knowledge of Jesus Christ as our Savior and Redeemer. Please, I implore you to feel what you feel right now and to act upon those feelings and accept the Lord's challenge to lay all of your worldly cares upon His lap.

After Paula's death, there was a long period of time on auto-pilot; many things I did don't make sense to me now. I told you I wouldn't reiterate on her death again. Guess what; I will write about it again and again and again until I am done, and you feel what you can about the most traumatic event in my life. My father died ten months after Paula, and I was in Maine at his funeral, and many photographs were taken of me. I was 270 pounds when Paula died, and I found myself getting bigger. Up until seeing the photographs of me at Dad's funeral, I had no idea. I looked at myself in the pictures and wondered who that massive man was. In my eyes, I saw defeat for the first time. I had been brought to my knees and couldn't sleep well, was overeating and indulging to kill the pain that I felt. Many times, I asked for anti-depressants and was told that I wasn't depressed. Boy, did I fool those doctors. I hadn't been on a scale in a year, so I decided to get on one of those scales that you pay for at a truck stop. 427 POUNDS! I was in shock and decided that I would swim the weight off and started swimming with my Vice-President, Brian. I found out that President Monson swam for exercise, and I saw President Medina and Bishop Whipple at the pool, so I knew I was on the right track. At the time I didn't know that I had become diabetic, and a sore or ulcer formed on my leg. I thought it was from the vein stripping. I soon found out that the ulcer had absorbed a staph infection. One morning, we were swimming when my leg swelled and became red and really hot to the touch. Brian said I needed to go to the hospital. I went immediately, and it was a good thing as I had about twelve hours to live! I would have died that night had I not gotten put upon a battery of intravenous antibiotics. None of them seemed to work. A disease specialist came and changed the antibiotic several times as I was within one day of amputation of my leg. The red had gone past my hip into my abdomen, and the doctors said that if things didn't change they would have to amputate.

I prayed and called Brian to give me a priesthood blessing, and within four hours, the doctors were amazed that the staph infection began to recede down my leg and eventually disappeared. It took two weeks of antibiotic drips, shots, and oral batteries to rid my body of the infection. A blood test showed me to be diabetic, and that was a shock; however, I was grateful to be alive and to have my leg. In Psalms 107:19-20, my dilemma is explained: "Then they cry unto the LORD in their trouble, and he saveth them out of their distresses. He sent his word, and healed them, and delivered them from their destructions." I felt overwhelmed with grief and loss, and now I was in the biggest struggle of my life, not to leave my five children parentless and alone.

Psalms 30: 1-4 explains the transition I went through when I hardly had recollection: "I will extol thee, O LORD; for thou hast lifted me up, and hast not made my foes to rejoice over me. O LORD my God, I cried unto thee, and thou hast healed me. O LORD, thou hast brought up my soul from the grave: thou hast kept me alive, that I should not go down to the pit. Sing unto the LORD, O ye saints of his, and give thanks at the remembrance of his holiness."

In Psalms 30:5, the Joseph Smith translation states, "For his anger kindleth against the wicked; they repent, and in a moment, it is turned away, and they are in his favor, and he giveth them life; therefore, weeping may endure for a night, but joy cometh in the morning." I needed these things to wake me from my prideful slumber. Have you ever thought of life ending tomorrow? How would you want to be remembered? What would your legacy be? I want my children to be married in the temple and to live Gospel standards and to know that God and His son Jesus Christ live and are available for advice and that there is a prophet on the Earth today, even President Thomas Spencer Monson, who will guide them if they listen, take heed, and apply their teachings to their lives. Those teachings are by his life's example and in general conferences in October and April every year. I think of the feeling I have when I listen to President Monson and his counselors and apostles, and it can be summed up by Psalms 55:6: "And I said, oh that I had wings like a dove! For then would I fly away and be at rest." And Psalms 56:13: "For thou hast delivered my soul from death: wilt not thou deliver my feet from falling, that I may walk before God in the light of the living?"

I feel as if I can walk on air, and I leave this existence when I absorb scriptures from the past and the present as I listen to the Lord's representatives and special witnesses speak wisdom and impart it unto my soul. I know that the general authorities are messageurs to us all, and as it states in Psalms 86:7, "In the day of my trouble I will call upon thee: for thou wilt answer me." Many answers to my prayers, promptings, and spiritual impressions are addressed in general conferences by the general authorities' talks.

Psalms 103:3-5 tells you who to seek forgiveness from: "Who forgiveth all thine iniquities; who healeth all thy diseases, who redeemed thy life from destruction; who crowneth thee with loving kindness and tender mercies; Who satisfieth thy mouth with good things; so that thy youth is renewed like the eagle's." Jesus Christ is the fountain to all exaltation and righteousness, and I'm grateful for His example and the life he freely gave to me and for me. Again, you shouldn't only cry unto the Lord when you lie upon your death bed. In Psalms 107:6 again: "Then they cried unto the Lord in their trouble, and he delivered them out of their distresses." Death-bed repentance—have you ever cried unto a God you don't know is there? Have you ever prayed daily and awaited counsel from the ultimate Messageur? The Holy Ghost is the Messageur of choice and with the priesthood; the right to act in God's name restored, we are armed with the ability to change and transform the world preparatory for Christ's Second Coming ONE SOUL AT A TIME!

Many times, throughout my books, I will bounce from one time in my life to another. Understand, spiritual things are on a timeline; however, awareness comes many times after hardship, trial, and tribulation. Until you receive the gifts, it will be hard for you to remember in retrospect the path you traveled and the messages you received from beyond. Looking backward helps you make sense of things that didn't make sense to you at the time of their occurrence because of missing discernment or just not being ready to listen to the still, small voice.

One of the most life-changing experiences, or what I would call my conversion and change of heart, happened in Norfolk, Virginia, in a warehouse on the comer of Twenty-Sixth and Llewellyn, the ghetto where I lived towards the end of one life and the beginning of another. I can hardly express my gratitude to my Savior Jesus Christ and my Sister Sharon for sending the missionaries to me, and for mailing me a copy of the Book of Mormon that an unseen spirit put my hand on the night I'd decided that I'd had enough of the drugs and alcohol: November 6, 1994, at 6:36 p.m.

David speaks to the Lord from a cave and asks for help and protection like I did in Psalms 142: "I CRIED unto the LORD with my voice;

with my voice unto the LORD did I make supplication. I poured out my complaint before him; I shewed before him my trouble. When my spirit was overwhelmed within me, then thou knewest my path. In the way wherein, I walked have they privily laid a snare for me. I looked on my right hand, and beheld, but there was no man that would know me: refuge failed me; no man cared for my soul. I cried unto thee, O LORD: I said, Thou art my refuge and my portion in the land of the living. Attend unto my cry; for I am brought very low: deliver me from my persecutors; for they are stronger than I. Bring my soul out of prison, that I may praise thy name: the righteous shall compass me about; for thou shalt deal bountifully with me."

Joseph Smith, while in the sacred grove, plead similarly when he asked the Lord to deliver him from his enemy, and suddenly a pillar of light appeared and two beings, one pointing to the other, saying, "This is my Beloved Son, hear Him."

Once you die, your spirit awaits to be reunited with your immortal body to be judged. That period of waiting is either in Spirit Paradise, where those who have received the Gospel and lived it await, and the other Spirit Prison, where those who didn't receive it and live it **wait.** You can help those who have passed without the knowledge by doing vicarious ordinances in the temples of our Lord. Ralph Waldo Emerson states how I feel about what happened up to and including that night in the warehouse that changed my life and my progenitors' life and all who would meet me now, then or in the future, when he stated profoundly, "With the past I have nothing to do; nor with the future. I live now." I know as you do or **will** that Jesus Christ lives and that the Priesthood of God has been restored to the Earth, that the Book of Mormon is true, and that Joseph Smith was the first prophet of this dispensation of time and that today Thomas S. Monson holds all the keys restored and leads us today while standing in counsel with the Savior, Jesus the Christ.

That night in the ghetto when I prayed for the Lord to show Himself to me as I plead and explained how I couldn't live this way anymore, an unseen being lifted my arm and placed my hand backwards on the headboard on a dusty Book of Mormon that my sister Sharon had sent me months before that I hadn't cracked open once. I picked up the book and began to read. My conversion and change of heart occurred all at once in that night of suffering and awakening. Of course, the conversion process continued as I have explained with other such experiences and still is happening today as I struggle with obedience and faithfulness with activity in the church and financial crises. You, too, will feel the hand of fellowship and love extended to you when you cry out to the Lord, and when you're ready, the Teacher **will** appear. He's been there all along, you just couldn't see Him until you asked for His presence and His presents. A moment must occur where spontaneous combustion takes place where you open your mind and spirit to the Almighty God who created you.

In the Book of Mormon, Moroni explains how all is as it was and <u>educates</u> you as to what is required on your part to partake of eternal blessings and life. Moroni 7:28-38 reveals, "For he hath answered the ends of the law, and he claimeth all those who have faith in him; and they who have faith in him will cleave unto every good thing; wherefore he advocateth the cause of the children of men; and he dwelleth eternally in the heavens. And because he hath done this, my beloved brethren, have miracles ceased? Behold I say unto you, nay; neither have angels ceased to minister unto the children of men. For behold, they are subject unto him, to minister according to the word of his command, showing themselves unto them of strong faith and firm mind in every form of godliness. And the office of their ministry is to call men unto repentance, and to fulfill and do the work of the covenants of the Father, which he hath made unto the children of men, to prepare the way unto the children of men, by declaring the word of Christ unto the chosen vessels of the Lord, that they may bear testimony of him. And by so doing, the Lord God prepareth the way that the residue of men may have faith in Christ, that the Holy Ghost may have place in their hearts, according to the power thereof; and after this manner bringeth to pass the Father, the covenants which he hath made unto the children of men. And Christ hath said: If ye will have faith in me ye shall have power to do whatsoever thing is expedient in me. And he hath said: Repent all ye ends of the earth, and come unto me, and be baptized in my name, and have faith in me, that ye may be saved. And now, my beloved brethren, if this be the case that these things are true which I have spoken unto you, and god will show unto you, with power and great glory at the last day, that they are true, and if they are true has the day of miracles ceased? Or have angels ceased to appear unto the children of men? Or has he withheld the power of the Holy Ghost from them? Or, will he, so long as time shall last, or the earth shall stand, or there shall be one man upon the face thereof to be saved? Behold I say unto you, nay; for it is by faith that miracles are wrought; and it is by faith that angels appear and administer unto men; wherefore, if these things have ceased, then has faith ceased also; and awful is the state of man, for they are as though there had been no redemption made."

It's simple to have messages from beings from the other side as long as you have faith and allow the Holy Ghost to reach you through the willingness and discernment you'll attain by living faithful to these principles available only in Jesus Christ's church. You can be of another faith; however, if you're like me, the only reason I was Catholic was because my mother, was along with two thousand years of my ancestry. I didn't even know how my religion related to Jesus Christ, and I never felt the Spirit or read the scriptures or had a testimony of the truthfulness of what I didn't even know I believed. I had no questions and no answers. When the time, came my mother became a member and tried to share the Gospel with me, and I laughed at her as I felt any church that took away my freedoms wasn't for me. What I found later was my so-called freedoms were like a ball and chain that actually were bondage to addiction and to a way of life that condemned and separated me from the messageurs and the life I could be leading with better standards and direction. I now have that life—how about you?

The hardest thing for me was to believe that I could be forgiven for all the indiscretions of my past. David had the same problem in Psalms 25:6-7 when he pleaded, "Remember, O LORD, thy tender mercies and thy loving kindnesses; for they have been ever of old. Remember not the sins of my youth, nor my transgressions: according to thy mercy remember thou me for thy goodness sake, O LORD." Baptism is symbolic and real as a means of starting anew. Psalms 54:7 reinforces the process by saying, "For he hath delivered me out of all trouble: and mine eye hath seen his desire upon mine enemies." It's as simple as leaving one life behind and walking into another—like changing clothes, taking off the dirty and putting on the clean, the cloak of righteousness and garments of armor and shield from the sins of the world to endure to the end for exaltation and eternal life in the realm of Jesus Christ and His Father.

Psalms 69:12 refers to Job in the footnote and reminds me of my past life: "They that sit in the gate speak against me; and I was the song of the drunkards." Life is hell; I've heard, and I experienced my own hell that I created myself and saw no way out. Jesus Christ through angels and ministers showed me the portal of escape and the realization of a better life behind the curtain of misery that veiled my eyes from sight and allowed me to focus on what matters in this life—peace, joy, and happiness—and brought to pass the immortality and eternal life of man occurred for me. I'll never forget the feeling that Psalms 77:1-4 brings me: "I CRIED unto God with my voice, even unto God with my voice;

and he gave ear unto me. In the day of my trouble I sought the LORD: my sore ran in the night and ceased not: my soul refused to be comforted. I remembered God, and was troubled: I complained, and my spirit was overwhelmed. Selah. Thou holdest mine eyes waking: I am so troubled that I cannot speak."

I found it interesting that according to footnote 3a, "complained" means "meditated." So, in ancient Hebrew, complaining means meditating. Don't you find that interesting? Meditation and sincere prayer are what open the door to revelation and administration with the ministering of angels along with visitation of assigned messengers, or for my purpose messageurs, for the message is URS as you will not receive inspiration for the church or the human race, only yourself, your family, and those over whom you have stewardship and those who are set apart to do so. In gratitude I, like David, express thanks, me through this work and David in Psalms 86:13: "For great is thy mercy toward me: and thou hast delivered my soul from the lowest hell." That sums it up for me.

One day, in Springville, Utah, I was in my favorite restaurant, Ginger's Cafe, a health food place where many spiritual realizations have occurred for me. I was sitting at a window seat eating my pumpkin soup, waiting for my smoothie and yellow fin tuna sandwich when I received a phone call and was talking about my frustrations with my organizations leadership styles with my partner in another entity. Just then, I hung up, and my food arrived, and I took a sip of my Emerald Isle smoothie. It was heavenly. While I was waiting, I went and had a double ginger shot and a double wheatgrass shot and sat down. After my food arrived, two gentlemen of odd athletic physique given their age, appearing to be seventy or better, came up to my table and began to review things in my life that no one knew. I was fascinated and thought I should give these guys a card, so I asked them their names. I didn't realize until after how unusual it was for total strangers to know things about my life that no one else knew. It felt totally normal as we conversed, and it never crossed my mind how these men knew details about my life. I asked what their names were. The first said, "I am John," and the second said, "I am James."

I immediately asked where Peter was, and they turned to walk away. I asked, "Are you the sons of Zebedee, the brothers of thunder?"

John turned and smiled, and they left the restaurant. As soon as they went out the door, they disappeared. I knew at that point that I had seen the apostles, and I thought to myself that I must have disappointed by being unprepared for their visit. I will be next time; I am now prepared. I've always wanted to meet John the Beloved and the three Nephites, all selfless souls who chose to remain and tarry on this earth. The Lord granted me my wish; I guess I was ready. These are not normal occurrences for everyone, and I sometimes wonder why I've been so blessed with visitation. I firmly believe that all is possible with the Lord. I did shake John's hand, and it was flesh. Then they were gone.

Jesus Christ set an example of how to commune in both worlds simultaneously. Psalms 113:6 speaks of Him: "Who humbleth himself to behold the things that are in heaven, and in earth!" I share with your things that are sacred to me that the Lord has asked me to share; understand these are my experiences, and I lie not, nor embellish.

Alma 38:10-12, 14 will impart to you how I must be careful: "And now, as ye have begun to teach the word even so I would that ye should continue to teach; and I would that ye would be diligent and temperate in all things. See that ye are not lifted up unto pride; yea, see that ye do not boast in your own wisdom, nor of your much strength. Use boldness, but not overbearance; and also see that ye bridle all your passions, that ye may be filled with love; see that ye refrain from idleness. Do not say; O God, I thank thee that we are better than our brethren; but rather say: O Lord, forgive my unworthiness, and remember my brethren in mercy—yea, acknowledge your unworthiness before God at all times." I am only as good as the Lord empowers me to be and can only do what He wills. When I go contrary to that, the Spirit is grieved. I still make mistakes; I am, after all, only mortal at this moment. Time still escapes me without these experiences at different interims based on my obedience and spirituality at any given time. Also, understand that if these visits were constant, we'd be in the millennium with the Savior reigning in the absence of earthly opposition and adversity caused by Satan and his angels which constantly reign with terror here on Earth.

To every action or occurrence, there is opposite reaction and many times obsessive re-occurrence until shock or tragedy allow you to step outside your reality and entertain a different level of existence. Acting on a goal requires ownership and perseverance. Reacting, or living a life adapting to others' actions without initiative, creates a victim mentality. My terminology is ACTSYS versus REACTSYS for the purpose of this trilogy. ACTSYS is your action system, and it is based on your ideals and usually has patterns that both accelerate some aspects of your life and hinder others. Your REACTSYS contains bias and protection mechanisms and peer influence with tradition that can create impotence and inability to change, adapt, and be aware of things unseen. Neural-linguistic programming is an example of nonverbal communication skills that, I believe, border on telekinetic messaging, which is the form of communication of the subconscious and the SPIRIT. Being prompted requires being aware, and being aware means living in another dimension while being in the world but not of the world. *The Psalm of the Messageur* mentions saying yes today. "No today" must become "KNOW TODAY." If your mind and body are not one with your spirit and you are closed off to communication, neither the Lord nor I can help you. Being impenetrable, cynical, and pessimistic is a horrible existence, and loving your neighbor as yourself fails in both instances. You've heard in

Proverbs in the Bible that you reap what you sow. Now you know what it means. Cantankerous, miserable, hurt, paranoid humans are reactors and not actors in their own life. Many just seek the negative attention and loneliness to which they've condemned themselves. I've been there; I hope you're not, but if you are, wake up and smell the roses before you're lying beneath them wishing you'd used your mortal probation in a more edifying and legacy-leaving manner and that you had not left your offspring ignorant to repeat the same mistakes you made by either not practicing what you preach or, worse, preaching one thing and living another as a hypocrite. The Holy Ghost will not reside with a person who constantly belittles and criticizes others while doing nothing of worth themselves.

Become an ACTION-taker with an ACTION SYSTEM and carry on. Cease to be a wayward son or daughter, and step up to the plate, swing, and keep swinging. If you don't get a hit, change your stance and do more batting practice. Four single base hits are as good as a homerun and even better in many instances. Give the Lord what He deserves and stop squandering your mortal existence. Stop being a spectator—or worse yet a spectacle—and purify yourself through the atonement of Christ. Then open your mouth and help others to the light through the waters of baptism and the covenants of the sealing ordinances in the temples of the Church of Jesus Christ of Latter-Day Saints. Someday you'll thank me, and we can sit down together around the dinner table of our Lord. Thank Him instead of whom I write, even Jesus the Christ. It's ironic that I was born in 1961, and on page sixty-one, I am now at the age of fifty years young, able to share about my rebirth and yours. The word "remember" is used 118 times in the Book of Mormon, and I use it a lot. However, if you live in the past, tomorrow becomes yesterday and today just another excuse. Live life today and start anew, no matter how old or young you are. With open arms, the church invites you to come unto Christ, no matter what your religious background, and partake of the living ordinances restored by the Living Christ. Be present and accept the presents of He who created you and stand in His presence again. Do not put off or procrastinate the repentance process. If you've ever wanted to lose weight, the Lord is there to shoulder your burden. It's time for you to put down the backpack of sin and live again. Remember, He never said the road would be easy; He said it would be worth the journey.

Psalms 119 TETH:71-72 reads, "It is good for me that I have been afflicted; that I might learn thy statutes. The law of thy mouth is better unto me than thousands of gold and silver." In footnotes 71a, "afflicted" cross references "chastening," and I've been there many times, however, gratefully, not yet as Job. If we weren't important to God, would he waste all this time and effort? Psalms 144:3-4 says, "LORD, what is man, that thou takest knowledge of him! Or the son of man, that thou makest account of him! Man is like to vanity: his days are as a shadow that passeth away."

Doctrine and Covenants 123:12-14 restates the dilemma: "For there are many yet on the earth of all sects, parties, and denominations, who are blinded by the subtle craftiness of men, whereby they lie in wait to deceive, and who are only kept from the truth because they know not where to find it—Therefore that we should waste and wear out our lives in bringing to light all the hidden things of darkness, wherein we know them; and they are truly manifest from heaven—These should then be attended to with great earnestness." Now, you know why I sit here and beat up this computer one finger at a time as I will wear out my life and actually extend it bringing others to the knowledge and blessings of the Gospel of Jesus Christ. Remember, the Lord giveth, and the Lord taketh away. First, I will share Doctrine and Covenants 121:34-46.

Before I share this very important scripture; I want you to know that when I say, "The Lord giveth, and the Lord taketh away," I mean that life goes through cycles, and oscillations naturally occur as a result of your awareness at any given time as a byproduct of your daily routine and your level of dedication and obedience to messages, both as the sender and a recipient. People and life situations come and go constantly like the tides. How you react and goal-set with action will determine whether you ride the wave or get rolled up in it, swept and whisked away by every wind of doctrine. In Doctrine and Covenants 121 starting with verse 34 and going to the end, you read, "Behold, there are many called, but few are chosen. And why are they not chosen? Because their hearts are set so much on the things of this world and aspire to the honors of men that they do not learn this one lesson—That the rights of the priesthood are inseparably connected with the powers of heaven, and that the powers of heaven cannot be controlled nor handled only upon the principles of righteousness. That they may be conferred upon us, it is true; but when we undertake to uncover our sins, or to gratify our pride, our vain ambition, or to exercise control or dominion or compulsion upon the souls of the children of men, in any degree of unrighteousness, behold, the heavens withdraw themselves; the Spirit of the Lord is grieved; and when it is withdrawn, Amen to the priesthood or the authority of that man. Behold, ere he is aware, he is left unto himself, to kick against the pricks, to persecute the saints, and to fight against God. We have learned by sad experience that it is the nature and disposition of almost all men, as soon as they get a little authority, as they suppose, they will immediately begin to exercise unrighteous dominion. Hence, many are called, but few are chosen. No power or influence can or ought to be maintained by virtue of the priesthood, only by persuasion, by long-suffering, by gentleness and meekness, and by love unfeigned; By kindness, and pure knowledge, which shall greatly enlarge the soul without hypocrisy, and without guile—Reproving betimes with sharpness, when moved upon by the Holy Ghost; and then showing forth afterwards an increase of love toward him whom thou hast reproved, lest he esteem thee to be his enemy; That he may know that thy faithfulness is stronger than the cords of death. Let thy bowels also be full of charity towards all men, and to the household of faith, and let virtue garnish thy thoughts unceasingly; then shall thy confidence wax strong in the presence of God; and the doctrine of the priesthood shall distill upon thy soul as the dews from heaven. The Holy Ghost shall be thy constant companion, and thy scepter an unchanging scepter of righteousness and truth; and thy dominion shall be an everlasting dominion, and without compulsory means it shall flow unto thee forever and ever."

I have misused the priesthood a few times and found this to be true—the heavens withdraw themselves—and I was left to take the brunt of punishment that I could have easily avoided had I not suffered with vain ambition, pride, and the false feeling of power exercised in anger. The priesthood is the authority to act on God's behalf here on the Earth, and it only works when you do it His way. When the heavens withdraw themselves, you will be left to wonder what happened, remembering no compulsion or usurping unrighteous dominion over others. I was left alone, and all my earthly possessions disappeared as they lost value to me; they became worthless. In Helaman 13:29-39, the process is explained for those who doubt: "O ye wicked and ye perverse generation; ye hardened and ye stiff necked people, how long will ye suppose that the Lord will suffer you? Yea, how long will ye suffer yourselves to be led by foolish and blind guides? Yea how long will ye choose darkness rather than light? Yea, behold, the anger of the Lord is already kindled against you; behold, he hath cursed the land because of your iniquity. And behold, the time cometh that he curseth your riches, that they become slippery, that ye cannot hold them; and in the days of your poverty you cannot retain them. And in the days of your poverty ye shall cry unto the Lord; and in vain shall ye cry, for your desolation is already come upon you, and your destruction is made sure; and then shall ye weep and howl in that day, saith the Lord of Hosts. And then shall ye lament and say: O that I had repented, and had not killed the prophets, and stoned them, and cast them out. Yea, in that day ye shall say: O that we had remembered the Lord our God in the day that he gave us our riches, and then they would have not become slippery that we should lose them; for behold, our riches are gone from us. Behold, we lay a tool here and, on the morrow, it is gone; and behold, our swords are taken from us in the day we have sought them for battle. Yea, we have hid up our treasures and they have slipped away from us, because of the curse of the land. O that we had repented in the day that the word of the Lord came unto us; for behold the land is cursed, and all things are become slippery, and we cannot hold them. Behold, we are surrounded by demons, yea, we are encircled about by the angels of him who hath sought to destroy our souls. Behold, our iniquities are great. O Lord, canst thou not turn away thine anger from us? And this shall be your language in those days. But behold, your days of probation are past; ye have procrastinated the day of your salvation until it is everlastingly too late, and your destruction is made sure; yea, for ye have sought all the days of your lives for that which ye could not obtain; and ye have sought for happiness in doing iniquity, which thing is contrary to the nature of that righteousness which is in our great and Eternal Head. O ye people of the land, that ye would hear my words! And I pray that the anger of the Lord be turned away from you, and that ye would repent and be saved."

If you will not heed my words and my counsel, please heed the Lord's and that of His Prophet. I hope that the peace which I have been led to by a series of messageurs will lead you to the iron rod, the word of God, and that you will hold fast to it and endure to the end.

Helaman 5:45-51 tells you who the source of all truth and comfort is: "And behold, the Holy Spirit of God did come down from heaven, and did enter into their hearts, and they were filled as if with fire, and they could speak forth marvelous words. And it came to pass that there came a voice unto them, yea, a pleasant voice, as if it were a whisper, saying: Peace, peace be unto you, because of your faith in my Well Beloved, who was from the foundation of the world. And now, when they heard this they cast up their eyes as if to behold from whence the voice came; and behold, they saw the heavens open; and angels came down out of heaven and ministered unto them. And there were about three hundred souls who saw and heard these things; and they were bidden to go forth and marvel not, neither should they doubt. And it came to pass that they did go forth, and did minister unto the people, declaring throughout all the regions round about all the things which they had heard and seen, insomuch that the more part of the Lamanites was convinced of them, because of the greatness of the evidences which they had received. And as many as were convinced did lay down their weapons of war, and also their hatred and the traditions of their fathers."

You must begin to recognize a pattern that applies today, the same as these things applied since the beginning of man. The Lord beckons you to listen if your ears are open and your mind in tune with the messageur. I liken this process unto a wave from the ocean and call the next analogy "The Wave".

Fascination with waves started for me at an early age; I have been on many beaches from Maine to South Carolina over the last forty-five years and spent six months in Hawaii last year on three different islands. I've grown to appreciate the relentless tides that come in, ebb, roll, and crash upon the beach, bringing gifts from the sea, and then return with more force, dragging sand and your legs, if you're not careful, in the undertow. Once, while in Hatteras where the Atlantic Rift and the Atlantic current are close to shore, friend from Ireland and I nearly didn't overcome the undertow swimming frantically to make it to shore.

We were almost overtaken by the feeling of swimming as hard as we could but sitting still. Oceans and beaches can be different colors and temperatures, which is obvious immediately. The variable that is unknown is the configuration of the terrain under the water, which has a huge bearing on how the undertow affects objects in the water. At Cape Hatteras, the shore drops off over near the campground by Bubba's Barbecue thousands of feet straight down on the Atlantic shelf and creates an undertow that neither my friend nor I were prepared for. I yelled, "Swim as hard as you can; we're being swept out!" Fortunately, we were able to exert enough effort to overcome the riptide and come ashore on the waves.

The sound of the beach is amazing with the birds and the smell of salt along with the feeling of the sand beneath your feet and the smell of sunscreen. When your body surfing and you go beyond the third wave crest, you hardly notice that you're being swept away. As fun as the ride in can be, the ride out can be a lot faster and deceiving. The quiet message of the ocean weaves is peaceful and relaxing—and on occasion, *too* relaxing as the water going out is much stronger than the water coming in and crashing loudly on the shore, the crest of the wave up high and the undertow down low. Sometimes, you can be so impressed with the loud wave crashing in that you may fail to recognize that your feet, like your world, are eroding away beneath without your noticing. The scriptures and spiritual messages are much like the waves. They come, and they go constantly whether you're aware of them or not and regardless of whether you're there to see it or not. Many times, the message is softer and less loud and occurs on the way out instead of the way in. You must be aware of both and appreciate and respect that the things that happen that you may not be conscious of will many times be the message you should listen to instead of the ebb tide. The riptide or undertow must be equally addressed, or tragedy can and will occur. Being one with the Holy Ghost assures you of this gift of receivership that only comes when you know that the obvious and the not-so-obvious are of equal importance.

When you are confused and being swept away by every wind of doctrine, pay attention to the only giver of truth and the Messageur, the Holy Ghost. He will guide you and keep you on the safe and eternal path and keep your ship on a steady course, helping you to avoid the treacherous coral reef or sudden depth changes that affect the surface and yet are unseen. You may not believe that unseen things will affect you. I know they will, and I know of the importance of having the gift of the Holy Ghost conferred upon you by the laying on of hands by one holding the authority to do so, even the Melchizedek Priesthood. To navigate this life and return safely to shore, this is the most important advice I can give you: Live worthily to receive promptings and messages from the Holy Ghost, and work day and night on opening the channels of communication so as to better recognize how the Spirit of the Lord communicates with you, as each of us is unique in that respect. Sometimes you can hear the wave and miss the message.

In Psalms 144:11-15, David counsels, "Rid me, and deliver me from the hand of strange children, whose mouth speaketh vanity, and their right hand is a right hand of falsehood: That our sons may be as plants grown up in their youth; that our daughters may be as cornerstones, polished after the similitude of a palace: That our garners may be Ml, affording all manner of store: that our sheep may bring forth thousands and ten thousands in our streets: That our oxen may be strong to labor; that there be no breaking in, nor going out; that there be no complaining in our streets. Happy is that people, that is in such a case: yea, happy is that people, whose God is the LORD."

Do you feel and see the link between the wave and what David just said? Selah. Have you noticed that in Psalms LORD is all-capital letters? These are subtle things, and life is and will be your workbook and your study guide. The answer key is provided by the Holy Spirit of God. First, you must find the page and tune in to His frequency—frequency being the key word here—often.

A Columbian with whom I worked on the island of Oahu loved surfing, and one day out off of Diamondhead, he caught a perfect wave as he was with a group that allowed him to be in line, if you know about surfing politics. He rode the wave as far as he could, and then he was swimming out to get back in line for another run. A local native Hawaiian was paddling on his board standing up and said, "Hey, bra, you not going back like that?"

My Columbian friend asked, "What do you mean? I just had a great run."

The local said, "Look at your foot, bra. It's bleeding, ya?"

Ivan looked down and saw the flesh hanging off his foot as he had stepped on jagged coral after his run and mangled his foot. Bleeding like that attracts sharks. Ivan had to go ashore and get stitches from his wife, who is a doctor from Thailand. Psalms 91:12 explains how things can be seemingly going well when you're actually bleeding below unnoticeably: "They shall bear thee up in their hands, lest thou dash thy foot against a stone." Had that local not seen the problem, there may have been tragic results.

You must be willing to listen to messengers who observe things you can't about yourself and listen, take heed, and adjust your behavior accordingly. I shared a Book of Mormon with a gentleman from Baltimore, a man who had just graduated in a ministry last week. I bore testimony to him of many principles of the Gospel yesterday, and he said he had asked some friends and done some research and was going to return the book without reading it. I told him that had never happened to me before. He just wrote a book about the section of Acts in the Bible, and having already outlined my third book as *Your ACTSYS, Your Sphere* and using Acts as an example of doing what you have been taught as the apostles went forward and did after the Savior left them and visited the peoples on the American continents prior to His ascension to the Father, I asked him, "If you knew that there is a church on the Earth today that Jesus Christ Himself is the head of, would you want to be a member of that church?"

This was the same question that Jim Y. asked me that day at his house in Middleburg, Virginia, when I responded, "Well, yeah, Jim. That's a no-brainer."

This individual, Steve, had no response, and I further testified that even if I'd published all my books and was a millionaire and blessed the human race who read them, they would not hold a candle to the Book of Mormon and the principles and power laid forth therein. This was not a coincidental meeting; however, Steve still had his agency to reject the message and me, the messageur, and so do you! However, I would challenge you to thoroughly investigate with the missionaries and read the Book of Mormon and do as it direct in Moroni 10:3-5. Like Ivan, you'd hate to go out and catch a wave amongst the sharks after having been warned that you are wounded, wouldn't you?

The world is very noisy with the wind of confusion driving you to and fro. It would behooveth you to heed my warning and that of the elders that you may experience peace, joy, and happiness in this life. Psalms 107:23-31 explains this process of being tossed and then saved as I have been led to the Gospel of Jesus Christ by messageurs of Spirit and of flesh: "They that go down to the sea in ships, that do business in great waters; These see the works of the LORD, and his wonders in the deep. For he commandeth, and raiseth the stormy wind, which lifteth up the waves thereof. They mount up to the heaven, they go down again to the depths: their soul is melted because of trouble. They reel to and fro and stagger like a drunken man and are at their wits' end. Then they cry unto the LORD in their trouble, and he bringeth them out of their distresses. He maketh the storm a calm, so that the waves thereof are still. Then are they glad because they be quiet; so, he bringeth them unto their desired haven. Oh, that men would praise the LORD for his goodness, and for his wonderful works to the children of men!"

Heavenly Father, Jesus Christ, and the Holy Ghost live and love you! Fear is of the devil; don't be caught playing for the losing team. Remember to pray and listen for an answer, to establish communication with the Lord, and to live worthily to house His Spirit so you may know when and where your messages and messageurs come from. Psalms 65:6-8 further quantifies, "Which by his strength setteth fast the mountains; being girded with power: Which stilleth the noise of the seas, the noise of their waves, and the tumult of the people. They also that dwell in the uttermost parts are afraid at thy tokens: thou makest the outgoings of the morning and evening to rejoice."

I believe the outgoings are prayers. The footnote 8a for "tokens" cross references "signs," and I believe the signs are the incomings that return from the prayers. You shouldn't seek signs; however, when they come, you should be prepared to recognize their source and to receive them and discern the message and take ACTION like the Apostles did after seeing firsthand the Savior in ACTION. The next book will address this; remember, when the student is prepared the instructor will appear.

You may feel at this point that the song and the chorus is redundant, and maybe you're growing weary of the same old story. Don't! There's a reason for repetition, and there's a reason why David, a king in the line of the Savior, sings the psalms over and over and over. I will do the same. Singing the same old story and the song has its benefits.

Psalms147: l-7 tells of the gathering that is taking place: "PRAISE ye the LORD: for it is good to sing praises unto our God; for it is pleasant; and praise is comely. The LORD doth build up Jerusalem: he gathered together the outcasts of Israel. He healeth the broken in heart, and bindeth up their wounds. He telleth the number of the stars; he calleth them all by their names. Great is our LORD, and of great power: his understanding is infinite. The LORD lifteth up the meek: he casteth the wicked down to the ground. Sing unto the LORD with thanksgiving; sing praise upon the harp unto our God..."

Do you think that all the scriptures were written for the people of that time? I promise you that the message is more applicable today in our society as we approach the Second Coming of our Lord than it ever was, and I challenge you to keep consecrated oil with you, so you are not like the five virgins who failed to prepare for the bridegroom, and even more importantly hold a temple recommend. If you do not know what these are, ask the missionaries of the Church of Jesus Christ of Latter-Day Saints. They'll be happy to explain when you're ready to listen and obey the Lord's servants.

It says in Psalms 37:11, "But the meek shall inherit the earth; and shall delight themselves in the abundance of peace." This is not the earth that you now live in, but an earth devoid of Satan and his followers with Jesus Christ in a millennial reign prior to the resurrection where all men will be reunited spirit with body for the judgment and dispersion into eternal life in the kingdoms prepared for us based on our righteousness and obedience and our willingness to endure to the end. Either you act on this now and become baptized to begin your journey, or someone will do it on your behalf in the temple and hope that the same spirit that you left here with in mortality will not hinder your eternal progression. Are you **willing** to take that chance? If you are, then I may be wasting my ink. Repent and be baptized into the Lord's only true and living church upon the face of the earth of which Jesus Himself is at the helm through His Prophet on the earth, even President Thomas Spencer Monson.

Psalms 83:18 lets you know the source: "That men may know that thou, whose name alone is JEHOVAH, art the highest over all the earth." And when feeling afflicted, visit Psalms 88:7, "Thy wrath lieth hard upon me, and thou hast afflicted me with all thy waves. Selah." Come into the fold and hear the hidden message in the riptide as currents of rivers within oceans flow and ride the wave of eternal life in the presence of your family, past, present, and future, in a sphere of love in the company of your Heavenly Father, Eloheim, and His Son Jehovah of the Old Testament or Jesus Christ. And the chaos and turmoil will disappear as it states in Psalms 89:9: "Thou rulest the raging of the sea: when the waves thereof arise, thou stillest them." David addresses God's firstborn Son being greater than he and all kings.

As you may have noticed, the wave is symbolic of communication; the wave is sent ashore constantly just as messages from above, and then the wave recedes bringing with it all that is not deposited on the beach. As the tide becomes high, the water gets closer and when the tide gets low the water is further away. We are only six hours from one or the other as the seascape is constantly changing while most things appear to remain the same. Psalms 93:3-5 explains in relative terms who's in charge. "The floods have lifted up, O LORD, the floods have lifted up their voice; the floods lift up their waves. The LORD on high is mightier than the noise of many waters, yea, than the mighty waves of the sea. Thy testimonies are very sure: holiness becometh thine house, O LORD, forever."

Do you have gratitude for this moment in time and gratitude for the lessons of the past and look forward to the tomorrow that you are creating today? Yes, TODAY! Yes, TODAY! Yes TODAY! Live in the now and adjust your ACTSYS, or system of action, towards the Lord, and do all you can to teach and raise children for a better tomorrow

TODAY. Read the Book of Mormon TODAY. Pray TODAY. LISTEN TODAY FOR AN ANSWER. Look for and ask for guidance through the messageur, even Jesus Christ through His Holy Prophets, servants, angels, and those who tarry today in immortal bodies on His errand, and most of all establish a house of prayer and refuge for you and your family, for nothing you can do in this life will compensate for failure to live His example and impart that to all with whom you come in contact.

I am about to enter a very sensitive issue that plagued me for years with an inability to forgive and forget. I call it my tarring and feathering in Independence, Missouri. As you may know, many in the church were persecuted and driven from their homes in Missouri, caused by some members who fell away being used by Satan to misinform Lilburn J. Boggs, the governor of Missouri at the time, which caused the extermination order against the early saints. I was in Jefferson City when we met with Governor Carnaughan and his wife to be part of the Mormon Pioneer Trail Exhibition. The church leaders gave them their genealogy, and you should have seen Governess Carnaughan's jaw drop when she was told her great-grandmother was a member of the Church of Jesus Christ of Latter-Day Saints. The Heart of America choir lined the stairs spiraling up and sang hymns in the Capital Building. Up until 1976, when the extermination order against Mormons was rescinded, it was legal to kill a Mormon in the state of Missouri, and in 2002, it almost happened to me.

I had just had surgery on my left leg and had thirty-two staples in my leg and also had a hernia repaired. I was resting at my house when my brother showed up on drugs and alcohol, filling my foyer with obscenities. Knowing I could do nothing in my condition, I asked him to leave, and he wouldn't, so I made one of the biggest mistakes of my life and called 9-1-1 and the Independence police department. I saw my brother grab my van keys where all my tools were and run out the front to take my van and pawn everything, just like he'd done the week before with my other tools in the truck I provided him. I threw my crutches down and went after him to stop him as this happened immediately after I'd hung up the phone. I leapt into the step van before he could start it and held him down and told him to give me my keys. The police showed up and said, "Police! Come out of the truck."

I turned for a split second, and Kevin grabbed a hammer. I turned and held his arm, so he couldn't hit me with it. The police officers tore my bib overalls off trying to pull me out. While holding Kevin down, I told them that I was the homeowner, and I had called. They said to let go and come out. Kevin was still holding tightly to the hammer. I let go of his hand and turned quickly to exit the van, so he wouldn't hit me, and the officers started macing me in the eyes and telling me get on the ground. I told them that I'd just had surgery while they continued to empty two cans of mace down my face and chest. I told them I was the homeowner and that I couldn't get on the ground. They then hit me with their night sticks on the staples and ruined my left leg forever; it almost needed to be amputated a year later. While my wife who is now dead watched from the library window, they arrested me and dragged me down the driveway in front of all my neighbors, who didn't see a thing later when questioned by the Gestapo. I had tried to cast Satan out of my brother before the police had come. My brother's face contorted in anger and his voice changed, and Satan himself or one of his angels said, "That's not how it works!"

I saw my brother's body deflate as the evil force jumped into Officer McPhee from the Independence Police Department from Independence, Missouri. He later lied in court, and his companion told the truth, which is rare if you know how the fraternal brotherhood works. I had to make bail for calling 9-1-1 for help and was sitting in a hospital. You should have seen McPhee's face when he saw my leg; it will never be right. He pulled his fellow officer aside, and they made up charges of feloniously interfering with the arrest of an officer. I was facing twelve months in jail and a fine for doing nothing, and the judge wanted me to do a plea bargain. I put my foot down and said, "I have done nothing wrong, and these officers have lied." I was not guilty! The judge banged his gavel, and the case was dismissed. The prosecuting attorney whom I had visited at home already knew of my intent to bring suit against the city, and he must have informed the judge. All charges were dropped, and I eventually was led to drop the lawsuit as I was told I'd have to move out of Missouri or face a lifetime of harassment.

The spirits that were in Missouri raping, pillaging, burning, killing, and driving the saints out of their homes and property in the middle of winter still exist. I've seen them in Palmyra and Independence and while moving the paintings by Glen Hopkinson and Liz Swindle from fireside to fireside. I know that the adversary doesn't want you to read the Book of Mormon and that he will use ignorant friends and religious leaders and all necessary means to hinder Jesus Christ's kingdom from growing. He's fighting a losing battle. Which side are you on? Bishop Partridge was tarred and feathered on the streets of Independence not far from where I lived, and I know the persecution continues today. They burned the printing office, and the mobs later killed Joseph Smith and his brother Hyrum in Carthage Jail. Great lengths are taken by Satan on this earth to deceive you into thinking that evil is good. Standards of conduct in society and media are deteriorating at an accelerated rate. Technology is increasing the rate of Elijah's work of exposing the entire human race through genealogy work to the sealing ordinances and all other covenants and ordinances necessary to create eternal families and prepare for the Lord Jesus Christ's Second Coming. These things can only be done in the temples of our Lord.

Psalms 94:20-21 says what I tried to explain on the previous page: "Shall the throne of iniquity have fellowship with thee, which frameth mischief by a law? They gather themselves together against the soul of the righteous and condemn the innocent blood." Injustice prevails as much today as it did in the early days of the Church. Psalms 115:4-8 tells you why: "Their idols are silver and gold, the work of men's hands. They have mouths, but they speak not: eyes have they, but they see not: They have ears, but they hear not: noses have they, but they smell not: They have hands, but they handle not: feet have they, but they walk not: neither speak they through their throat. They that make them are like unto them; so is everyone that trusteth in them."

Injustice is served by your legal system where the wealthy buy their way out, and many times the best way to spur your economy is to grow medicinal marijuana or open another prison. Great strides are being made in many areas of your life; however, the chasm is growing wider between good and evil, and tolerance for immorality in our media and acceptance of evil as good will bring the calamities that have been foretold to the forefront. Brace yourself; repent, be baptized, and endure to the end. If you are prepared, you will not be caught up in the frenzy, and you will look forward to a return to values and to the commandments. Psalms 59:12 speaks of those who use position or injustice to prevail and prosper: "For the sin of their mouth and the words of their lips let them even be taken in their pride: and for cursing and lying which they speak." I feel sorry for those who must make a dishonest living and lie for their paychecks—don't you? In Psalms 82:2, Asaph asks, "How long will ye judge unjustly, and accept the persons of the wicked? Selah." Also, Psalms 83:3 states, "They have taken crafty counsel against thy people, and consulted against thy hidden ones." I forgive all in Independence who were part of my demise, even myself.

As for those who are adversaries in that area and all others, I will share a lengthy warning in the entirety of Psalms 109: "HOLD not thy peace, O God of my praise; For the mouth of the wicked and the moth of the deceitful are opened against me with a lying tongue. They compassed me about also with words of hatred; and fought against me without cause."

Joseph Smith translates verse four. The King James Version states, "For My love they are my adversaries: but I give myself unto prayer." Joseph Smith translation states for this same verse, "And, notwithstanding my love, they are my adversaries; yet I will continue in prayer for them."

Verse 5 continues, "And they have rewarded me evil for good, and hatred for my love. Set thou a wicked man over him: and let Satan stand at his right hand. When he shall be judged, let him be condemned: and let his prayer become sin. Let his days be few; and let another take his office. Let his children be fatherless, and his wife a widow. Let his children be continually vagabonds and beg: let them seek their bread also out of their desolate places. Let the extortion catch all that he hath; and let the strangers spoil his labor. Let there be none to extend mercy unto him: neither let there be any favor to his fatherless children. Let his posterity be cut off; and in the generation following let their name be blotted out. Let the iniquity of his fathers be remembered with the LORD; and let not the sin of his mother be blotted out. Let them be before the LORD continually, that he may cut off the memory of them from the earth. Because that he remembered not to shew mercy, but persecuted the poor and the needy man, that he might even slay the broken in heart. As he loved cursing, so let it come unto him: as he delighted not in blessing, so let it be far from him. As he clothed himself with cursing like as with his garment, so let it come into his bowels like water, and like oil into his bones. Let it be unto him as the garment which covereth him, and for a girdle wherewith he is girded continually. Let this be the reward of mine adversaries from the LORD, and of them that speak evil against my soul.

But do thou for me, O God the LORD, for thy name's sake: because thy mercy is good, deliver thou me. I am gone like the shadow when it declineth: I am tossed up and down as the locust. My knees are weak through fasting; and my flesh faileth of fatness. I become also a reproach unto them: when they looked upon me they shaked their heads. Help me, O LORD my God: save me according to thy mercy: That they may know that this is thy hand; that thou, LORD, hast done it. Let them curse, but bless thou: when they arise, let them be ashamed; but let thy servant rejoice. Let mine adversaries be clothed with shame, and let them cover themselves with their own confusion, as with a mantle. I will greatly praise the LORD with my mouth: yea, I will praise him among the multitude. For he shall stand at the right hand of the poor, to save him from those who condemn his soul."

I'm glad I prefaced this Psalms with forgiveness. Psalms 14 is the perfect scripture to continue making my point against the adversary and those who follow him, "THE fool." I just noticed that this psalm has a complete translation in Joseph Smith's translation and I'll use it here: "The fool hath said in his heart. There is no man that hath seen God. Because he showed himself not unto us, therefore there is no God. Behold, they are corrupt; they have done abominable works, and none of them doeth good. For the Lord looked down from heaven upon the children of men, and by his voice said unto his servant, seek ye among the children of men, to see if there are any that do understand God. And he opened his mouth unto the Lord, and said, Behold, all these who say they are thine. The Lord answered and said, they are all gone aside, they are together become filthy, thou canst behold none of them that are doing good, no, not one. All that they have for their teachers are workers of iniquity, and there is no knowledge in them. They are they who eat up my people. They eat bread and call not upon the Lord. They are in great fear, for God dwells in the generation of the righteous. He is the counsel of the poor, because they are ashamed of the wicked, and flee unto the Lord, for their refuge. They are ashamed of the counsel of the poor because the Lord is his refuge. Oh, that Zion were established out of heaven, the salvation of Israel. O Lord, when wilt though establish Zion? When the Lord bringeth back the captivity of his people, Jacob shall rejoice, Israel shall be glad."

As I prepare to delve into the most tragic period in my life since joining the church, I am preparing myself and you for what is to come, which has been the predecessor to most of my recent difficulties and definitely a motivating factor to writing these books in case I, too, slip through the veil unexpectedly. My children must learn from my mistakes and do better with their children as I feel that my conversion to the Gospel has and will help them. I hope to leave a legacy of service and love.

David complains about his enemies and their transgressions, and so do I. Psalms 35:14-20 suggests his frustration: "I behaved myself as though he had been my friend or brother: I bowed down heavily, as one that mourned for his mother. But in mine adversity, they rejoiced, and gathered themselves together: yea, the abjects gathered themselves together against me, and I knew it not; they did tear me, and ceased not: With hypocritical mockers in feasts, they gnashed upon me with their teeth. Lord, how long wilt thou look on? Rescue my soul from their destructions, my darling from the lions. I will give thee thanks in the great congregation: I will praise thee among much people. Let not them that are mine enemies wrongfully rejoice over me: neither let them wink with the eye that hate me without a cause. For they speak not peace: but they devise deceitful matters against them that are quiet in the land."

And David felt in Psalms 57:4, "My soul is among lions: and I lie even among them that are set on fire, even the sons of men, whose teeth are spears and arrows, and their tongue a sharp sword." Brothers and sisters—and *you* are my brother or my sister—remember the cunning of the evil one. Sometimes when you least expect it, in your time of need, those closest to you may betray your confidence and sell you out. The ultimate example is Jesus Christ, whom Judas betrayed and Peter, fulfilling Christ's prophecy, denied thrice. Peter repented and felt remorse, and he was given the lead of the Apostleship and worked great miracles in the similitude of the Savior in Acts, a section of the Bible that will be integrally weaved in my next book, *Your ACTSYS, Your Sphere.*

There are things that happen in your life that throw you into a tail spin, and relatively speaking, individually, some are universal. You may cope differently than I do with certain situations. With the many self-inflicted traumas that I've suffered and all the setbacks of the past, some which I discuss and some I don't, I thought I'd pretty much seen it all. One night I was out with the missionaries teaching a single father and his two children in Independence. We stayed a little late as the Father had committed to baptism, and I felt a prompting to go home to my wife. The missionaries said we probably needed to get home, so I could return to my wife. I told them there was no hurry as I thought to myself that my wife, having been a returned missionary, would be fine with my staying a little longer. If I had only known and listened to the message from the Spirit, I may have gotten home in time to save my wife from suffocating to death during an epileptic seizure. Instead, I came home, and the house was dark, the children asleep. Before I went upstairs, I decided to feed the woodstoves with logs to continue supplementing our heat through the night. My wife and I had plans that evening, so I went upstairs and checked the children's rooms and found them asleep. When I walked into my room, Paula was wrapped in a towel lying face down in the bed. I said, "Paula, what are you doing sleeping?"

I thought she had fallen asleep and was out cold. When I saw she didn't move, I rolled her over, and her eye sockets were blackish-purple and her face blue. Her mouth had been sealed in a puddle of blood from biting her tongue, and I immediately began cardio-pulmonary resuscitation while calling 9-1-1. They kept asking me questions to ɉkeep me on the phone as I was panicking, giving a priesthood blessing, and performing lifesaving techniques to the best of my ability. I remember saying on the phone, "I think she's dead!"

By the time the rescue team arrived, it seemed like hours, and I knew she was gone—my eternal companion and the mother to my five children was gone. The homicide detective kept me for questioning, and I was allowed to go to the hospital when they determined it was an accidental death. Bishop U. was there with me along with Ron when the doctor came in and pronounced she had passed. He told me I could go see her. When I went in to the emergency room and she lay there, I felt she wasn't there anyway, so I turned and walked away. The next time I saw her was at the viewing when she was walking around her relatives' backs. No one else saw her. She had said that it would take a funeral to get her entire family together, and it worked. I'm sure she didn't mean her own funeral. My children said goodbye during the open casket before the funeral and the internment. I was in shock for months, and things really still haven't returned to normal nine years later.

I've learned to cope and accommodate; I've been through another marriage and subsequent divorce; and now I'm waiting for a sealing clearance to be sealed to my third wife in the temple. Dana is a blessing to my family now, and I'm certain Paula and she will be great friends on the other side. She's a nurturing mom, and I believe she will fill the void in the children's lives.

Many things happened after this tragedy that caused me to be as Job. All of my earthly belongings were lost; I fell into bad credit and IRS debt; and a fall from grace has me in humble circumstances at this moment. Did I play a role in my demise? Of course; I'd be a fool to not admit that irrational decision-making and a lack of attention to detail and a subsequent embezzlement would have probably not happened had it not been for the derailment of my life. I won't blame anyone else for my demise, even though many of my "friends" and associates did, including many who should have been able to discern if they had looked past what appeared to be true. This is neither here nor there at this point as this is in the past, and today I live in the present.

Paula and I met through a series of non-coincidences, and she believed she might not find a man in this life. We met in Virginia and were engaged in Kirtland, Ohio, where the first temple in this dispensation of time was built and where all the keys of the Kingdom were restored through a series of visitations. The temple was abandoned like the temple in Nauvoo after great persecution and revelation caused the saints to leave. Life is an eternal round, and the beginning and the end of one era to another can be skewed with forethought and discerned with reflection and circumspection. One thing is sure: looking backward, many things are more understandable once removed from trauma, heartache, and grief.

Psalms 56:8 reads, "Thou tallest my wanderings: put thou my tears into thy bottle: are they not in thy book?" The footnote for book is the Topical Guide and references Book of Remembrance. This is why I have written this trilogy—so that out of my experiences and trials, you may find hope and guidance not to make the same mistakes, and to be able to slice the learning curve and avoid the bad while emulating the good, if that makes sense. In Psalms 94:17, you'll find the source of my inspiration to write this work: "Unless the LORD had been my help, my soul had almost dwelt in silence." Had I not found the Gospel of Jesus Christ, these books would not have been written. I think it's a shame when a member has inspiration and shares his or her talent, and one they look up to has the audacity to make a statement like, "Don't blame that on the Lord." After all, it says in the introduction that if there are mistakes, they are the mistakes of man, so I wouldn't blame an ignorant statement like that on the Lord. The Gospel is perfect; men are not.

After Paula's death, many came forth with visits that they'd had with her where she said something that caused them to think that she wasn't going to be with us much longer. Bishop Billings, God rest his tender soul and his wife's Ida Mae, came up to me in Sacrament the Sunday before she died while she was giving a talk. I was leaving to change Rebekah's diaper when Bishop Billings put his hands on my shoulders and said, "You know, I'm waiting to join my wife on the other side of the veil." I didn't know at the time that she would die two days later; the Lord used a seventy-nine-year-old man to be the messageur so that I would know and be warned. Remember, communication requires a sender and a receiver; however, if one is not tuned in, the message is still imparted. Listening has always been difficult for me, but with the constant companionship of the Holy Ghost, I have been blessed with a feeling that helps me to listen when it is vital to those over whom I am a steward. A message can be assigned, transported, delivered, and then confirmed by the messageur to the sender upon returning and reporting. The Lord sends messages to me, and they are always repeated three times in the exact same words, so many times the message giver is not the one who delivers the message. They are couriers sent from the Lord with His message and those Messages are URS and URS only, hence *The Psalm of the Messageur*. Tune in and listen, for you may walk to the beat of different drum than I, even though it should come from the same source. You'll need to read The Doctrine and Covenants in its entirety to understand how to discern who the sender is. To know the sender is to be a better receiver, and to discern will cause you to act, for without action the message is for naught.

Many times, in your life, you may feel isolated or misunderstood, especially when life-altering experiences, trials, and tribulations find your doorstep. Losses cause grief, and prolonged grieving periods can cause your receivership to be interrupted. This doesn't mean the Lord has abandoned you. It just may mean that, just as Job or David in Psalms, you are being tested. My experience with grief has been extensive. The first sign after a tragic occurrence is a feeling of shock. This is followed by a period of irritability, anger, resentment, and sometimes a self-created isolation from those who could help you speed through this phase. The third is depression, a sense of loss, deep, sorrowful feelings, and the ever-present "Why me?" syndrome. A Psalm of David, Psalms 27:9-12, explains feeling isolated: "Hide not thy face far from me; put not thy servant away in anger: thou hast been my help; leave me not, neither forsake me, O God of my salvation. When my father and my mother forsake me, then the LORD will take me up. Teach me thy way, O LORD, and lead me in a plain path, because of mine enemies. Deliver me not over unto the will of mine enemies: for false witnesses are risen up against me, and such as breathe out cruelty." David asks the Lord to teach him how to overcome his emotions during an extreme time of disappointment in his friends and family.

I've experienced the letdown of isolation during times of trial and tribulation when many are going through yours and their own, when they don't always show or even have compassion or a shoulder to lean on. During my wife's death and an embezzlement that destroyed my assets along with my father's death all within ten months, I felt like David, and I better understood what Joseph Smith suffered during periods of blame and persecution for things that happened beyond his control. Psalms 13 says it all: "HOW long wilt thou forget me, O LORD? Forever? How long wilt thou hide thy face from me? How long shall I take counsel in my soul, having sorrow in my heart daily? How long shall mine enemy be exalted over me? Consider and hear me, O LORD my God: lighten mine eyes, lest I sleep the sleep of death; Lest mine enemy say, I have prevailed against him; and those that trouble me rejoice when I am moved. But I have trusted in thy mercy; my heart shall rejoice in thy salvation. I will sing unto the LORD, because he hath dealt bountifully with me."

I have found gratitude through the mess. After all, if it doesn't kill you, it makes you stronger, RIGHT? Psalms 6 speaks of grief: "O LORD, rebuke me not in thine anger, neither chasten me in thy hot displeasure. Have mercy upon me O LORD; for I am weak: O LORD, heal me; for my bones are vexed. My soul is also sore vexed: but thou, O LORD, how long. Return, O LORD, deliver my soul: oh save me for thy mercies sake. For in death there is no remembrance of thee: in the grave who shall give thanks? I am weary with my groaning; all the night I make my bed to swim; I water my couch with my tears. Mine eye is consumed because of grief; it waxeth old because of all mine enemies. Depart from me, all ye workers of iniquity; for the LORD hath heard the voice of my weeping. The LORD hath heard my supplication; the LORD will receive my prayer. Let all mine enemies be ashamed and sore vexed: let them return and be ashamed suddenly." When your spiritual eyes are consumed with grief, it's hard to see the light at the end of the grieving gauntlet. Don't give up before the miracle occurs.

Remember to look for gratitude as David does in Psalms 31, and maybe you'll shortcut the isolation better than I did. Psalms 31:7-24 reads, "I will be glad and rejoice in thy mercy: for thou hast considered my trouble; thou hast known my soul in adversities; And hast not shut me up into the hand of the enemy: thou hast set my feet in a large room. Have mercy upon me, O LORD, for I am in trouble: mine eye is consumed with grief, yea, my soul and my belly. For my life is spent with grief, and my years with sighing: my strength faileth because of mine iniquity, and my bones are consumed. I was a reproach among all mine enemies, but especially among my neighbours, and a fear to mine acquaintance: they that did see me without fled from me. I am forgotten as a dead man out of mind: I am like a broken vessel. For I have heard the slander of many: fear was on every side: while they took counsel together against me, they devised to take away my life. But I trusted in thee, O LORD: I said, thou art my God. My times are in thy hand: deliver me from the hand of mine enemies, and from them that persecute me. Make thy face to shine upon thy servant: save me for thy mercies' sake. Let me not be ashamed, O LORD; for I have called upon thee: let the wicked be ashamed and let them be silent in the grave. Let the lying lips be put to silence; which speak grievous things proudly and contemptuously against the righteous. Oh, how great is thy goodness, which thou hast laid up for them that fear thee; which thou hast wrought for them that trust in thee before the sons of men! Thou shalt hide them in the secret of thy presence from the pride of man: thou shalt keep them secretly in a pavilion from the strife of tongues. Blessed be the LORD: for he hath shewed me his marvelous kindness in a strong city. For I said in my haste, I am cut off from before thine eyes: never the less thou heardest the voice of my supplications when I cried unto thee. O love the LORD, all ye his saints: for the LORD preserveth the faithful, and plentifully rewardeth the proud doer. Be of good courage, and he shall strengthen your heart, all ye that hope in the LORD."

You see that the Lord gives you exactly what you want according to your actions, and when you think you're cut off, most of the time it's by your own confusion, unless you've committed transgression or sin knowingly without repentance. Like I said earlier, life is an eternal round, and what goes around comes around. Forgive, for it is required of you. As for the Lord, He will forgive whom He chooses, and only the Judge of Israel in your area or the Bishop, whether you're a not-yet-member, a life-long member, or a convert, has stewardship over you given him by the Lord through His Priesthood line of authority.

Psalms 55:14 gives me goosebumps: "We took sweet counsel together and walked into the house of God in company." The House of God is the temple, and I pray that you and I will enter a temple in fellowship, soon, as a result of your reading the Book of Mormon and finding of its truth as I did and as others with whom you share will. Pay it forward; I know that proclaiming the Gospel is the most important thing that I can do for others while in this mortal life and after, the Lord willing. I have felt the absence of one life immediately and the start of another in the grieving gauntlet that only time will mask and never erase.

Psalms 88:8 and 18 may help you to know how I feel today while on my way to renewal of a new life in the absence of all my friends, family, and acquaintances from my past as a result of loss: "Thou hast put away mine acquaintance far from me; thou hast made me an abomination unto them: I am shut up, and I cannot come forth. Lover and friend hast thou put far from me, and mine acquaintance into darkness." I gave away control after I had none, and I testify that my demise was not entirely my own.

Enough of the grieving already; are you getting as depressed as I am? Do you see how easy it is to dwell in the past? Today, yes, today, yes, today—YES, TODAY, as my psalm becomes my motto. If I focus on the pain of the past, tomorrow becomes a by-product of yesterday, and today slips away, another opportunity given away instead of squandered on the past. I believe that half of my life, I have spent unnecessary time on worrying and reminding myself of pain and anguish while failing to relish the now-moments which become a reducing commodity. Many times, I've felt like, "What's the use?" and wanted to leave this existence. Had I done so, I wouldn't have found these sacred truths that have given me hope, peace, and happiness. Thank You, Jesus Christ, for all You've done for me. I've had to find gratitude and humor while exiting life's cyclones.

Psalms 94:12-13 seems like an oxymoron: "Blessed is the man whom thou chastenest, O LORD, and teachest him out of thy law; That thou mayest give him rest from the days of adversity, until the pit be digged for the wicked." I am in the restoration phase as Job in the last chapter and have finally surfaced, and my body, mind, and spirit are in the same realm. What a ride it's been; and I sing praises to the pilot, tire Holy Ghost. I have been whisked away by the Spirit of the Lord several times and taught and then returned to my mortal understanding; the key is to be grateful for the journey.

Have you ever heard that it is better to give than to receive? I've been on both ends of the stick, and I agree that it is easier to give than it is to receive. One requires a human doing that which is charitable while the other requires a human being able and willing to bless others by losing pride and allowing others to give to them. I promise that being the receiver is harder than being the giver, just like prayers offered up that become redundant and hurried where no time is given to receive an answer. Most have never received an answer to a prayer and believe that it doesn't happen. Try fasting and praying with the earnestness of Enos, and don't leave your knees until you receive an answer. A prayer doesn't have to be long or eloquent. Address your Heavenly Father and say, "I am grateful for…" As if you're talking to a respected friend, let the Lord know what you have to be grateful for. Then, include a (hopefully) shorter list after: "I ask thee for…" Then close in the name of Jesus Christ. I like to ask a question and wait until the Holy Ghost speaks to me with an impression, sometimes asking for confirmation after I have thought out in my mind exactly what I need answered. You'll be in awe when you do as directed in Moroni 10:3-5 and receive the answer that opens the door of ultimate communication and receivership from the constant companionship of the Holy Ghost.

Forgiving is possible when hate and misunderstanding are replaced with love and open communication. Forgiveness has always come for me after wasted time and effort holding a grudge which only seems to injure me and not the subject of my anger. The Lord forgives and forgets; the latter has been the most difficult for me—FORGETTING. I seem to drag on my suffering by continuing to tell total strangers the things that have been done to me that have caused me to struggle and need help. I drop that now and forget the horrible onslaught and urge you to not bring these things up to another human being as I KNOW it is my VANITY and PRIDE that causes this insanity. I'm done with yesterday and ready for a brighter today that will bring a better tomorrow. I apologize to all I have harmed or made afraid as a result of my PRIDE. I'm scalping the ticket to my past and seeking a new game to watch. Finally, I promise to forget those who have harmed me in my time of need, and I wish them the best. I pray that the Lord will confound me anytime I speak of the past except in a positive uplifting fashion. Thank you for indulging me through this process, and I hope you can find it within yourself to cleanse your pain, anguish, and resentment as I am doing. I call this process FOR-GETTING, for by forgiving, forgetting, and moving on, you can foretell that the things you'll be getting will change when you stop repeating the self-talk of the past and allow by gone to be bye, gone, once and for all (the spellings are obviously purposeful in my case). My wife Dana said the other day that every time we meet someone new, I talk about the same exact things from the past. Then I caught myself doing it, and I had a momentary lapse in my dysfunction, suddenly realizing she was right. That was and still is eye-opening. I thank her for her constructive criticism, and I thank the Holy Ghost for sending me to Caribou, Maine, where I could have down time long enough to write these books for my posterity and for you (but, most of all, for me). I have healed immensely and been given revelation as I have soaked myself in the scriptures and my subconsciousness like never before. Thank you, Eloheim and Jesus Christ and my best friend, the Holy Ghost, for helping me find myself again and for helping me find the purpose for which thou hast sent me here to this earth. I AM GRATEFUL! From now on, I will sing your praises to all men I meet through my example.

Mosiah has been one of my favorite sections in the Book of Mormon because it includes King Benjamin's speech prior to his death and is symbolic of a righteous leader leaving a legacy to his people, like Jacob, who is Israel, leaving a legacy and blessing to his sons who are the heads of the twelve tribes of Israel. My blessing to my posterity begins today, and believe it or not, I will need to read this trilogy to get a better grasp of what is contained herein as I have been acted upon by the Spirit throughout this seventeen-year process. Mosiah 3:5 and 9 elicit some confusion: "For behold, the time cometh, and is not far distant, that with power, the Lord Omnipotent who reigneth, who was, and is from all eternity to all eternity, shall come down from heaven among the children of men, and shall dwell in a tabernacle of clay, and shall go forth amongst men, working mighty miracles, such as healing the sick, raising the dead, causing the lame to walk, the blind to receive their sight, and the deaf to hear, and curing all manner of diseases. And lo, he cometh unto his own, that salvation may come unto the children of men even through faith on his name; and even after all this they shall consider him a man, and say that he hath a devil, and man shall scourge him, and shall crucify him."

The biggest necessary error in the history of man was the killing of the Son of God, and Heavenly Father knew it would happen because of the blindness, pride, and corruption of those in power in religion and state and their confusion at how to deal with all of the contradictions in their previous learning and interpretation. The chosen people were not ready for Jesus Christ, and neither is the earth ready for His Second Coming TODAY. Some of us are; however, some of the elect are also deceived by the cunning and craftiness of men, hence the need for a prophet and a dichotomy of communication through an ecclesiastical and Priesthood line of authority and guidance through transition. The Church of Jesus Christ of Latter-Day Saints is the means to the end of one era and the paradisiacal beginning of one thousand years of Christ's reign to close one book and open another.

Psalms 61:8 EXPLAINS BRIEFLY HOW DAILY INTROSPECTION AND REMEMBRANCE ARE NECESSARY TO RETAIN PROTECTION: "So I will sing praise unto thy name for ever, that I may daily perform my vows." I believe this is living an example through action and emulating the light of Christ while inviting all to come unto Christ through that example. I apologize for coming up short on most occasions. Psalms 75: 1 explains, "UNTO thee, O God, do we give thanks, unto thee do we give thanks: for that thy name is near thy wondrous works declare." All around you there is proof of our great gift, shall you squander your birthright or magnify it unto the children of men, yours first. Enter the covenant by being sealed for time and all eternity to your family now. Begin, act, persevere, and begin again to bless others once you have received the ultimate praise for good behavior. Then will you feel to sing, as David did in Psalms 95: 1, "O COME, let us sing unto the LORD: let us make a joyful noise to the rock of our salvation."

A minister of another faith said to me when I shared a Book of Mormon with him, "A lot of people are going to be surprised when they get to heaven." I felt he meant that many are deceived. I testified to him of the truthfulness of our church and that it was the only true church on the face of the earth and that Jesus Christ Himself was at the helm along with a prophet here on earth, Thomas Spencer Monson. I asked him, "If there were a church on the earth today that Jesus Christ himself were the head of, would you want to be a member of that church?"

He avoided the answer and said that he didn't want to offend me, to which I replied I did not own the propensity to be offended. He said that he had done some research on the church and spoken to some friends and that he wasn't interested. I asked him if he'd read the book which I testified was the most important book on the face of the earth and professed that a man would get closer to God by abiding by its precepts than by any other book. He said he would not read it because he believed only in the Bible. Bible, Bible, we have not the need for another bible.

"The Book of Mormon is another witness of Jesus Christ and His dealings with the peoples inhabiting the ancient Americas," I explained, "and the sticks of Judah as discussed in Ezekiel is the Bible and the sticks of Joseph is the Book of Mormon."

This man wrote a book and a study guide on the same section of the Bible that I will discuss in my third book. This isn't for everyone, even though it is; some are not ready or have found a path alternate to that of the Savior. At least I exposed him to it. My work is complete until he asks again, and he will ask. You must gain a knowledge of this and save your children from the search and the pain and anguish of a life devoid of the principles of a righteous standard of living. "Lo, children are an heritage of the LORD: and the fruit of the womb is his reward. As arrows are in the hand of a mighty man; so are children of the youth. Happy is the man that hath his quiver full of them: they shall not be ashamed, but they shall speak with the enemies in the gate."

Ah! From the mouths of babes—how our children could teach us if we only knew how and when to listen. And the reward of life is happy offspring armed with correct teachings as it says in the next Psalms 128: 1-3: "BLESSED is everyone that feareth the LORD; that walketh in his ways. For thou shalt eat the labor of thine hands: happy shalt thou be, and it shall be well with thee. Thy wife shall be as a fruitful vine by the sides of thine house: thy children like olive plants round about thy table."

My parents' parents suffered horrific, unusual tragedies that left indelible impressions upon my parents that in turn left impressions on me that without the Gospel being imparted (and still with some struggles) may have continued for generations. I am grateful to be a hub for positive change, and I thank Jesus Christ for getting my attention and making it impossible for me to be confused. I know that He lives and stands at the right hand of the Father and speaks to a prophet on earth today, even Thomas Spencer Monson, and that the Book of Mormon is true. Joseph Smith is the first prophet of this dispensation and all the Keys of the Priesthood restored here on earth were given through him by multiple visitations, and he saw in the sacred grove God the Father and His Son Jesus Christ who is our Savior. The sacred and holy work that goes forward in the temples is necessary for exaltation and eternal life in the presence of the Father and of the Son and of the Holy Ghost. I pray that I may continue to make a positive role model and father for my children and a better husband to my wife. I know that as I seek the Spirit for proclaiming the Gospel, I will continue to help others to the light, and I pray that the Lord will lengthen my stay on the earth as he did for John the Beloved, the three Nephites, and many others whom He deems necessary to accomplish His work here among mortals to bring to pass the immortality and eternal life of man as it states in the Book of Moses in The Pearl of Great Price.

Psalms 25:1-4 reads, "UNTO thee, O LORD, do I lift up my soul. O my God, I trust in thee: let me not be ashamed, let not mine enemies triumph over me. Yea let none that wait on thee be ashamed: let them be ashamed which transgress without cause. Shew me thy ways, O LORD;

teach me thy paths." I have been conveyed by the Spirit and been in the Celestial Kingdom to experience what it feels like. I know that the Lord showed me things to remove all doubt. I have been dead and returned while experiencing separation and reunion of the spirit and my body. I know that when you die, you live, leaving the tabernacle of clay to be reunited at the resurrection to be judged and placed in a paradise you lived to be in. However, to live in the presence of the Savior, you must be sealed and have received the ordinance of baptism only by one holding the Levitical Priesthood which is the Priesthood of Aaron.

That path on the Appalachian Trail that lead me to that gnarly peak where I talked with a man about the Savior and walked into another path with white stones to an altar having been conveyed by the Spirit for three miles without walking is an experience I'll never forget. Has my calling in election been made sure? I'm not positive; however, after that day, I knew that salvation was mine to lose. The Messianic Psalm of David, Psalms 40:9, says it all, and may I sing at the top of the mountains: "I have preached righteousness in the great congregation: lo, I have not refrained my lips, O LORD, thou knowest." I have committed to the Gospel of Jesus Christ and am in the world but not of the world. Since my baptism and confirmation, and even in that warehouse in Norfolk where my conversion began, I have been on the Lord's errand. Mistakes I've borne, mine and others, but unwavering has been my testimony.

My testimony to not-yet-members such as my brother has been met with mixed reception. My brother, Kevin, said in Independence that I was so righteous that I would end up like Job; that turned out to be prophecy. Kevin is still caught up in the addiction scene, and I've found it hard to forgive him many, many times. I've finally decided to tell you of our hardships together and close the book on the past. When Kevin was little, being one and one-half years younger than me, I used to protect him. When I was too scared of my father, when he was beating my mother, Kevin would stand up to him from a young age. I was totally emotionally, mentally, and physically brutalized by my father, being the oldest, and couldn't wait to get away from him; we left in the night in our pajamas with Mom and never came back. Kevin and my sisters, Sharon and Angie, were very traumatized by this, and it would affect their lives and still does to this day as I'm sure you already concluded, mine most of all.

I noticed something yesterday about the word psalms that may interest you. When you split the word up, it is "P.S." and "alms," one meaning a note after the fact and another meaning giving of alms, which is an offering. When you sing after something has occurred, as David did, you hope for forgiveness and gain appreciation for what is to come. A psalm is an offering after the fact, and so is *The Psalm of the Messageur*. Back to Kevin: we went separate ways after the divorce. My mother worked swing shifts as a nurse and went to school while taking care of four of us in a townhouse in Centreville, Virginia. I swam at the local pool and was involved in many activities that were illegal, and so was Kevin. The only difference was that Kevin smoked cigarettes and decided not to work out or play sports. He started hanging around full-time the people I would hang around part-time. We really had no discipline or standards, even though Mom tried to instill her sense of Catholic morality in us.

Kevin wrecked my new Kent racer on a gravel road and scarred his face up badly. He was with Chris Jones, his friend, and that was my last bicycle, after losing so many to theft before that. I wasn't much of an example as a big brother as I was selfish, hurt, and confused about my life. We moved to New Hampshire when my Mom got a position at Littleton Hospital and said she was moving back to her home state to spend more time with family. I don't remember spending any time with her family the whole time we were there. I was so much into football, basketball, pot, and girlfriends; I hardly remember anything except indulging myself in beer, drugs, women, working out with weights, and running. Kevin wasn't around me much as he hung with a different crowd, even though we were doing similar things. He played football his freshman year and did really well as a running back and as a linebacker. Then the teachers started asking him why he wasn't more like me, and he quit school after failing and being held back. I don't know what he did with his time after that, and I really didn't care much as we grew further apart—me, the partying jock, and him, the dropout smoker. We'd hang out sometimes and party together even though his friends were different, but that's about all we had in common.

Then Mom got a job in Washington D.C. and decided to leave for Virginia. I decided to stay with my coach and my girlfriend and my life. My family went on without me to Virginia and lived while I finished my senior year in hopes of athletic and academic scholarships. My partying became excessive and began to get me in trouble while distorting my priorities and putting me around a bad element of people. Two of them killed a homosexual, and the FBI dragged me out of school for questioning even though I wasn't involved. We had a party and stole a big bottle of blue Valiums and took a bunch. I decided I could jump over a stair landing down to the floor below and rolled my ankle on the top of a step. We were heading to state finals in basketball, where I was supposed to play, and the coaches found out about the incident and benched me. I really couldn't play anyway as my mental condition had caused me to make irrational decisions. I turned down all my New England scholarship offers and ended up going to Virginia Tech on grants and government loans as an in-state student since my Mom was a resident. The partying grew greater as I used the money I made selling drugs to support my lifestyle, buy my books, and support my many habits. I walked on and off the football team, and most of my life has been spend walking on and walking off of many things in rage and irrationality.

My junior year, I got a call from my mom, and she said it was about Kevin. I asked, "Is he dead?"

She said, "No, he's killed someone, and the news cameras are in my front yard right now!"

I told her I would leave school and come home, but she said that she would handle everything and that I should stay in school as there would be nothing I could do. To date, this was devastating to me, and I remember crying in a public speaking class and giving the presentation on my brother. I stopped caring about everything and got deeper into drugs and alcohol 24/7. I felt so guilty about not being there for my brother and my family that I became totally out of control and began selling to anyone I could find so as to drown my sorrows. I forgot that what I was doing for all these years was illegal and went wide open and got caught after selling an acquaintance cocaine that turned out to be a DEA agent on a sting operation. I take full accountability for my actions and would spend twelve more years in the throats of addiction while running some very successful legitimate businesses in various parts of Virginia. I'm not going to go off on a tangent drink-alogue or drug-alogue. The blessings of the gospel have rid me of my addictions even though some of my behavior and character flaws remain. Kevin and I have gotten together many times in business as he was doing better than I when he got out of prison and married money. When I got sober and Kevin didn't was when we parted ways. Many times, he would come to rescue me from a drug house or a party, and I wouldn't leave with him. He cares about me and I about him; it's just so hard. He was the perpetrator that Satan possessed who tried to steal my truck. That caused me much hardship. However, it was partially my fault as everything in my life has been. I take full responsibility for my rights and my wrongs. Today, the right far outweighs the magnitude of the minor mistakes that I take care of each week when I partake of the sacrament. I had custody of my brother's son, Jesse, for eight years. Now Jesse's back with his mom, and I hope he will share the gospel with his mom, Debbie, and my brother and his father, Kevin. I know Kevin's health has been failing and that he still drinks and drugs today at the age of forty-nine. We all have scars from the past, but they're much easier to deal with in the Gospel and sober than they were before. I'm living each day to the fullest and trying to get back in the best shape of my life to increase my energy, vitality, and life expectancy as I have a wife and four children to live and provide for. I want to live life to the fullest today the with the hope of a brighter tomorrow for all who I come in contact with and myself. I can even forgive a date rapist like Eric for what he did to my sisters. Eric was our neighbor in Burke, Virginia, and Kevin's friend, and he later became my friend. My sisters asked my mom why Kevin and I never did anything about Eric raping them as he had to so many other young virgins.

My mom asked me, and I was in shock as my sisters had never told me. I don't know if Kevin knew or not. I believe it was good for Eric that we didn't know. I forgive you, Eric; I hope my sisters can. I hope the Lord will forgive you or that we can meet, and I can share the Gospel of Jesus Christ with you. Psalms 69:12 states, "They that sit in the gate speak against me; I was the song of the drunkards." I cannot begin to tell you the horrors of my life's decisions prior to my sobriety and membership in the church.

Do not begrudge others. Do not be a grudge to others, and do not hold a grudge for others. It will consume your happiness, and instead of inflicting pain on the culprit, you become the recipient. What an eye-opening revelation. Psalms 25:18-21 further explains the process of forgiveness: "Look upon my affliction and my pain; and forgive all my sins. Consider mine enemies; for they are many; and they hate me with cruel hatred. O keep my soul and deliver me: let me not be ashamed; for I put my trust in thee. Let integrity and uprightness preserve me; for I wait on thee." I know that the atonement of Jesus Christ has worked on my behalf and that today I stand forgiven for all wrongs I have done and that I await the Second Coming of Christ to be reunited with my loved ones in the Celestial Kingdom after the resurrection of the righteous.

There have been many in and out of the church that have said things that were not helpful. I believe an anxiety exists when living in the world and not being of it. Peace, joy, and happiness in this life and the life to come are what they appear to be; it's just that many in a position of influence in and out of the church lose focus as they are human. The optimum situation to be in is to have all that you need financially so as to escape scrutiny and misunderstanding along with the judgment that doesn't exist in the church but is at every turn with human members caught up in confusion of how to live in this world but not be of it. LOVE means unconditionally caring, listening, and imparting of your substance to others. I can give of my labor for free, even if I don't have disposable income, and I do. When I serve others, I forget my pains and challenges, and so can you. It requires stepping out of the hamster wheel rat race and finding meditative time to reflect on real priorities and reading scriptures daily while praying for help, guidance, and a way to sustain yourself and your family. I have been betrayed, belittled, and led astray by those who should have been trusted in their positions. Psalms 41:7-9 relates just how I've felt: "All that hate me whisper together against me: against me do they devise my hurt. An evil disease, say they, cleaveth fast unto him: and now that he lieth he shall rise up no more. Yea, mine own familiar friend, in whom I trusted, which did eat of my bread, hath lifted up his heel against me." Sometimes, I've been treated as a disease or an inconvenience and made to leave my own fellow church members as a result of their persecution and lack of understanding while giving service begrudgingly and for the wrong reason. I would challenge members of the Church of Jesus Christ of Latter-Day Saints to hold their tongue when speaking ill of others. It can be very hurtful and has been to me and to Job and to David and to the Savior himself, who was betrayed by those who should have shown love instead of mobocracy, corruption, and pride of position and financial status along with politics and peer pressure.

Psalms 101:7 says, "He that worketh deceit shall not dwell within my house: he that telleth lies shall not tarry in my sight." The discernment usually comes in hindsight; even though there are indicators of one's lack of integrity, sometimes the layers of protection confuse even the mantle upon the man trusted to judge. Personal opinion has no place in the judgment of wrong. Relying upon the Lord would bring much greater results with far less pain, loving kindness and understanding rather than irritation and a feeling of being inconvenienced. Remember, there if not by the grace of God go you. Don't think for a moment that because of prestige, power, and financial clout that you may be immune from being the one you misjudge or in many cases the one that you judge in righteousness.

The interesting thing is that I continue to follow the path the Lord lays in front of me and go where He tells me to go audibly three times. No matter the hardship, I go and am continually questioned by those in and out of the church feeling that what I do makes no sense. If the Lord's errand makes no sense to you, then so be it. I wish you well in your worldly endeavors. I shall go forth as Lehi and Nephi of old, continuing to make no sense to those who know not the workings of the Spirit. I apologize not for doing what the Lord commands me to do, and neither should you. It is better to be misunderstood in the Lord's service than to be understood while not in His service. Psalms 119: GIMEL makes me feel right: "Deal bountifully with thy servant, that I may live, and keep thy word. Open thou mine eyes, that I may behold wondrous things out of thy law. I am a stranger in the earth: hide not thy commandments from me. My soul breaketh for the longing that it hath unto thy judgments at all times. Thou hast rebuked the proud that are cursed, which do err from thy commandments. Remove from me reproach and contempt; for I have kept thy testimonies. Princes do also sit and speak against me: but thy servant did meditate in thy statutes. Thy testimonies also are my delight and my counsellors." I shudder to think of the things that Jesus Christ and his Spirit have taught me before men ever mentioned or the scriptures iterated. I am so grateful for Thy intervention on my behalf and for the tender mercies which Thou hast extended to me and my eternal family here on earth and in the life to come. Let me be understood by those who would receive Thy message and misunderstood by those in the world except when Thou sees fit to pluck another soul from the gall of iniquity. May I be ready with a copy of the Book of Mormon and worthy to house Thy Spirit so as to deem recognizable Thy Spirit as I carry Thy great message to the children of men and my own immediate family. You, the reader, now have a responsibility to ACT on the challenges you have been given and to share with others the Gospel or at least bring the missionaries to those you meet when feeling so prompted. Your ACTSYS, for example, will foretell of His coming. People are always watching us like they somehow know that what we have is good, so be on your best behavior.

Helaman 10:6-10 in The Book of Mormon explains the sacredness of the authority of the Melchizedek Priesthood and its sealing power bestowed upon the prophets and sealers in the Temples of our Lord: "Behold, thou art Nephi, and I am God. Behold, I declare it unto thee in the presence of mine angels, that ye shall have power over this people, and shall smite the earth with famine, and with pestilence, and destruction, according to the wickedness of this people. Behold, I give unto you power, that whatsoever ye shall seal on earth shall be sealed in heaven; and whatsoever ye shall loose on earth shall be loosed in heaven; and thus, shall ye have power among this people. And thus, if ye shall say unto this temple it shall be rent in twain, it shall be done. And if ye shall say unto this mountain, Be thou cast down and become smooth, I shall be done. And behold, if ye shall say that God shall smite this people, it shall come to pass."

There is a type of this thing from the Old Testament, and here we are thousands of years later, still trying to figure out what these true events have to do with us today. Is there any hope? I never read scriptures when I was Catholic. A whole new world was revealed to me as I likened the real-life experiences of people in the past to my life. The actual medium and timeframe disappeared when I realized that God and His Son Jesus Christ were speaking to me about my circumstances and that wisdom and happiness could be found by learning from others in the past the path to happiness in this life and what happens when you choose to live contrary to revealed truths and principles. Universally, actions and consequences remain similar throughout history. Remember the Lord and be happy or forget Him and be miserable. You have a choice, don't you?

In the Book of Mormon, 3 Nephi 10:14, after the Savior's death, many prophecies were fulfilled, and Nephi writes, "And now, whoso readeth, let him understand; he that hath the scriptures, let him search them, and see and behold if all these deaths and destructions by fire, and by smoke, and by tempests, and by whirlwinds, and by the opening of the earth to receive them, and aft these things are not unto the fulfilling of the prophecies of many of the holy prophets." By raising your voice in prayer and song and by reading the scriptures with the discernment of the Holy Ghost, which allows for communication and proper fitting interpretation, you may learn the wisdom of those who already know the relationship between earth-life death and life hereafter. The mysteries of Christ are contained in the books which have been revealed, especially the King James Version of the Bible translated in crucial spots by Joseph Smith, the Book of Mormon, the Pearl of Great Price, and the Doctrine and Covenants. You may have the truth of all things by reading the Book of Mormon. If you haven't picked it up, read it, and prayed about it, then I've wasted my ink. Again, start now! Read it; pray about its truth and call the missionaries from the Church of Jesus Christ of Latter-Day Saints. They're in the phone book. Do it! If you're a member and you think you know all there is to know and have a testimony, think again. Pick it up, read it, and pray alone and with your family. Share it with your friends and help others to come unto Christ and to be sealed for time and all eternity in the covenant of the everlasting priesthood which only exists with its power and authority in this church and in this church alone. I had a minister from Baltimore tell me the other day that that was a bold statement, and I asked him if he'd read the book I gave him. Read it now.

There are other revealed scriptures as I have referred to you throughout the first book and this one; however, your understanding will be significantly increased by reading the Book of Mormon first since it is directly from Christ and only translated once by the gift and power of God. Acts 8:39-40 explains how one can be conveyed and literally become invisible when the Lord sees fit: "And when they were come up out of the water, the Spirit of the Lord caught away Philip, that the eunuch saw him no more: and he went on rejoicing. But Philip was found at Azotus: and passing through he preached in all the cities, till he came to Caesarea."

So, this man was baptized by water and received the gift of the Holy Ghost apostolically, and Philip was conveyed away to work elsewhere, or he slipped to another kingdom and proceeded to do the

Lord's will, reappearing in Azotus. This is literal; sometimes, when you haven't experienced something, your mind will interpret it in a way that makes logical sense, thus destroying the meaning of the event and the significance in parlaying a message in the realm of possibility, hence when the student is ready, the teacher—the messageur—will appear.

I have recently been accused of self-aggrandizement when I share my experiences. If I have offended anyone or you, I apologize. It is my intent to carry you away into a new world which has been made known unto me by a series of visitations and promptings along with vistas of beauty which have been revealed, along with coinciding hardships and many times, on my part, misunderstood guidance only remembered in hindsight. I love you as the Lord loves me, and I wish to impart my love the only way 1 know how—by sharing about my path to eternal precepts on a journey that is continual. Boasting and boisterous behavior comes from insecurity on my part and has no place in this work, so discount these feelings and read beyond and between the written word to find the true meaning of my words and the message of prompting to follow in the footsteps of the Chosen One, even Jesus Christ. Two of my favorite movies are *Meet Joe Black* and *The Secret Life of Noah Dearborn*. Watch both of them, and you will see how I yearn for a quiet mind that would allow me the peace of pursuing that which I love, creating work both physical and spiritual that will leave a lasting indelible legacy to you and my progenitors. As Sandler would say, "Run silent, run deep." I promise you, the reader, that from this day forth, I will make an effort to use my words both spoken and written more wisely, for certainly it truly is better to be silent and be thought a fool than to speak and remove all doubt. The tongue can, in many instances, be mightier than the sword. At least the sword brings finality to the mouth where the verbose one lives on to continue suffering.

I would much prefer to be a better listener and to have been led to many courses on the subject in sales to learn empathic listening skills. Non-verbal communication fascinates me even though I will simultaneously speak while using neural-linguistic programming. Communicating with the end in mind and setting an agenda are important. I write in this fashion not to deceive but to edify and call forth the spirit to witness to you as it has to me that Jesus is the Christ and that the Priesthood has been restored to the earth and that the Book of Mormon is another witness of Jesus Christ and his sacred atonement was for all and not just for those in the Holy Land. There is a prophet today on the earth who holds all the keys of the Priesthood of God as prophet, seer, and revelator, even Thomas S. Monson. Since Joseph Smith, the first prophet of this dispensation, these keys have been passed in succession and by solemn assembly as each prophet has gone through the veil to the other side. When Heavenly Father and Jesus Christ appeared to the boy or young man in the sacred grove, the rock that was cut from the mountain without hands began to roll forth, never to be removed from the earth again until His Second Coming.

Listening is an art and requires ongoing response and questions which allow participants to know that you have heard and understand what is said. Listen, answer, ask a question, listen, answer a question; many times, dialogue is not spoken, and this is most effective in moments of prayer and meditation. Know that the most important messages are relayed in this fashion and come in a form that is individually known by Jesus Christ as He knew you before you were born and knows how to best get your attention.

Psalms 12 speaks to me. It reads, "HELP, LORD; for the godly man ceaseth; for the faithful fail from among the children of men. They speak vanity everyone with his neighbor: with flattering lips and with a double heart do they speak. The LORD shall cut off all their flattering lips, and the tongue that speaketh proud things: Who have said, with our tongue will we prevail; our lips are our own: who is lord over us? For the oppression of the poor, for the sighing of the needy, now will I arise, saith the LORD; I will set him in safety from him that puffeth at him. The words of the LORD are pure words: as silver tried in a furnace of earth, purified seven times. Thou shalt keep them, O LORD, thou shalt preserve them from this generation forever. The wicked walk on every side, when the vilest men are exalted." In the world, many times, evil seems to prevail as Satan's angels walk in the shadows and beside evil, selfish individuals who seem to prosper from abusing others and controlling decisions that change your life. Their time is coming to a close, and for that I am grateful.

Conspiring men earn their reward as it says in Psalms 81:12: "So I gave them up unto their own hearts' lust: and they walked in their own counsels." The Lord withdraws His Spirit from such and leaves them to their short-term reward. It is my hope that as you read Christ's words and the words of His Apostles, you, too, will be baptized in the true church. Christ's voice can be heard through the Holy Ghost when you have it conferred upon you by one holding the Priesthood of Melchizedek and receive the Holy Ghost as your constant companion. Psalms 95:7 explains, "For he is our God; and we are the people of his pasture, and the sheep of his hand. Today, if ye will hear his voice." Listen after praying using the proper order of prayer you will learn from the missionaries of the Church of Jesus Christ of Latter-Day Saints.

You must reinvent yourself with repentance and be baptized by one holding the Priesthood of Aaron as even the Savior did when He sought out John, his cousin, to baptize Him as only he could, having had the Priesthood of Aaron conferred upon him in the office of a priest. If you are a member and HAVE DONE THIS, SEEK THE TEMPLE COVENANTS AND ENDURE TO THE END. Avoid pornography and divorce if at all possible. Live worthily to hold a recommend and visit the temple as often as your situation deems possible; partake of the Sacrament worthily by arriving seven minutes early and asking for forgiveness for specific sins and attend the entire three-hour block and keep the Sabbath holy. In my first book, *Howning Your Sphere*, I stressed the importance of setting goals and using your ACTSYS in the direction of your goals, one step at a time: learn to crawl, then walk, then run. Living the principles of the Word of Wisdom will help.

Once you do these simple things long enough, you will begin to feel as the sons of Mosiah did in Mosiah 28:3-4: "Now they were desirous that salvation should be declared to every creature, for they could not bear that any human soul shall perish; yea, even the very thoughts that any soul should endure endless torment did cause them to quake and tremble. And thus, did the Spirit of the Lord work upon them, for they were the very vilest of sinners. And the Lord saw fit in his infinite mercy to spare them; nevertheless, they suffered much anguish of soul because of their iniquities, suffering much and fearing that they should be cast off forever." When faced with the reality that you've been wrong your whole life in the way you have lived, thinking to eat, drink, and be merry, feeling that we just die in the end anyway, and suddenly being faced with an existence after this life based on how you fared, here can be a huge slap in the face or what I called a wake-up call. I, too, was the vilest of sinners, and felt that if I could be forgiven and start over, it would truly be like being born again, except that I would know better the things to do and the past things to avoid. When you're born into this world, you are made to forget the pre-existence where you lived before.

My goal now is to attain a sealing clearance to bring my wife Dana to the temple to be sealed for time and all eternity to me and my family. We met on the Latter-Day Saints mingles site. I was looking one night at profiles when I felt impressed to go to a section that I hadn't noticed previously, new accounts. I looked through, and right at the end I saw a ninety-nine-percent match from Nova Scotia and immediately emailed her, knowing that she was the one by the Spirit. We talked on the phone for hours, many times until I had to plug my phone in and call back because my battery would go dead. On faith, I mailed her an engagement ring before I ever met her. I flew up to Halifax to meet her family and church leaders and wasn't allowed into Canada over college transgressions; Dana and I only met in the airport for three and a half hours. We had to tell her mom that she was going to marry a convict. I'd never been called that before, but given the circumstances, I could do nothing but offer to withdraw the engagement. And if the adversary could do any better, then it turned out that I needed to get permission from my previous wife, whom I'd divorced, to be able to go to the temple and be married. This is another tiling for which I had to humbly offer up a withdrawal as Dana had waited all these years to marry so as to be married in the temple. I'm still waiting, two years later, for the sealing clearance, and we are married. We were married civilly by Bishop T. in Kolob Ninth Ward in Springville, Utah. We then went to Hawaii for six months with the five children, including Jesse, who would later self-destruct back to Norfolk, Virginia, and his real Mom. This turned out to be good for all. After I worked for a Columbian surfer in the solar business and a gay CEO's son who turned out to be part of the Mafia, importing antiques and who knows what else from Saudi Arabia and Japan; I'd had enough of the islands. They were a nice place to *visit*.

We came back to Nebraska as I was delusional in thinking I could get a wealthy country boy to back me in a service business or get my books published through some people I'd sold an e-commerce program to in Lincoln. They tried to be our friends, but I guess we weren't ready, and the piano they gave my daughters turned out to be the final boost to get us enough gas money to go to the Field of Dreams and then on to Maine, where we are now, unemployed and living off the state and the church welfare program. You might feel as if you shouldn't walk my path, and you have every right; however, the best is yet to come, for I know that all of our struggles have been for a reason. It is so I could see my character defects that still exist even though the Lord has forgiven me. I must truly forgive and forget the past and live today and change myself, reinventing Michael Durgin for the millennium to come.

Jesse's in Norfolk, Virginia. I love him like he's my son, and I gave him the only four-hundred-dollar watch I'd ever owned and put him on a plane that my Mom paid twelve hundred bucks for to send him as a project shy of Eagle Scout and a teacher in the Aaronic Priesthood. I heard he's doing well. We have the four children: my son Isaiah, thirteen, and my daughters, Elizabeth, twelve, Naomi, eleven, and Rebekah, ten. Dana and I are waiting for the clearance, and we don't know how we'll get to Boston when the time comes. The Lord will provide. Dana and the girls are going to Canada for a couple weeks to get Dana's passport renewed, and the Bishop has lent us his car for her and the girls to go. Isaiah and I will make the most of our time together without money at this moment. We're fasting and praying today for a maintenance position to open in Limestone at the MSSM School, and Dana's buying food with food stamps to bring to Canada to lighten the burden on her family's food bill. You might say things are awful humble. I needed to suffer to keep my mouth shut and to stop talking about the past. It is pride that keeps me talking about successes that seem fleeting as if only yesterday. Hope comes today for a better tomorrow. I'll watch my two favorite movies and ask the Lord to make me dumb, so I may listen better, not as John the Baptist's father was made dumb but in a way that allows me to speak when appropriate and become a man of few words. I pray for this NOW.

"Heavenly Father, I am grateful for the gift of intellect and corresponding gift of gab that has provided for me in sales in the past. I ask Thee to quiet and make wise my mind and temper my mouth and tongue so as to be perceived as a better disciple of Christ. I pray that Thou wilt honor my fast by helping me to provide for my family and provide assistance to others as Steve in Fort Fairfield did even from the pantry, being of another faith and one under Christ. The bishop and the church have expended much on my behalf since becoming a single father of five and since failing to find sufficient employment to provide for basic necessities. For this, Lord, I am grateful, and I ask Thee to bring our sealing clearance forward and proper employment, so I can provide for my family. For this, and all other things thou see we stand in need of at this time, please help us to recognize Thy hand and for me to do things Thy way and not begrudgingly. Silence my mind and my tongue while allowing me to preach the Gospel and may Thy will on behalf of me and my family be done and may Dana and the girls return home safely and unharmed from Canada. I ask these things in the name of Thy Son and my Redeemer, even Jesus the Christ, Amen."

Psalms 84:3 again reads, "Yea, the sparrow hath found a house, and the swallow a nest for herself, where she may lay her young, even thine altars, O LORD of hosts, my King, and my God."

And Psalms 86:11 says, "Teach me thy way, O LORD; I will walk in thy truth: unite my heart to fear thy name." Fear in the scriptures means to respect and revere when talking about fear of the Lord.

The most important university of higher learning on the earth is the temple. Psalms 65:4 states, "Blessed is the man whom thou choosest, and causest to approach unto thee, that he may dwell in thy courts: we shall be satisfied with the goodness of thy house, even of thy holy temple." All truth is given in the temples of our Lord. I have spent much time in these holy edifices, and much wisdom has been imparted and many ordinances on my behalf, on my family's behalf, and for many whom I have yet to meet. I have asked the Lord, as John the Beloved and the three Nephites did in the past, to allow me to tarry and not taste of death until I can reach more people with this glad message. I have squandered many opportunities to share the Gospel, especially as I am currently set apart as a Mission Leader and have been consumed by my stress, financially. I am ready to prosper again and to be humble without being compelled to do so. When He is ready, I shall exit this existence as billions before me, however in an exalted state, to live with my family and friends for ever in a state of never-ending peace. Enos said it better in Enos 1:27: "And I soon go to the place of my rest, which is with my Redeemer; for I know that in him I shall rest. And I rejoice in the day when my mortal shall put on immortality and shall stand before him; then shall I see his face with pleasure, and he will say unto me, ye blessed, there is a place prepared for you in the mansions of my Father. Amen."

In small things are great things brought to fruition. The Greek word "Aitia" defines a legal cause of action. If I have caused anything in yours to change, then I have succeeded. If not, I have still succeeded; maybe you just haven't looked at these works in the right frame of mind. Hopefully, you will be ready even if the seeds I have planted remain dormant for a while. You could avoid a lot of heartache by implementing these principles before it becomes a necessity. If your cause to act isn't there yet, it will be, and in your time of need, just as when I was in the warehouse in Norfolk, hopefully a Book of Mormon will be within reach. If not, when you're ready, the missionaries will knock on your door, and a self-fulfilling prophesy will have been fulfilled by one who lived it before and so on.

In the following pages, we will focus on the temple blessings and the fact that your body is a temple that houses your spirit and how you must keep your body clean and free from addiction to feel the truth of all things and to be approachable by the Spirit of our Lord. I was in sobriety and working the twelve steps of recovery when the Spirit of Christ approached me at the Washington, D.C., temple in Kensington, Maryland. My brother-in-law and my sister, Sharon, had brought me there to see the Christmas lights, and while walking up the hill and pondering the sights, intervention occurred, and leaves were swirled in my direction as well as a corresponding message from the Lord, which said, "Let Satan out, and let me in." Three times it was reiterated to me in the form of commandment in a piercing, still voice, so overpowering.

After the Savior's death many prophecies were manifested. In 3 Nephi:3-15, it says, "And it came to pass that while they were thus conversing one with another, they heard a voice as if it came out of heaven; and they cast their eyes round about, for they understood not the voice which they heard; and it was not a harsh voice, neither was it a loud voice; nevertheless, and not withstanding it being a small voice it did pierce them that did hear to the center, insomuch that there was no part of their frame that it did not cause to quake; yea, it did pierce them to the very soul, and did cause their hearts to bum. And it came to pass that again they heard the voice, and they understood it not. And again, the third time they did hear the voice, and did open their ears to hear it; and their eyes were towards the sound thereof; and they did look steadfastly towards heaven, from whence the sound came. And behold, the third time they did understand the voice which they heard; and it said unto them: Behold my Beloved Son, in whom I am well pleased, in whom I have glorified my name-hear ye him. And it came to pass, as they understood they cast their eyes up again towards heaven; and behold, they saw a Man descending out of heaven; and he was clothed in a white robe; and he came down and stood in the midst of them; and the eyes of the whole multitude were turned upon him, and they durst not open their mouths, even one to another, and wist not what it meant, for they thought it was an angel that had appeared unto them. And it came to pass that he stretched forth his hand and spake unto the people say: Behold, I am Jesus Christ, whom the prophets testified shall come into the world. And behold, I am the light and the life of the world; and I have drunk out of that bitter cup which the Father hath given me and have glorified the Father in taking upon me the sins of the world, in the which I have suffered the will of the Father in all things from the beginning. And it came to pass that when Jesus had spoken these words the whole multitude fell to the earth; for they remembered that it had been prophesied among them that Christ should show himself unto them after his ascension into heaven. And it came to pass that the Lord spake unto them saying: arise and come forth unto me, that ye may thrust your hands into my side, and also that ye may feel the prints of the nails in my hands and in my feet, that ye may know that I am the God of Israel, and the God of the whole earth, and have been slain for the sins of the world. And it came to pass that the multitude went forth, and thrust their hands into his side, and did feel the prints of the nails in his hands and in his feet; and this they did do, going forth one by one until they had all gone forth, and did see with their eyes and did feel with their hands, and did know of a surety and did bear record, that it was He, of whom it was written by the prophets, that should come."

The real messageur, the only one I direct you to find using this work as a medium to get you to the Book of Mormon, the missionaries, and to the waters of baptism to follow Christ's example.

This could be the end of this book, but it's not. Today, I found myself anew, with new life and motivation and tears of appreciation for the process of life and appreciation for renewal in my career as I move to Florida to get back in the game. Thank you for your help, even though you don't know me yet; by writing for you, I have been healed and made whole. As all messageurs come from the dust through the living, I wish to let you know that the past, the present, and the future are one in Christ and that he will come soon to rescue the world in its current state of wonder and from the adversarial elements that embitter you.

There are fifteen men currently called as prophets, seers, and revelators, and they are the First Presidency and the Twelve Apostles of the Church of Jesus Christ of Latter-Day Saints. We can get closer to the Lord and His work in the temples of His Church which dot the earth. In John 16:12-13 of the New Testament, the Savior explains, "I have yet many things to say unto you, but ye cannot bear them now. Howbeit when he, the Spirit of truth, is come, he will guide you into all truth: for he shall not speak of himself: but whatsoever he shall hear, that shall he speak: and he will shew you things to come. In the absence of the Savior, His Spirit of truth or the Holy Ghost who is a separate individual in the Godhead helps us to the truth many times through physical manifestations as the action arm of Heavenly Father and His Son Jesus Christ. Proverbs 3:13 states, "Happy is the man that findeth wisdom, and the man that getteth understanding."

Prior to beginning the final book of this trilogy, *Your ACTSYS, Your Sphere*, where I will focus on the effect of action on your circumstances, I WISH TO DISCUSS MORE ABOUT temple worship and of its importance. Psalms 119:19 is how I feel after having been converted: "I am a stranger in the earth: hide not thy commandments from me." The footnote, HEB sojourner, i.e., not of this world for stranger, says it transpired yesterday and felt comfort that the Lord is in charge and that I'm ready to resurface and do my part, again in the Tampa area of Florida. My gratitude is arrived.

In Psalms 100:4-5, the cup is full: "Enter into the gates with thanksgiving, and into his courts with praise: be thankful unto him and bless his name. For the LORD is good; his mercy is everlasting; and his truth endureth to all generations." And Psalms 33:3 says, "Sing unto him a new song; play skillfully with a loud noise." And Psalms 40:3 states, "And he hath put a new song in my mouth, even praise unto our God: many see it, and fear, and shall trust in the LORD." Psalms 98:5 urges, "Sing unto the LORD with the harp; with the harp, and the voice of a psalm."

Psalms 144:9 reads, "I will sing a new song unto thee, O God: upon a psaltery and an instrument of ten strings will I sing praises unto thee."

Many times, like General Washington did, you must burn the ships and go forward, never looking back except to acknowledge the experience bringing the current wisdom that causes action. And with action, faith, determination, and focus, all that you were sent here to find and accomplish will lie in front of you like a rolling scroll. Psalms 71:18 reads, "Now also when I am old and gray-headed, O God, forsake me not; until I have shewed thy strength unto this generation, and thy power to everyone that is to come."

Psalms 47:6-7 says, "Sing praises to God, sing praises: sing praises unto our King, sing praises. For God is the King of all the earth: sing ye praises with understanding." It is with a new understanding I move forward from conversion to endurance with joy and happiness after having my eyelids opened from eight years of grieving and loss mismanagement. Psalms 81:1-5 reads, "SING aloud unto God our strength: make a joyful noise unto the God of Jacob. Take a psalm, and bring hither the timbrel, the pleasant harp with the psaltery. Blow up the trumpet in the new moon, in the time appointed, on our solemn feast day. For this was a statute for Israel, and a law of the God of Jacob. This he ordained in Joseph for a testimony, when he went out through the land of Egypt: where I heard a language that I understood not."

Joseph's brothers sold him into slavery and threw the coat his mother had made him in tatters because they were jealous of his position, being so young and yet chosen over his older brothers. The Lord knew of his mission in Egypt and what he would do for others before he was cast out and sold as a slave. The Lord knows your mission.

Your Actsys, Your Sphere

REINVENTING YOURSELF IS VERY PAINFUL. After all, if you could have done it and gotten where you wanted to be and become who you want without all the pain, emergency, and trial upon tribulation, you would have, wouldn't you? Recently having been in an eighteen-wheeler as a student actually driving constantly for thirty days to get my training after receiving my Utah CDL-A commercial driver's license, I had time to meet with messageurs from the other side while at C.R. England's training facility in West Valley, Utah. I'd always wanted to meet the three men who tarried after having been called as disciples by Jesus Christ after His resurrection and subsequent visit here on the American continent prior to ascending to His Father. I have met Nephi and his first and second counselors and had time to listen to their wisdom on my behalf, also having met Matthew, a young man also on a quest to find a career in trucking after having been disappointed with his computer graphics and web design efforts. He has offered to publish my works on Kindle, and I have offered him half of my entire revenue that will be generated as a result of our non-coincidental meeting during our driving education classes. None of us would have met, including Reagan, an entrepreneur and hockey player from Lethbridge, Alberta, with whom I will soon start a logistics company called Zion Logistics, had it not been for constant promptings to go to this driving school to change our stars and find something that works in this down economy, having lost all hope in our abilities previously developed to provide for ourselves and our families.

While in Maine, during my last set of trials, this trucking ad kept coming up; I even spammed it, and it wouldn't stop. Having sold mentoring packages during my stint as a high-end phone salesman to many truckers, honestly, the thought of becoming one and divorcing my family had never entered my mind. Having to believe through untold hardships that my talents as a builder and plumber were no longer marketable viable skills, I decided to pursue the last thing on earth that I thought I would: becoming a full-time independent contractor behind the wheel of a mobile university called a tractor trailer. I told my wife that I would move us to the Hurricane, Utah, area to get out of the snow, and if no job appeared through diligent effort on my part, I would take the plunge into the logistics/trucking industry. Of course, the thought of my being gone ninety percent of the time and her being alone with the four children wasn't appealing, but the idea of income and what it would provide outweighed the need to stay on government and church-assisted welfare.

I made plans to move and sought a moving trailer after exhausting all alternatives. Suddenly, after having realized that no trailer existed within our budget, I had the idea of buying a van for under a thousand dollars, taking the drive shaft out, towing it as a trailer, and selling it when we arrived in Utah or using it as a work truck. I put a hitch on the Ford conversion van and began to take the drive shaft off and the bumper to install the hitches that mysteriously became available for ten cents on the dollar from an old man named Chief. We set a date to leave and asked the bishop to pay our bills, so we could depart as no work opportunities had presented themselves in Maine.

I painstakingly planned with my wife a route that would get us three thousand miles without mountainous terrain as I quite honestly didn't know whether my three-quarter-ton towing a one-ton van full of a ton of our belongings would even make the trip on level ground and at what speed we would be able to travel and whether the brakes the bishop helped me install with rotor and discs on the front of the Ford would even be able to stop us.

We mapped out miles and incremental destinations, estimating expenditure on fuel and food and the money we would need to pay to rent a house upon arriving, and we figured we had a surplus of four hundred dollars. Boy, were we wrong! I call the following "The Mountain Analogy."

We planned the perfect trip, avoiding mountains and installing trailer lights on the van so I could hook them to my trailer hookup from the Ford and have brake lights and signals along with running lights for safety. We sold everything that wouldn't fit and packed the Savana, hooked it to the Ford, and drove off towards Utah, not knowing what lay ahead. We didn't plan on hotels except for one night. We made a decision to stop at a Knight's Inn in Springfield, Massachusetts, for a night and after a robbery attempt by the hotel management flunkies, we left, having wasted sixty-nine dollars and only sleeping for one hour. Imagine waking the children after one hour of sleep after having been in the van for two days and telling them we had to leave! The thieves followed us to the highway, and I drove four hours away before stopping to sleep. After another day on the road with four children and two cats, for which my wife made harnesses so that they could be walked, we stopped at a La Quinta, which is a great place in Indianapolis where they have security to watch your trucks and a great continental breakfast. We were rejuvenated, and all was well until we were in Texas and heard a pulley let go. I prayed that we'd make it to the next exit, but we didn't. I pulled over, put my emergency flashers on, popped the hood, and saw the disintegrated bearing on the tensioner pulley, which was gone. Just then, a Texas roadway assistance unit showed up as if sent to us, and the nice man not only went and got the part but paid for it with his credit card and provided a crucial tool, and the assistance to get us back on the road. We thought we were done with adversity at this point.

We were on our sixth day and close enough to decide whether to go another day to Vegas and then go north to St. George and to Hurricane; this would have cost us the two hundred dollars in gas and another day, making us unable to meet our financial commitments, so I looked on the map and saw Highway 89, a straight diagonal shot to Hurricane that would save us a lot of time, or so I THOUGHT!

I failed, on the tail end of the trip, to see the elevations of over ten thousand feet. For some reason, I thought everything was desert and didn't even see or think of the mountains. It was a beautiful trip going up to Lake Jacob at times looking at eight-thousand-foot drop-offs without guardrails and praying as the Ford would slow to under five miles an hour, trying to pull the weight over the mountains. It was horrifying, and my wife was crying and praying that the transmission didn't let go; miraculously, angels must have lifted us over the peak. We reached the summit and a gift shop/gas station and stopped to cool the engine and transmission for an hour and decided that downhill would be easier; the only thing I failed to remember was that the new brakes would hardly be sufficient to slow the van on the seven-percent downgrade for ten miles. Tragedy struck as the brakes caught on fire, and as I used the ice water from our cooler to put out the fires, I realized that this was one of the most foolish things I had ever done in my life besides the Expedition episode on Sundance in Provo. I used first gear and made it.

Who you were sent here to be. Important to recognize is the fact that when you think you've arrived at your destination, it may just be a robber in disguise waiting to rob you of the rest and rejuvenation you would have required to follow in the Savior's footsteps had you listened or even asked at that point where distance and expenditure would have been far wiser than taking a shortcut based on what seems to make sense, disseminating all meticulous planning by yourself and others and removing your protection while exposing you and your loved ones to cavernous dangers while overgrowth hides the way and the path you should have trodden. If this is confusing, great—you're beginning to understand.

When you are confused and focused at the same time, you have arrived. Writing your *youlogy* is much easier than writing your eulogy; the first is done while you're living, and your legacy is created by the positive attributes that others, including your children, will teach to progenitors. The second someone else close to you writes upon your passing through the veil into the next life and you're done, a legacy is for the funeral and the newspaper and goes away as fast as it came. Youlogy has life and experience and is imparted through example; eulogy is imparted through assignment and past tense instead of present. I prefer to write my own accomplishments into future generations myself rather than waiting until after life as my impact will have greater reach. How about you? Your ACTSYS, or action system, speaks so loudly to others that what you say is much less important, and your SPHERE of influence follows as example is imperative to impart wisdom. I recently traveled to Salt Lake City to join the best mechanical contractor in the state of Utah this week and to leave trucking as things really didn't go as planned. Even Matt, my Kindle publisher, blew me off and still has copies of my two books and won't answer my phone calls. In the process of taking action, things will not always go as planned; however, looking at each setback as a set-forward will increase your radar and perception and allow you to adapt and escape discouragement. A pupa escapes a cocoon and develops through stages to maturity to fulfill its creation, becoming a pupil or student while going through a series of changes and a natural progression, survival is instinctive. Sometimes, the P.U. pill is hard to swallow; it stinks having to swallow your pride and admit ignorance to become vulnerable and teachable. Even the Apostles were men and had their issues struggling with what the Savior meant in His teachings.

The actions of the Apostles Paul, Peter, James, and John, along with the other eight, were motivated by their need to continue the work which they had been taught by their mentor, Jesus Christ, and of course the promptings of the Holy Spirit along with much grief and confusion. This confusion would increase after their death and be misconstrued and fed upon by corrupt men to gain influence and monetary advantage over the ignorant and still is today. If you fail to open the scriptures during this process, you will reap a diminishing result. As you read Psalms section 106, you will see in verse 2 where David asks, "Who can utter the mighty acts of the LORD? Who can shew forth all his praise?" I've just felt the Spirit, and my eyes are wet and my bosom warm. You see the small letter "a" as a preceding and superimposed above the word "acts," which, in the King James Version of the Bible, will compel you to look at the bottom of the page and reference Jacob 4:8 in the Book of Mormon.

If you have yet to read the Book of Mormon, then stop here and read it from cover to cover before proceeding. It took me seven days at approximately eighty pages per day to read it the first time, and I have since read it and studied it for eighteen years daily. If you are a student of this book, proceed to Jacob. In it you will read that no man knoweth the works and mysteries of the Lord save it be revealed to him. I testify that you must be a student of the scriptures to open the window of understanding to fully reckon the lessons herein. Otherwise, what is to come will be difficult and perhaps unprofitable to you. I challenge you now to do something different and feel the Spirit to search the standard works that are revealed to man through the restoration of the Priesthood of God through the Church of Jesus Christ of Latter-Day Saint missionaries, whether you join the fold or not, and you will be blessed to understand what is to come in this final motivational work of my trilogy.

In Acts 1:1-5, all the Savior taught through His atoning sacrifice is discussed. The twelve Matthias, having been called to replace Judas, are commissioned to be witnesses. They were assembled and asked to wait for the promise of the Father which is the Holy Ghost. John the Baptist had baptized by water, and they would receive the promise so as to baptize with the Holy Ghost. In Acts 4:31, they were assembled, and the place was shaken, and they received the Holy Ghost and spoke with boldness as they sold all they had and consecrated their lives to the work ahead of them. Their *why* had been established; has yours?

In Acts 1:13-26, Peter speaks of Judas and the purchase he made with money of iniquity and how his bowels burst there, and that Judas's bishopric would be filled by another. Would you feel slighted upon your replacement after such a gross violation of confidence? I've often wondered about Judas and whether he was foreordained to betray Jesus, and I believe he was not and that even though someone would have done it, it didn't need to be, nor was he compelled to be the culprit. The field of Aceldama, or field of blood, was to be desolate as spoken of in Psalms by David, and the Holy Ghost fell upon about 120 of them. In Acts 4:20, it states that they could not speak the things which they have seen and heard. On occasion and at the right time and place, these things that happen can be spoken of; however, casting your pearls before swine can be dangerous, and you must rely upon the Holy Ghost to know when to share these things. Many who do not receive promptings from the Spirit will say hurtful things like, "Don't blame this on the Lord!" and I have witnessed such blurts from those in positions that should have known better.

The word "remember" is used 118 times in the Book of Mormon for a reason, and in the introduction, it states if there are mistakes, they are mistakes of men, and these would be easily forgotten had they not come from leaders who were trusted. Unlike Brigham Young, I have witnessed gross errors on the part of trusted leaders and have forgiven but taken years to forget. They pay eventually, and no one is perfect. Peter stood before the high priest and told him that he listened to God rather than man and taught what the Spirit directed, and the priests were cut to the heart and sought to slay them; I believe that some men are put in charge of others who are later found to be doing wrong and teaching incorrect doctrine and misjudging some members into inactivity. God bless them in their bitterness, and restore their faculties, and reveal their serpent. Verse 20 of Acts 4 is again restated for what is written: "For we cannot but speak the things which we have seen and heard." This same scripture which I misunderstood on the previous page comes to light. See the difference; feel the difference? In Doctrine and Covenants 30:1, revelation speaks to David Whitmer and rebukes him for having relied on and feared 10,0011 men instead of relying on the Lord like he'd ought to have. Section 26, verse 16 of Acts recounts Saul's visit from Christ on the road to Damascus and how he was asked to witness to others. I had a similar experience at the D.C. temple, even though the visitation was to get my attention first, and it instantaneously changed my life. These things do happen; if not to you, maybe you were never bad enough. You must become void and empty for a moment to perceive things of the Spirit and be ready to receive promptings from the Holy Ghost, to receive light and knowledge as Joseph Smith did in the grove of trees in Palmyra, New York.

I love You; I thank You; forgive me. Or better: I love THEE; I thank THEE, please forgive me and allow me the freedom of a new life with renewed purpose and forgiveness of all. If this sounds odd to you, you may not be ready yet. Keep reading and learn from "Preach My Gospel" from the missionaries. I had a fellow named Ray in Independence,

Missouri, say to me once, "I don't need some nineteen-year-old punk kids to teach me about God!"

The Spirit immediately retorted through me, "Ray, neither did the Sadducees and Pharisees in the temple in Jerusalem when a twelve-year-old boy taught them. His name was Jesus Christ." Ray was in church the next Sunday.

Your Actsys (Action System)

MANY FACTORS WILL WORK ON you, from environment to associations, but none will be of more influence than your motive coinciding action. Without constant guided action, you will not attain orbit or influence through revolving influence. Increasing your surface area of exposure will make you more vulnerable, which in turn will leave you open to impressions and guidance from a source outside yourself which is omnipresent. Indecision and inaction will have the opposite effect. You must have an end in mind and a plan to begin with and then act while being always on the lookout for messageurs and promptings. The Apostles had more faith in Christ's absence, and you must exercise what Jesus taught. You have the power within to shine and to fulfill your purpose; do it, or forever live in regret—which is a sin, by the way. Be a light and not one who snuffs out others' candles.

I have shown you my goals, and some have evolved, and some have remained constant. For instance, the goal of weighing 205 pounds has had many years to finally appear in the form of my juice fast and a permanent change in how I look at food. I often wondered if Christ actually fasted for forty days or if it was like in other scriptures translated from Hebrew with forty days in them, which means "a long time." Denying food usually, for those of us who overindulge, would seem like the last thing we would do; we'd starve to death. If you're anything like me, you have your food storage stored in your body to last longer than you should. I've visualized myself walking the stages of TV personalities, explaining my books and the individual true stories of those permanently altered and improved by them. I've visualized what I look like and what I'm wearing on these shows. Unlike Napoleon Hill, I've been given permission to publish these things while still living instead of being hindered by relatives who say this is too controversial. Enough about me; let's get on with the parallels between the Apostles of Christ and how what they did will resemble what you do when you're ready.

In Joppa, Tabitha was raised from the dead by Peter, the same Peter which denied Christ thrice prior to the cock crowing thrice. He had made mistakes in his life, and what seemed to throw him into ultimate despair upon his return to the work made him strong in his faith that he could perform the way his Savior had while in the body. This is in Acts 9:36-43, and Peter tarried just like James and John the Beloved, along with the three Nephites. I will tarry also; however, I want my epitaph to read something besides, "Fat man who could have lived longer and better with his family had he conquered his FOOD ADDICTION."

Many demons will hinder you, the greatest of which are your appetites and passions that contradict your goals. I have struggled immensely with peeling the layers away on my onion to lose the excess attitudes in my life. Once living in abundance and then suffering trials and tribulations that led me to let go of all material possessions and be reduced to squalor, I now have a perspective, not of a martyr but of an awakened soul seeking to express myself while providing for my family. As of late, I have realized that until my temporal house is in order, I will struggle to help others as my fulltime attention is upon helping myself, and I'm okay with that. How about you? I understand that my approach of motivating you through scriptural accounts and my own in comparison is unique; I believe that the only way to act with decisiveness is to learn from the things of the past so history does not repeat itself at your expense like it has with me. Positive light will inevitably be balanced with equal doses of darkness just like night and day. Both can be productive and counter-productive, the key being to weigh in the favor of positive productivity in action to yourself, your family, and to others once the first two are in order. Oscillation will occur periodically and require you to adapt and reset while creating your own positive environment again; nothing is permanent, and flexibility can come from a series of stretches that leave indelible lessons. See my point? Liken this to yourself. Can you remember when a paradigm shift or event permanently changed your direction and how hard you tried to return to a previous place and time only to find that what you remembered wasn't there anymore?

Pondering and wandering aimlessly are only separated by a determination to align your actions with your goals; this is my greatest struggle as I seek to publish this trilogy. It's eighteen years in the making with many more books to come; I await and demand fulfillment of my goal of doing my part to expose the wisdom that I am attaining daily and putting my goals into action while avoiding the plague of seeking advice from others who are just as screwed up, if not worse, than I am in their struggle to find sufficient rest in their niche.

Back to the scriptures, to stay on task with my outline: Acts 4:34-35 states that the Apostles sold and received the proceeds from all who were converted and of one mind at that time, having received the Holy Ghost so that no one would be in need going forth to proclaim the Gospel. I have been the recipient of many of my previous offerings of late in the form of food orders and bills paid by the church and must repent for my lack of gratitude and vain pride through the process, for as it says in the Bible, "Are we not all beggars?"

In Doctrine and Covenants 107:14 and 68, the Priesthoods are explained and also how the office of the Bishop is responsible for temporal things; I have put white hair on many bishops' heads and hopefully equal blessings upon the same as they have helped me and my family since tragedies have struck. I will very soon bless many in return with the proceeds of this trilogy along with my favorite charity, my wife and children. Tithing and fast offerings do not pay clergy in the Lord's true church but do go to build temples and meetinghouses along with maintenance while the latter, fast offerings, provide for the hungry and the needy all over the world. The proclamation "You shall know them by their fruits" seems applicable here, and like the Savior, being rejected and persecuted, we, too, are misunderstood and belittled by those who would be better served joining the fold. The Melchizedek Priesthood is explained in verse 8 of the Doctrine and Covenants as administering to all spiritual needs. I have found that attending to spiritual needs is almost impossible when the basic temporal needs of food and shelter are lacking; therefore, you see the Lord's balance in His true church.

In Acts 21:8-10, four virgins in the book of Philip prophesied, and a Prophet named Abagus came down and made Paul to know that he would be bound and imprisoned by the Romans. What power would cause a man who was Saul of Tarsus, a Jew on assignment from the Sadducees, converted on the road to Damascus, and now an Apostle to subject himself to torture and perhaps death? What force and what authority would motivate such selflessness? This is what has been revealed for 180 years as countless missionaries of the Church of Jesus Christ of Latter-Day Saints have gone forth at their own expense to testify. If you've made it this far through my works, you're probably already a member; if not, it's high time you became one with the fold as Saul found on the road. You must get on the path first.

Your actions and motives as expressions of your major goals and purposes reflect who you will be in the process of changing and becoming who you are. You must first be in orbit so your Actsys, or the center around which you revolve, is your standard in your sphere of influence. Get moving and stop being a slow-moving target for those who already are on their path. Doctrine and Covenants 100:5-6 reads, "Therefore, verily I say unto you, lift up your voices unto this people; speak the thoughts that I shall put into your hearts, and you shall not be confounded before men; For it shall be given you in the very hour, yea, in the very moment, what ye shall say."

And in verse 7, it states to declare Christ's name in solemnity and meekness in all things; many times, boldness borders on arrogance. If I offend anyone with my approach, I apologize. In Acts 21:21, Paul went into James, and the elders were present and said that they must forsake the law of Moses and do away with the zealous, absolute way of doing things. Christ had fulfilled the law, and these things needed to be discontinued while forgiveness through Christ's atoning sacrifice had replaced all that was for the Jew and the Gentile previous to His coming. In the Book of Helaman, a section in the Book of Mormon, 5:6, Helaman sees Nephi and Lehi looking to the sky with light shining from their countenances seeming to speak to an unseen being, thirty years before His birth. This had been happening in all areas of earthly existence since the beginning of man, and yet today we still call it miraculous or deny that it did, does, or ever will happen just because we haven't personally seen it.

I was born in Japan. Have you ever been there? How do you know it even exists? Get my point? I testify that when the Lord can trust you and knows you hear His voice and follow His commandments, these types of "miracles" will occur in your life and become prevailing.

Stephen was an HONEST man who confounded the Jews in the synagogues of Jerusalem, and his face appeared as the face of an angel to them. He was stoned to death. Have you ever wondered why martyrs were killed by those in offices of INFLUENCE? Corruption covers the face of the earth today, and greed has robbed the elderly of their life savings or a great portion of it while bad mortgage and investment firms have profited at our demise while rejecting God and Jesus Christ in a country under God and indivisible with liberty and justice for all. It's time for the Lord to come a second time and establish true, honest governing bodies with true principles and cast Satan and his angels from leadership here and throughout the world. Then and only then will we know happiness. In verse 8 of Acts 23, it clearly states that the leading faction of the Jews, the Sadducees, didn't believe there was a resurrection, but the Pharisees confessed that there was, and angels and spirits not only existed but had appeared. I believe this was the Lord's purpose in converting Saul of Tarsus to become Paul the Apostle, him having been a Pharisee.

My reason for discussing these gentlemen of the past is that I, too, have experienced similar conversion experiences as only the Lord knows; there may be those or even you who would refute that such things occur. As for me, I cannot deny what I have seen and heard regarding the ways of the Lord and His Father, Eloheim. My reason for inspiring the multitude through my writing is because of a commandment to bring my experiences to you so as to help you realize that Jesus is the Christ, that He lives, and that He administers to us today through a Prophet, even Thomas S. Monson, and has done such since the beginning of the last dispensation of time starting with Joseph Smith. That said, Joseph through the power and authority of God did translate a sacred work called the Book of Mormon, a cornerstone in Christ's restored church. His priesthood has been restored, both the Levitical or Aaronic and the Melchizedek, to administer unto the temporal and spiritual welfare of the church and its members, indeed to all mankind when needs arise. The work of exaltation has begun on the earth with the building of temples that dot the earth, where the work of perfecting all the human race is taking place today. Christ visits these hallowed halls, and angels frequent these sacred edifices. Christ also regularly visits His Prophets,

Seers, and Revelators for our behalf. All of this started with a young boy's fervent prayer in Palmyra, New York, in the early eighteen hundred. Now it is almost fourteen million members strong with fifty thousand missionaries plus serving in all corners of the world sharing the First Vision, the Book of Mormon, and the message of the restoration of the Gospel of Jesus Christ prior to His Second Coming.

My wife just called to make an appointment with the dentist for the children and a doctor's appointment for me as I have had some swallowing/breathing difficulties twice. My father died of throat cancer, so I thought I'd get it looked at. We found out there's a copay, and we don't have it, so she had to cancel the appointment. You must understand—and I'm sure you do—how life can get in the way of all things that are good, and it will. Why do you think it's taken me eighteen years to compile and come forth with this, most of which happened at various turning points in my life? Mine in comparison to those written about in scripture are important to my children and for generations to come even though they may pale in significance or magnitude to things written for all men. Don't misunderstand me; if you read the Book of Mormon first and then my books, you would be better served, and you, too, will go through your own refining process, whether you get on the path now or we help you to decide whether to do it later through our work in the temples.

In Acts 5:5-12, Ananias and his wife both give up the ghost when confronted with their having lied to the Lord. In section 4 of Acts, verses 5-12, you will see that Peter and John stood before the high priests, and they marveled at their abilities as one of the healed men stood before them. Later they would be delivered from prison by an angel. The Apostles, no doubt, were doing the unfinished business of their Master, Jesus Christ. The Gospel was rejected and taken from the earth to be restored at a later date as I had just discussed. You and I are expected to take the message forth to those around us through example and to succor those who stand in need without becoming suckers in the process. My therapy is in these pages, and all is not well in my life—whose is? I'm coping and dealing with issues and following the Spirit as I struggle with money and poverty in my own way. The harder I try, the worse it gets; so, should I quit, crawl up in a hole, and die, or keep moving forward towards my destiny? I choose the latter. I am acting by writing these books and driving a tractor trailer, doing a siding job, and consulting for a week in Salt Lake City. Now, I'm on a juice fast to fix my major goal, my health, energy, and sexual ability and to support my wife and children. So, for now, I'm going running for the second time in fifteen years. Wish me well!

I said something that may or may not be true in your life but has permeated mine. You may notice that the thing you worry about constantly presents itself over and over again in different forms, and there's nothing worse than knowing this and being a victim of your own doing. I call this group of three books my TRYOULOGY because until you've tried yourself and converted to the spiritual side of life, these experiences will seem like they are fairytales based on your temporal existence and all you've been told they may indeed be. The apostles had to go forward and try the Savior's methods and believe that the same Spirit with which he healed would work for them as they followed promptings to accomplish His goals; however, their goals were similar and had been acted upon by Jesus Christ as the Exemplar. I am not one of these men, but I have experienced similar things, and you will, too, once you become aware of your potential to do good. A man asked me, as I have asked so many in the past, what I did for a living, and I blurted, "I'm a licensed builder in six states and a master plumber, and I do HVAC, and electrical work."

Before I could finish, Charles said, "Well, don't be a know-it-all."

I thought, *but he didn't let me finish*! I realized then that I'm constantly saying the same things due to my current financial insecurity and my lack of belief that these books will be published and benefit myself, my family, and mankind in general. I'm a broken record. How about you? Do you find yourself setting goals to do something you really want and then defeating your purpose by living in the past?

Remember that when you live in the past, tomorrow becomes yesterday, and nothing changes. I finally can practice what I preach. These books are written for me. Someone on the other side wants me to know that playing the same scratched record will only yield to the point of the scratch repetition of verbal responses and correlating action to support the things that you don't want but talk about constantly. What a vicious cycle; I'm free. I will get these books published, and I will. I am a writer; all I have to do is put this accomplishment at the forefront of every conversation, prayer, and interface, and the Lord will manifest it in the exact way that I want and need. Your goals will be accomplished in the same way. It's high time for a change in focus. I finally get it and had to write three books to realize that my lack of belief, all of my faith promoting experiences, has hindered my progress and been detrimental to my goals and my family. How about you?

It's time to create a new record of results through action and focus in the direction of my goals. I am 195 pounds; my TRYOULOGY is published; I am saving sixteen hundred dollars per month; and I have gained wisdom through this process. Why does it have to take so long? It seems there is a realization period in between setting goals and accomplishing them. You will see the delay and realize why many times, you and I give up on or forget our goals because we're unwilling to wait long enough for them to materialize and unfold and that they do eventually, without notice, if you're willing to wait. The phrase "Thy will be done, and thy timeframe be used" comes to mind.

Manifestation of goals happens based on actions over time and a constant focus. Now, do you see the parallel between scriptural accounts and your own life? Aren't you experiencing the same things these predecessors did? Does history have to repeat itself? Why are we still barbarians, killing each other over greed? Why can we not raise ourselves up above ancient ways? You can; I can. The individual soul is more important than the accumulation of all because change happens to each of us individually before the whole intelligence or majority will change. You and I must change, and the process continue and be taught through your progenitors. Face it—we've had the knowledge and methods for thousands of years, and action has not won over fear yet. Even my life has been hindered by ignorance and a cowardly lack of perseverance. I'm ashamed and sorry, and that's enough. I have found higher ground and seek to guide you to that realm of peace, joy, and happiness in this life. I am no longer a scratched and broken record. As of today, I cease to be unwise. Thank you for bearing with me. I hope you will do some selfless soul-searching as a result of my trials, tribulations, and morphing process.

Just do it now! Say YES TODAY, YESTODAY, YESTODAY. Change YESTERDAY today and find the hope and manifestation of a best tomorrow. Begin evolving and revolving around your own ACTSYS and cease to be an enemy unto yourself. If you're confused, reread the entire TRYOULOGY again and be obedient to the promptings.

In Acts chapter 3, Peter and John go to the temple and in the name of Jesus Christ heal the lame man in front of the temple as his parents had left him there to beg for alms. Christ's example and their belief along with the faith of the lame man provided the environment for manifestation; it was belief and action of all parties at the temple that provided the environment for the lame man to be healed. You and I must do what is required to manifest the good in our lives. Are you getting it?

In 2 Nephi 25:20, it is stated that, "There is none other name given under heaven save it be this Jesus Christ, of which I have spoken, whereby man can be saved." The priesthood is restored to the earth, and if you haven't met with the missionaries of the Church of Jesus Christ of Latter-Day Saints yet, then put this book down and call them so you can be taught; otherwise, all of my work has been in vain on your behalf. However, the seed is planted. Now it's up to you to provide the fertile soil for gestation of these ideas. Who knows? Maybe you'll write about your experiences as I have.

One thing is certain: corrupt rulers will always be ignorant of such things as their wealth and control over people is contrary to the Spirit of the Lord, and adversity and misery comes to citizens subjected to such. Today, the U.S. is slipping into the abyss of corruption and control by losing freedoms through fear tactics planned and orchestrated by corrupt politicians and wealthy men, and certainly we will and are suffering from the usurping of unrighteous authority by those who wield the sword of the Gadianton robbers. This always has been and always will be until the Savior alone rules the world at His next coming, where Satan will be bound, and one thousand years of temple work will commence on behalf of all humanity. You may think that I speak an unfamiliar language and that the scriptures are confusing. Acts 2:4 explains, "And they were filled with the Holy Ghost, and began to speak with other tongues, as the Spirit gave them utterance."

My son, Isaiah, is fourteen years old and he thinks I speak in tongues as his ability to listen has been fogged by puberty. He's very intelligent, and when he informed me that he was getting an "F" in history class, I was baffled as he had informed me that he sought to be a history teacher/ game designer/ non-homework-doer. I reminded him of his goal and asked him how he thought he'd teach something he didn't even care to try in and that he could have gotten a 22% without even being in the class. Then I realized that I was guilty of the same thing.

I had been talking about the same horror story for nine years since my downfall and had lacked the belief in myself to get this book finished and published and corresponding royalties established as being a writer is my goal. I have been writing since I can remember and have yet to publish my TRYOULOGY. Now I will finish it and align my goals, beliefs, actions, speech, and focus into publishing my work.

I say YES today; how about you? Is there something you're wanting to do yet lack the resolve or, worse yet, ask other people for their advice that are more screwed up than you are? Remember, YOUR DREAM is exactly that, and asking those who have failed to live or realize theirs is the last thing you want to do. Finding a mentor, however, is helpful in the process of becoming a mentor and coach yourself.

Even the apostles struggled with believing the Savior had risen from the dead. In Acts 10:40-41, THE Bible states, "Him God raised up the third day, and shewed him openly. Not to all the people, but unto witnesses chosen before of God, even to us, who did eat and drink with him after he rose from the dead." Jesus Christ knew the resurrection would occur; he said it, died, and did it. He asked the apostles repeatedly why they could not do the things He did when they could. Faith, belief, and life's experience had showed them they could not do these things that they thought so miraculous. Later, after the Savior's death, resurrection, and ascension after visiting the American continent, they did accomplish similar "miracles" through faith. The faith of the lame, however, was the faith of the dead required to live again or another will need to restore life. Have you ever let your dreams die and given up on them? DON'T. When are you too old to live and do what you want? There is no such age.

The adversary will discourage you through other humans who've lost their way. Surround yourself with positive, like-minded people who allow you freedom of expression as you reciprocate to them and allow free-flowing "miracles" to occur in your YOULOGY group. I talked to my sister, Sharon, and we shared an idea she had and acted on it while discussing product names, packages, and ingredients for marketing. We also discussed visualizing being at my book signing for TRYOULOGY, and while talking to her, I visualized a certain design of the cover—very unique and never before done. Now I must conclude this series of experiences as I'm about thirty percent through the outline. I will complete this work in the next couple of weeks, and it will be published. Then I will work on the new candy product with Sharon and begin another chapter of action in my life and write a book about the development of a life-changing, all-organic candy and an entire line of health products. I will not reveal the names of the products or what they're made with as I have had other inventions in the past misused by those with whom I have shared and later developed for their profit when I confided in them for financial help in doing the same. I share with you as ideas and action perpetuate a constant progress. I challenge you to start acting on your dreams now. Put this book down, and touch, feel, taste, and envision your dream and purpose in this life. Write it down with an action-oriented, time-framed incremental plan, STARTING NOW. Share your idea with a total stranger without getting specific and read your elevator pitch to yourself morning and night and move in that direction with a daily course of action and correlating accomplishment. It's that simple. There are still principles I will cover and a very intense scriptural section on charity. Then I will expect success stories and opportunities to coach and mentor one on one.

You will remain open to revelation and correlating actions by others to help you gain momentum centrifugally inward towards your ACTSYS. I am not going to explain scriptures to you or the process any further. Like the apostles in Jesus Christ's absence, I must rely on your diligence at this point and your subsequent conversion to help you to do as I have done; otherwise, I have imparted my wisdom to no avail. I will suggest you go to the following scriptures that will help you take action. Remember to read between the lines and to liken the verses in the standard works to your life and not to get caught up in the intellectual pursuit as it will prove futile.

The following list will help: Acts 3:17 JST, Doctrine and Covenants 6:21, Mosiah 26:30, Alma 5: 1-15and 21, Acts 3:20 JST (JST means Joseph Smith Translation in the King James Version of the Bible), Acts 7:37, 1 Nephi 22:20, and Doctrine and Covenants 1:14-16 along with Doctrine and Covenants 133:63.

READ these and ponder on their purpose in my travels and how you may apply the principles discussed therein in your pursuits. Revelation has always come to me three times personally and one time in conference with church leaders through the Holy Ghost. The Holy Ghost is required to testify of truth, and when you feel the burning in your bosom the first time, you will know it without a doubt. Then it will behooveth you to act and progress to keep the channel open and on. You alone must walk this path that has been walked by millions before you and certain to be ventured by millions in the future. It will be personal and unique. In other words, you probably won't experience the same things I have and certainly not the same way. In this way, you are incurably unique as a one of a kind creation of your Heavenly Father. Read about Psalms 68:27 and the subtrahend at the bottom of the page referring to the Hebrew reference to Benjamin and Adam Ondi Ahman, along with Doctrine and Covenants 123:12. When you, the pupil, are prepared as a sojourner, the messageurs will suddenly appear as those whom you will perceive are not of this world when they actually are. They will impart wisdom to you. Next, I will discuss the importance of example.

As you see on the insert after page twenty, I HAVE HAD VAST TRAINING AND EXPERIENCE. So how do I end up not being used or put to work? I've thought it's the bad economy or the fact that my credit was destroyed by the IRS, or—gosh, it could be the background from 1983 now that the TSA has taken our freedom and molested our mothers and children in airports to "protect us." I wonder what's next and who really controls all of our financial losses and communist random increases in fuel prices.

My goodness, we're being robbed and have no bearing on who gets elected! Other than that, I maintain optimism in myself and my abilities to assimilate into a productive life once again. My Youlogy has barely begun; the best lies ahead. I have decided to finish this book differently than the previous two and publish them as soon as possible as attracted by focus, goals, and action. I must survive and provide for my family in the interim. I am grateful for the sixteen hundred dollars a month that I receive due to my wife's death and for the church's help and the government's help with food on the local level. I hope to rub on instead of rub off by my example. I am currently not where I want to be, but I'm gaining momentum of purpose by accomplishing my goals—progress, not perfection.

I'm seeking to stop sizing others up as to what they can do for me. I am unknown here in Hurricane and was asked why I moved to so many places. Was I or am I a serial killer? I just met this guy this morning, and rather than be offended, I explained the circumstances and promptings that have led to my actions. I wonder if he would have asked the Savior and the apostles that question for leaving JERUSALEM!

I HAVE FOUND THAT ACCEPTING OTHERS FOR THEIR DECISIONS IS EASIER THAN QUESTIONING THEIR MOTIVES. Now you may read several scriptures in this order and see if they correlate in your mind as they did in mine: Helaman 10:6-10, Acts 8:39-40, Doctrine and Covenants 88:81, Acts 1:8-9, Doctrine and Covenants 100:11, Alma 17:2-3, Mosiah 28:3, Acts 4:20, Acts 23:10-12 and 26 about the Apostle Paul, and Helaman 16: 1-5, 5 being where Samuel foretold.

It's YOUR SPHERE or world and your responsibility to adapt and share or, in other words, to have CHARITY. When this word comes to mind, you might think of freeloaders or people who don't work or are lazy. I believe that there are many ambiguous ways of defining the word charity. I am told it is the pure love of Christ. What does that mean to you? You could probably come up with another abstract definition. I believe charity to be selflessness without martyrdom, in other words, doing your best to provide for yourself and your family first and then to share your surplus with others. I call the law of consecration, where you are willing to give your all for the building up of Christ's church, a sacrifice. Paying ten percent tithing can be difficult if you've never done it or have fallen out of the habit. Giving until it hurts in fast offerings for the poor every month by not eating two meals and fasting for twenty-four hours and giving a generous offering on top of the ten percent can be very difficult when your own family's needs are not being met. I've found through difficult times that many things I have spent my money on over the years were not wise and that I overindulged myself in food and all things when I should have been saving. Also, I have been thinking wrongly and not optimistically, seeking to provide in any environment I've been in, feeling defeated as doors closed that were always opened before. I have head trash, too. When your brain and your wallet are broken, it's hard to maintain optimism. I'm finished with the belly-aching and ready to move on with my aspirations. I just want you to know that we all struggle with something; that's what keeps life interesting and engaging.

Again, I will make a list of scriptures to read to help you understand charity better: Acts chapter 2, Acts 21:4 and 9-11, Acts 11:27-28.

The second list on charity is as follows: Mosiah 3:5-6, Acts 13:34-37, Alma 22:3-11 and15.

The third cluster of scripture is: Acts 8:14-17, Acts 4:4 and 32-35, Doctrine and Covenants 51:3, and 36:7.

List four is the following: Acts 5:14 and 4:31-37, Doctrine and Covenants 68:3-4, and 3 Nephi 11:28-30.

The next cluster of five is: Moses 7:18 in the Pearl of Great Price; Topical Guide, look up "unity," Doctrine and Covenants 49:20, Acts 5:1-11, Acts 6: l, and Doctrine and Covenants 83: l-6.

The sixth scripture chain is: Acts 2:45; Topical guide look up "welfare," Acts 11:22-24, Doctrine and Covenants 19:34; Topical Guide look up "family."

String seven begins with: Acts 5:16-25, Acts 12:7, Moroni 7:29-33; Topical Guide look up "angels," ending with Acts 16:26.

The final scripture to help explain the utopian word charity is Mosiah 28:3.

NOW share this list of scriptures exactly as delineated and reap the pleasure of educating and converting others. The ultimate charity was the selfless sacrifice of Jesus Christ as a vicarious offering for all mankind; we cannot approach this, and we don't need to. You and I can do our part by imparting information and service.

NOW, when you are done, read the TRYOULOGY again and highlight; take notes and ACT on all counsel, both given and received. READ the scriptures and do the same. Psalms 81:12 and Acts 7:42, along with Romans 1:28, will help motivate you. FEEL the meaning as it may have nothing to do with what's written and yet everything to do with what's written.

Contradictory? NOW you're beginning to understand. Remove the earthly screen and allow a flow of information in and out of the Heavenly portal that is opened when you receive the gift of the Holy Ghost after baptism by the Priesthood of Aaron as Christ did to set the ultimate example and to be THE EXEMPLAR. READ and REREAD the Book of Mormon; the Pearl of Great Price, the Old Testament, and the New Testament. Highlight and follow the footnotes on prompted subjects and learn of the eternal round contained and shared amongst these books. Journal your OWN journey as YOU HOWN YOUR SPHERE; receive sacred messages from YOUR MESSAGEURS; and create YOUR ACTSYS of perpetual motion and centrifugal force. Learn to centripetally shed all that is dark and remain in the light. Journal what happens every day; I have not done that since the tragedy of my wife's death and have relied on recollection that may have been more detailed had I not been a hypocrite. Are we not all hypocrites when our ACTIONS do not ALIGN with our GOALS? Acts 1:10-11 and Acts 13:43 will further expound and solidify upon my confession.

When my son Isaiah was three years old, he loved taking my thirty-foot tape measure and stretching it out and hearing it snap when it retracted. He had no idea how to use a tape measure for its designed purpose and didn't care. Are you in the same boat with Isaiah with spiritual things? I prefer to measure my progress temporally and spiritually, and at the moment I am progressing. I FEEL NO GUILT OR SHAME. I renew my covenants made in the temple and at baptism and live worthily to stand in front of my Savior at the judgement seat, and it's never over. The Greek word "aitia" means a legal cause of action. My hope is that His work and my life will inspire others to act and to take the path less traveled and guide others to be converted to THE GOSPEL OF JESUS CHRIST and to walk in a light with a countenance improved by the knowledge of the ATONEMENT. ADIEU until we meet again. Bless you.

Appendix

While you are *Howning Your Sphere*, remember that you must become transparent to be understood, for your example will be seen and your reputation will be based on your ACTSYS, or your action system. I love the triangle as in the Greek alphabet it is the letter delta, which means change. Like on an isosceles triangle, there are two legs and a diagonal line that connects them called the hypotenuse. One leg is vertical and one horizontal, and they are sometimes in different planes. The change doesn't take place and the triangle isn't defined until the shortest path is established between the ends of the legs by the hypotenuse.

There are several ways for you to arrive at your destination. You can take the long way on the path, following the legwork on two perpendicular lines only to find termination at both ends, or you can execute a plan with action to find the shortest distance from where you are to where you want to be. When you're on the path of perpendicular legs, you lack the vantage point that comes from looking down from higher ground that makes it easy to see the path of least resistance and the way to affect change. Today, I went to the Timpenogas temple and had trouble finding it. The Spirit told me to turn and go up the mountain, and after elevation increased, I was able to see right where the temple was. That's what goals with intent will do. They allow you to reach higher ground and change your perspective. In this case, altitude determines attitude.

Your incremental ACTSYS will ultimately determine your rate of success or failure.

Washington Irving said, "Great minds have a purpose; others have wishes." Little minds are tamed and subdued by misfortune, but great minds rise above them. While journeying through trials, some have the ability to suffer positively. Now, you know the key is your reaction and focus. This is much easier said than done—bull, it's much easier done than said! You seem to inherit justification, oriented, fabricated phrases to make you feel better about your incapacity to cope with tribulation. You will see this pass as you read and implement the principles contained herein.

Harriet Beecher Stowe said, "When you get into a tight place and everything goes against you, 'til it seems as though you could not hold on a minute longer, never give up then, for that is just the place and time that the tide will turn." That is when you must arouse your faculties and raise the bar of expectation of recovery and, through belief, anticipate momentum through your system of action in the positive. Your results will be attributed to the alignment between your intentions, your actions, and the things you speak. To maintain perpetual motion around your ACTSYS, you must begin to realize the power within yourself to act in accordance with your life's intentions and adjust all your efforts and means in that direction. Prepare for success by believing first, visualizing and perpetuating the creation of the world you choose to be part of, and your sphere of influence will appear and attract support in a miraculously manifested way. Empowerment comes in this way.

The intention here is to complete this work by February 5, 2011 and give it away in the form of an e-book and follow with seminars and one-on-one coaching in person and online, depending on your needs and intentions. This is to debut on April 23, 2011, to be followed by two more books to complete the trilogy: *The Psalm of the Messageur* and

Your ACTSYS, Your Sphere. The seminars will be custom-tailored and interactive so as to address the particular audience's needs. To establish your ACTSYS, a record and ongoing evaluation will be kept tracking progress or the lack thereof. There will be a daily record kept of progression so as to document improvement, and evaluation of the program will be through video testimonial before and after transformational documentation.

In Dr. Seuss's *Horton Hears a Who*, he speaks of an elephant named Horton who hears a Who from a speck of dust which turns out to be a world unto itself with a thriving community called Whoville. No one but Horton knows they exist. Horton goes to great lengths to protect these beings he cannot see. Horton's discovery came when he heard, "We are here, we are here, we are here!" Many of us, maybe even you, go through life trying to let others know that we are here. Maybe few are willing to acknowledge you because you have failed to create your sustainable individuality and a world that exists that only you can hear. This is why positive affirmation and self-talk with corresponding aligned actions put your brain and spirit in line with your intentions. First, you must become aware and then act. Providence will work in your favor and allow you to become a creator and leave that legacy to all who hear you from your world, and your brain will cause you to act in harmony with your measurable goals. Jesus Christ said it best in Hebrew when He said, "Talitha cumi," which means arise. You must arise and arouse your faculties to fully develop your talents while on this sphere so as to fulfill yourself and those you become a steward over. Mentors are those who have done these things and teach others to do likewise. You may ask, "How do I write goals that are specific, measurable, attainable, reproducible, and time-framed?" What you have just read is my example in real life of just that. ENJOY!

Printed in the USA
CPSIA information can be obtained
at www.ICGtesting.com
CBHW071459100724
11292CB00040B/485